ISSUES:

Exercises in Political and Social Decision-Making

Fourth Edition

Edited by

Phyllis Botterweck

Gregory Publishing Co.   Wheaton, IL 60187

Design and Production: Gregory Publishing Company
Typeface: Times
Typesetting: Gregory Publishing Company
Cover Art: Sam Tolia

ISSUES:
Exercises in Political and Social Decision-Making

Fourth Edition, 2000
Printed in the United States of America
Translation rights reserved by the author
ISBN 0-911541-45-4

To My Sons,
B.G. and Brian

Contents

Preface

In 1978, the first edition of *ISSUES: An Exercise in Political and Social Decision-Making* was published. It is now time for the fourth edition. The stories of *ISSUES* have stood the test of time. The stories, and the issues surrounding them, are as relevant today as when they were first written.

For those of you new to *ISSUES*, allow me the opportunity to convey to you the philosophy of the textbook. It is difficult communicating to students the complexities of the world. Few truly understand the decision-making process and how it applies to the problems of government and society. This is particularly disconcerting since they will soon be called upon in their adult years to grapple with the age-old problems of poverty, racism, crime, political morality, internal security, foreign relations, taxation, the national debt, shrinking resources, global competition, and many others. Therefore, it appears crucial to find a way to more fully illuminate these problems while, at the same time, providing students with a method of resolving them in an effective and responsible manner.

Also, students need to assume part of the responsibility for their own education. At some point in life we must all become our own teachers. As humans we tend to learn best those lessons we teach ourselves. As such, the true role of the teacher in the learning process is that of a facilitator, helping the student down the road of discovery.

This text utilizes a teaching methodology that fulfills this purpose. First, it provides the student the opportunity to become his/her own teacher by defining problems, gathering information, and resolving them in some orderly decision-making process. Second, the teaching methodology employs a technique interesting enough that students are induced to seize the opportunity to teach themselves.

For this edition there are eighteen selected cases. Though fictionalized, each case parallels an actual problem in life. The student will be given information regarding the situation, the characters, and the events; but the student must provide the solution. In *ISSUES* there are no endings, there are only problems—problems that will excite and problems that will anger. But above all else, the problems in *ISSUES* will be frustrating. For frustration lies at the threshold of knowledge. In the immortal words of Professor Wattenburg, a fictionalized character in one of the cases, "Press forward. Your reward awaits!"

Phyllis Botterweck
Editor, Gregory Publishing Company

The Window

Anthony Puccini stood staring out the eleventh-floor window into the night. Behind him sat the mayor, his political chieftains, the superintendent of police, and Martin White, Director of the Affirmative Action Program. In front of him lay Williamsburg, a city torn with rage and civil disobedience. Over the horizon, flames leaped into the darkness, illuminating the skyline of the massive metropolitan community. In the streets below people huddled in small groups, pointing, gaping, and shouting childishly as they watched the ghetto burn from a safe distance. And everywhere the sounds of sirens were heard, racing desperately back and forth across the city.

It was Williamsburg's first riot. Tens of thousands of angry blacks and Puerto Ricans streamed into the streets in a carnival of rioting, looting, and burning. While those inside frantically considered their options, Puccini watched the city, mesmerized by the chaos.

Like Martin White, he, too, was new to his job as deputy superintendent of police. But very much unlike any of the others, street violence was not new to Anthony Puccini. Long ago, in another city, he had encountered it. It was a memory he had deliberately chosen to forget. But now, like a haunting ghost seeking resurrection, it beckoned him. He closed his eyes tightly, shutting off the shouting voices behind. Immediately, the events of that August night sprang to the forefront of his consciousness, dancing in images as vivid as the evening past.

It was hot. Yes, so hot, he recalled. The burning buildings turned what could have been a mild summer night into an inferno. He could see himself clearly now, crouched behind a stack of garbage pails seeking protection. He was new to the force and frightened. He crouched lower. A bead of sweat slithered down the length of his face and neck before disappearing beneath the dark blue collar. Across the street, through the smoke, he caught sight of a lone figure, small in frame, standing against a store window. He took his eyes off the man for a brief second to wipe his forehead. Suddenly, there were sounds of breaking glass. He turned back, searching for the man. He had vanished. He reached for the radio. Pressing the button, he whispered in a muffled tone, "This is K-39; do you read, M-4?" Nothing. Again, he repeated the message. Finally, much to his relief, came the response.

"This is M-4. What is your message, K-39?"

Again, he pressed the button. "This is K-39. I am presently located in the vicinity of 43rd and Eliester. Possible 9-18. Back-up unit requested."

"Negative, K-39," squawked the voice over the radio. "All officers presently detained. Proceed with caution."

Puccini froze. He could scarcely believe his ears. Surely they wouldn't let him, a rookie, go in alone after a suspect. Even veterans were discouraged from taking such action.

"K-39, this is M-4; do you copy?" The voice on the other end of the radio barked back the message a second time. He had forgotten to respond.

Pressing the button again, Puccini acknowledged the message. "M-4, this is K-39; message received."

"10-4, K-39." It was the last communiqué he would receive that night. Puccini carefully made his way to the squad car less than thirty feet away. Replacing the radio, he reached up for the 12 gauge. The way his hands were shaking, he'd have to use his shotgun. Looking back to the store through the broken glass, he could see the outline of a man moving about. He wondered if the suspect was armed. He could feel the perspiration seeping through the back of his shirt. The material clung tightly to the skin. Starting to move forward, he hesitated. For a brief moment a desire to escape seized him. He could turn and walk away, he thought. It would be so easy. He'd simply wait and then radio back that the store had been burglarized, but no suspect had been seen or apprehended. No one would ever know the difference. He sighed, no one but himself. If he walked away from this one, it would follow him the rest of his career, and he knew it. He had to do it!

Carefully he made his way across the street to the front of the store. Never had he been so alert. His blood was surging like a blind, raging river. Every muscle in his body ached from the tenseness. Inside he heard a noise, like a....

"Tony!"

He turned quickly as if startled and found himself looking into the eyes of Tom O'Leary, the superintendent of police. The whole room was staring at him now.

"Oh, yes, sir. I'm sorry, sir. What was it?"

"Tony," O'Leary requested, "would you please get away from that window and join us. I didn't bring you here just to get a better view of the riot. I had hoped that you might be of some help to me."

"Of course, my apologies." Puccini crossed the room quickly and sank into a large, square-like, cushioned chair.

O'Leary continued, "Now, gentlemen, as I was saying, what we need is a strong affirmative stand. All night long we've been on the defensive, and we're getting nowhere because my men don't know what's expected of them. We've never encountered this type of wanton violence and looting. I've been out there half the night, and, I can tell you, it's just plain madness. We have to stop it, or it's going to get worse."

"And what is it that you want, Tom?" asked Ralph Hannon, one of the mayor's chief aides.

"I want," he stopped short. "No, let me rephrase that. I'm not the only one out there in the streets trying to stop this chaos. What **we** want," he began again, "is for this office, for the mayor and the city council, to come out, forthright, as a unified front with measures what will stop this sort of lawlessness dead in its tracks."

"And what type of measures do you as superintendent of police recommend?" inquired Hannon.

"A shoot-to-kill order."

"WHAT?" shrieked Martin White, leaping up out of his chair. "You want a shoot-to-kill order? Man, you must be mad!"

O'Leary stood his ground, "Quite the contrary, Mr. White; I believe it to be a very rational suggestion. In my professional opinion, it is the only action that will stop the violence."

"You can call it a professional opinion if you want, but I still call it sheer madness, and I suggest we dispense with the superintendent's recommendation immediately."

The mayor leaned back in his chair as if in thought while lighting his pipe. "Now wait, Martin," he finally commented through a cloud of smoke. "Let's hear Tom out. After all, that's why we're here, isn't it?"

O'Leary walked behind his high-backed chair. Resting his arms on its back, he began again, "It's really not as complicated as it sounds. It's simply a matter of fighting fire with fire, you know, to prevent it from spreading. Now, for all practical purposes, the riots are over for tonight. Sure, the fire department is still out there and the police are still trying to run down a few snipers, but, for the most part, it's over. For tonight, that is," he said, raising his eyebrows to qualify his statement. "But tomorrow night is a new night, and from the experience of other cities we can expect more of the same. That is, of course, unless we take action tonight. Now, tomorrow, all day long, the only topic that's gonna be discussed is the riots. It'll be spread all over the papers. It'll be on the tube, and all day long that's the only thing you'll hear on the radio. It'll be that way because that's the only thing people will want to hear about, including everyone who was in the streets last night. They'll be looking through every paper in the city, trying to find their own face in one of the pictures. That's exactly what we want, gentlemen, because when they pick up the paper, they're gonna see our message to them in bold headlines: MAYOR GIVES ORDER: SHOOT-TO-KILL. Let me tell you, there ain't no way anyone who's considering going out tomorrow night for a little burning and looting is not gonna stop and think twice about it. We'll be giving fair notice, and I'll bet you a year's salary right here and now," he snarled, "that if the order is given, your problem is over."

"And what if they still come out tomorrow night, Superintendent?" asked White indignantly.

"If that happens, which I seriously doubt, Mr. White, all I can say is that the city warned them."

White shook his head and groaned, straining to hold back the hostility he felt for O'Leary. Puccini sat alone, watching the confrontation between the two men intensify. Slowly but steadily, his eyes were drawn to the window.

Reaching up again to wipe the sweat from his eyes, he cursed. It was hot, too damn hot! Again from the inside of the store he heard the noise; only this time it was fainter than before. It could mean only one thing, he thought, calculating the movement of the suspect. He had to be moving toward the rear of the store. Now was the time to make his move through the door and into the building. He pumped the shotgun, chambering a shell. Dropping to the concrete, he pulled himself along the front of the store, avoiding the open window. Slowly he moved until he was at the door. Reaching up with one arm extended, he grabbed the handle and pulled. It was locked. Damn, what now, he thought. Quickly he considered his alternatives. He could go through the broken window, the same way the suspect had entered. No, he dismissed the idea. Against the light, standing up, he'd be too vulnerable. There was only one alternative left. He'd have to make his way around to the side of the building and enter through the rear door. It was his only hope to surprise the suspect. Again, he dragged himself along the concrete to the side of the store where an alley would lead him to the rear entrance. Bits and pieces of glass cut through his uniform, tearing at his skin. Wincing in pain, he moved steadily forward until he neared his destination. Then, in one hard jerk he rolled past the window and into the alley. Springing up, he ran toward the back door, which was elevated by a short staircase and a small wooden porch. His back was against the rough brick siding as he edged forward. Carefully, ever so quietly....

BANG! The sound of White's fist striking the mayor's desk startled Puccini.

"I don't care what you say. A shoot-to-kill order is not going to stop anyone from rioting. In fact, it's going to make matters worse. It's all the provocation they need to hit the streets again. It's like trying to put out a fire with gasoline. Man, don't you know anything? Those people...."

"Animals, not people, Mr. White. Only animals would do this," O'Leary said, moving to the window and throwing back the drapes even further.

"Well, maybe they're acting like animals because they've been treated like animals!"

"Don't try to wet-nurse me with all that liberal crap, White," responded O'Leary.

White threw up his hands in disgust. "What's the use of talking? You've been living the rich life so long, O'Leary, that the cholesterol is clogging your ears."

"Don't try to put me down. I've heard everything you've had to say. I just don't buy it, OK?"

"No, it's not OK, because you're messing with people you know nothing about."

O'Leary was beginning to get excited now. His eyes flared, anger swelling up inside his head. "Hey, I've been working the street for 35 years. Don't tell me I don't know who lives there!"

"I didn't say that. Sure you know who lives there—the niggers, the spics, and the white trash, right?"

O'Leary's face flushed deep purple. Anger flashed in his eyes, and the muscles about the massive jaw pulled so tightly he could barely speak. "You bastard, I...."

The mayor sprang from his chair moving between the two men. "Now, gentlemen, let's not forget that we're all on the same side. We'll never solve this problem fighting among ourselves."

"We're not going to solve it by shooting people in the street either," White interjected. "Listen," he said, calmer now. "The people running around out there in the streets aren't there because they're celebrating the joy of life. They're out there because they're angry. They've been cheated by landlords, lied to by politicians, and kicked around by the police for so long that they've reached the breaking point. Don't you see," he pleaded, "they're not criminals—they're victims."

"Victims," laughed O'Leary. "You call them victims! Man, you've been hanging around those crazy university professors too long."

"Hey, leave the university out of this, will you? This has nothing to do with university professors."

"The hell it doesn't. You've been reading their books so long, you don't know the difference between criminals and victims. You're all mixed up," he said, waving his hand above his head in short circular motions.

"And you're not, huh?"

"That's right—I'm not. You want to know why?"

White looked at O'Leary contemptuously but said nothing. Stomping heavy-footed over to White, O'Leary hissed, "Well, let me tell you, anyway. It's because I didn't get my education reading books. I got mine looking out the front window of a squad car. And out there it's easy to tell the victims from the criminals. In fact, Mr. University," taunted O'Leary, "I can give you a couple of good examples fresh from the streets tonight. Wanna hear em?"

"Not particularly," answered White.

"No, I didn't think so. You wouldn't want to hear about the 12-year-old girl trapped in the alley by a gang of your poor, angry, social misfits. What those animals did to her was so horrible that they decided to bring in a shrink right away. Of course, he had to wait until the doctors got through stitching her back together." O'Leary's eyes were fixed on White's. His breathing was deep and irregular. "And then there's Al Machy, who owns the neighborhood ma-and-pa grocery store on the corner of 5th and Larmine. For thirty years he's been on that corner, and during that time he's probably given away more food than he's sold. Well, tonight the same people that he has worked with, lived with, and tried to help all of his life burnt his store to the ground. I know, because I was there helping put it out. But then, you're really not interested in hearing about this, are you? What's the matter, White? Does it offend your sense of social liberalism?"

White was about to answer when he heard his name being called from the opposite side of the room. He turned from O'Leary to find Allen Paulson, an old and trusted friend of the mayor, speaking to him. "Mr. White?" he asked. "I'm curious about a remark you made earlier."

"Yes?"

Paulson casually chuckled while lighting his pipe. A puff of smoke rose about his head. "Surely, when you spoke about politicians lying, you weren't referring to this administration?" Again, he chuckled.

"Wasn't I?" responded White.

"Well, I wouldn't think so. After all, I can't recall any lies we've told anyone lately, other than those we've told to our wives." With that Paulson broke into a hearty round of laughter, as did most of those in the room. White stood expressionless.

"My God, do you really believe that those people out there are stupid? Don't you think they remember the grandiose promises this administration made to them in the last campaign? Now, what was that program called that the mayor promised?" asked White while putting his hands to his forehead as if trying to summon up a forgotten memory. "Oh, yes, it was the GREATER HORIZONS program, wasn't it?" His lips turned into a loose smile as the words rolled off his tongue. "Oh, yes, the GREATER HORIZONS program. Now, there were promises one could truly live by," he said caustically. "We were going to clean up the ghetto, provide new housing, build more recreational facilities, give better police protection, and create meaningful jobs to reduce minority unemployment, which the mayor himself said had swelled to 'epidemic proportions.' 'Minority unemployment swells to epidemic proportions.' Catchy phrase, isn't it? As I recall, that even caught the attention of the media and was reprinted in all the papers. Yeah," he drawled, "we really got the mileage out of that phrase." White walked to his chair and said, "C'mom, let's not kid ourselves. This administration hasn't made good on even one of the five major points in the GREATER HORIZONS program."

"But surely, Mr. White, you must admit that this administration isn't to blame. When we made those promises, we had no way of foreseeing the current economic conditions. With inflation spiraling higher and higher every day, it would be politically and economically disastrous to attempt such an ambitious program. Even the Feds have closed shop. We can't get a nickel out of them, and we sure as hell can't go it alone."

"Don't tell me," yelled White. "Tell the people out there in the streets. They're the ones that have to live in the ghetto. But let me warn you. When you do tell them, you'd better take some cops along, because they're not going to understand your economic theories or the neat little graphs you've made, showing why everyone else gets more and they keep getting less. The only thing they understand is that in spite of all the promises, they still live in conditions that are more crowded, dirtier, and more dangerous than any prison in this country."

"OK, you've been bitching all night. What's your solution?" asked Paulson. "And don't tell me to wait, because the damn city is burning."

"If you really want to stop the violence, you tell the people out there that you understand their problems and that you're gonna give them what they want and what they deserve."

"You can't do that," shouted O'Leary. "That strategy will only encouraged more violence. It's like rewarding a child for bad behavior. Before long he'll learn that he can have anything he wants simply by throwing a fit. The same is true out there. If we reward rioting now, we'll just get more of it whenever anything doesn't go their way. If you ask me, it's a damn poor precedent."

Before White could defend his proposal, Paulson took command of the floor. "You know, Mayor, we have to consider the political consequences of any decision we make. Six hundred thousand people live in this city. One hundred and fifty thousand live in the ghetto or near it. I think we should give serious consideration to what they want. And, of course, there's the national media. The whole country is watching."

"Votes!" cried White, as he raced to the window. Throwing back the drapes as far as possible so everyone could see, he said, "People out there are dying, and you're concerned about votes?"

"That's right. I'm concerned about politics because it's as much a part of reality as the violence in the streets. And just one more thing," Paulson said, pointing his finger toward White. "Once we make this decision, whether it be bullets or promises, we all back it publicly! You got that?"

White shook his head and mumbled a few words. Puccini sat watching White stare out the window. Reflected on the windows across the street, he could see flashing lights. The voices of those in the room grew fainter as he concentrated on the colors, red and yellow. He felt hot again.

Inside Puccini could hear the sound of furniture being shoved about. It reminded him of the sound garbage men make when tossing metal cans. Inside his chest he could feel his heart pounding away like a mad drummer. It was unbelievably loud, so loud he could hardly hear himself think. He felt faint, nauseated. Why did it have to be so damn hot, he wondered. Momentarily he felt paralyzed, unable to move to perform his duty. Swallowing hard, he tried to calm himself. He had to make his move now; the time was right. He glanced to the left. There were two doors. One was a flimsy screen constructed from cheap material. The other was a sturdy, solid, wood door with a triangular glass inlay. The screen was closed. The wood door stood slightly ajar. It was lighter outside than inside, so he couldn't see in. That meant the suspect would have the edge. Granted, it was a small edge, but in situations like this one even the slightest advantage could mean the difference between life and death. His hands were so wet he could barely keep the shotgun from slipping loose. Puccini's mind raced, searching for a way to counter the suspect's advantage. Speed, thought Puccini. Yes, with speed he could even the odds. Quickly he made his plans. With the handle of the screen opposite him, he'd be able to use the door as a pivotal point, first opening it and then swinging around it into the store with the full force of his weight. In his mind he could visualize it, just like when he was a kid running full speed one way, catching a lamppost with one arm and then spinning himself back in the opposite direction. Only this time he wasn't a kid, and it wasn't a game. He closed his eyes briefly. He wanted to swallow, but his throat was too dry. Slowly he moved his hand across the face of the screen to the handle. Running through his mind were the words of his instructor at the academy: quick movements attract attention; slow movements conceal. Closer and closer his hand moved to the handle until finally his fingertips touched it. He stopped. Then turning his hand palm up, he carefully slid his fingers beneath the metal loop—he had it. He was safe, undetected. Inside, the noise continued. With the barrel of the shotgun pointed up, the butt resting on his hip, he made his final check. Sliding his fingers alongside the trigger guard, he found the safety latch. It was off. He was ready to go. The muscles in his body tightened; then in one quick, continuous motion he sprang to the top of the porch while pulling open the screen. It was then, at that very instant, that the door moaned as the hinges pulled away from the casing. A fear like none that he had ever experienced permeated his body, for instead of moving forward he felt a sensation of falling. Instinctively, he reached back for the wooden railing, attempting to recapture his balance. It was useless. Moving too fast, he missed, thus slamming the entire force of his body into the rotting structure. He tumbled, head over heels, off the porch and into the alley below. His body landed with a heavy thud on the rough pavement. At that very moment a violent explosion shattered the night. Puccini's eyes widened in disbelief, but the pain shooting up from his mangled foot left little room for hope—he had shot himself. The shotgun lay just a short distance away; but before he could reach it, the back door swung open wide, and what appeared to be a young man carrying a cloth bag stepped hurriedly out onto the porch. For a moment the man stood searching the street, desperately trying to find his escape. It was then that he saw Puccini lying in the street on his back. The man panicked. Dropping his bag, he leaped down the stairs, tripping over the last step and rolling into a stack of garbage cans lined against the wall. Puccini rolled over onto his side and drew his service revolver while shouting, "FREEZE—POLICE!" The man stumbled to his feet in wild, jerking movements and started down the alley. Blocking his way was a tall chain-link fence. Puccini fired one warning shot high, screaming again for the man to halt. The man flung himself at the fence catching about half the distance to be scaled. Again Puccini yelled. Still the man climbed. Lowering the gun until the man's mid-back was in his sights, Puccini shouted his last warning. In another instant the man would be up and over the fence. He could feel the revolver heavy in his hand. His finger moved to the trigger....

"What?" Puccini said, as he jerked his head up to look at the mayor.

"I said, are you all right?"

"Oh...yeah...sure," he stammered. "Why do you ask?"

"Why! Because you're sweating so much. You must be soaked with perspiration."

"It's nothing," Puccini said, wiping his forehead with the back of his hand. "Just a little fever. Really."

"All right then. What do you think?"

"About what, sir?"

"About Superintendent O'Leary's suggestion."

Name _____

Read each statement before coming to class. To the left check whether you agree or disagree with this statement. After discussing the statement with your group in class, record the total number of members agreeing and disagreeing in the boxes to the right and explain your position in a few sentences below.

A D   A D
☐ ☐   1. Violence is a legitimate form of political action. After all, didn't our Founders use it   ☐ ☐
          against the British to gain their freedom.

☐ ☐   2. The attitudes of bleeding hearts like Martin White actually encourage civil   ☐ ☐
          disobedience.

☐ ☐   3. If minorities had waited peacefully for the government to end discrimination,   ☐ ☐
          they'd still be riding on the back of the bus.

☐ ☐   4. In most riot situations, police abuse their authority.   ☐ ☐

☐ ☐   5. People have no respect for the law today.   ☐ ☐

Name _____

☐☐   6. For some groups in our society violence is the only way to get the government to   ☐☐
listen.

☐☐   7. The trouble with minorities is that they don't realize you can't change everything   ☐☐
overnight.

☐☐   8. Politicians don't care about people; they only care about votes. Otherwise, they   ☐☐
would have cleaned up the ghetto decades ago.

☐☐   9. Giving in to the demands of the rioters would only encourage future violence.   ☐☐

☐☐   10. Allen Paulson is right. Even though Martin White may not agree with the mayor's   ☐☐
final decision, he has an obligation to back it publicly.

Name _____

If you were Tony Puccini, would you shoot the suspect in the alley? Why?

_____

_____

_____

_____

_____

_____

_____

_____

_____

_____

_____

_____

_____

_____

_____

_____

_____

_____

_____

_____

_____

_____

_____

Name _____

If you were Tony Puccini, would you advise the mayor to issue a "shoot-to-kill" order? Why?

_____

_____

_____

_____

_____

_____

_____

_____

_____

_____

_____

_____

_____

_____

_____

_____

_____

_____

_____

_____

_____

_____

_____

Hollowed Victories

A long, sleek limousine sandwiched between two late-model black sedans rolled to a stop in front of Tilden Penitentiary. The doors to the sedans opened, and a dozen men dressed in dark suits and sunglasses poured out onto the street to surround the limousine. An irregular bulge beneath the armpit of each was conspicuously noticeable. A moment later, Janet Watkins, a senior federal agent attached to the Department of Drug and Alcohol's War on Drugs, emerged from the lead car. The woman moved quickly over to the limousine and communicated a number of commands. Immediately, two of the agents raced up the steps to the large iron gates of the penitentiary and disappeared within. Others positioned themselves at various points around the grounds of the complex. Watkins, along with several other agents, remained behind to secure the limousine. Moments later, reports began to filter in from the others by means of a special communication system commanded by the senior agent. Carefully she surveyed the horizon one final time and, then satisfied, she reached for the door of the limousine and opened it slowly while visually maintaining her search for anything that might appear out of the ordinary.

From the end of cellblock B, the man could hear the crescendo of clatter sweeping toward him like a rising ocean wave making its way to the beach. Such a reception was reserved for special guests, and the inmates up and down the hall hovered up against their cell doors poking hand mirrors through the bars in an attempt to steal a quick glance at the approaching visitor. Darrin Waverly lie on his bunk. He already knew who the visitor was and why he had come. Taking a small package of paper from his shirt pocket, he separated a thin leaf and laid it on his chest in front of him so that his hands were free to search for the pouch in his prison trousers. Scooting back up against the wall, he carefully sprinkled a generous portion of tobacco onto the paper and then rolled it into a cigarette. When he looked up, he saw the warden and one of the prison guards standing in front of his cell. "Why, Warden Duffy. What brings you and Officer Friendly down here to the neighborhood?" he said curtly as he lit the cigarette.

"I understand that Officer Maak and you are having your troubles today," replied the warden.

"Officer Maak and I having trouble?" he responded with a puzzled expression. "No, I don't think so. I mean, we did have a conversation, but I thought it went quite well. Didn't you, Officer Maak?"

"Cut the crap, Waverly," replied the warden sternly. "You have a visitor."

Waverly sucked hard on the cigarette and watched as the red glow raced up toward his mouth. He held the smoke in his lungs as he flicked the spent butt into the open toilet. Looking back up at the warden, he opened his mouth, and his face disappeared into a cloud of heavy smoke. "Well, that's the problem," he finally said. "As I was telling Officer Maak here earlier, it's a damn shame, but my calendar for today is already filled up. Now, I'll be real honest with you. If that visitor was wearing a short skirt and tight blouse, I might be inclined to rearrange my time, but that's not the case, is it Warden?"

"You don't have a choice here, Waverly. You're going to see this visitor."

"Now that's a real problem," he sighed. "I mean, true enough, I am a prisoner, but I do have some rights of privacy, and the court isn't going to take kindly to those rights being abused. Isn't that what this place is all about, ya know, all that legal stuff about breaking the law?"

The warden stared intensely at the man, his eyes narrowing in anger. The thick swollen lips about his mouth slowly thinned as the muscles about his jaw coiled into a mass of hostility. Waverly watched in amusement, elated by the fact that he had elevated Duffy's blood pressure to a death threatening height. Suddenly Duffy's face relaxed. A coy smile exuded an air of confidence. It was as if Duffy knew he now held the high ground. Waverly sat up alert in his bed, anticipating a new play.

"Yeah," moaned Duffy. "You certainly know your legal rights." He paused while nodding his head. "I respect that in a man. Don't you, Office Maak?" he asked, turning to the guard who was even more confused by the sudden shift of Duffy's mood than Waverly. "Oh, by the way," he commented to the guard in an afterthought tone. "Have you informed Mr. Waverly of his change of residence?"

"Change of residence?" stumbled Maak.

"Why, yes," he replied, trying to induce cooperation. "You know, we talked about it yesterday."

"Oh, that," Maak finally replied playing along. "I didn't get around to it."

"Oh, well, I suppose Mr. Waverly will find out soon enough."

Waverly leaped out of the bed. "What change? Am I being transferred to another prison?"

"No. Just another cell," explained the warden, "gotta make room for all the other pushers coming in here."

Waverly was clinging to the bars of the cell. "Wait," he called after Duffy and Maak who by this time had turned and were making their way down the corridor. "Who's gonna be my cell mate?"

Duffy stopped. Turning, he reached into his vest pocket and withdrew a sheet of paper. He studied it for a moment as he ran his finger down the list. "Yeah, here it is. Inmate Duboris. Know him?" he asked Maak.

Maak's face screwed up into a contorted wince. "Whew," he replied in a heavy sigh. "Bad break, Waverly."

"Wait, wait," screamed Waverly. "You can't do this to me. Duboris is an animal. He's an insane lunatic. He strangled his brother-in-law in his sleep."

"Yeah, I know," answered Duffy, "but the counselors say he's made remarkable progress. Of course, there was the incident in the yard last week but still I...."

"Okay, Okay," capitulated Waverly. "I'll meet with him. But only if I stay here in this cell alone."

"That doesn't seem so unreasonable to me. Does it to you, Officer Maak?" Duffy commented smiling. "After all, cooperation does merit some consideration."

Waverly was handcuffed and then led through a series of checkpoints and down the corridors away from the visitation center. "Going first class, huh? Must be an important visitor," commented Waverly to Duffy who was leading the way. Duffy ignored the remark, realizing that the inmate already knew who was waiting for him at the other end. He was always amazed at the inmates' network. Often, they knew things before he found out. "Didn't think that I knew anyone that important," continued the chatter from Waverly.

Duffy stopped and turned back so abruptly that Waverly literally bumped into him. "Now listen," he said sternly to the prisoner. "Cut the crap, right now. You develop an attitude problem in there and you bunk with Duboris tonight, hear?"

"Me, an attitude problem?" taunted Waverly. "Cooperation is my religion."

"Yeah?" replied Duffy. "Then just make sure you don't have a sudden conversion while you're in there."

Duffy opened the door to his office, and the guard behind Waverly nudged him into the room. Waverly shot an angry look back at the man. Waverly stood looking around. Smiling, he replied, "Ya know, Warden, your place is a lot bigger than mine. Better decorated, too. Think we could trade?" No sooner had he made the comment than he was pushed into one of the chairs facing the warden's desk.

Duffy walked over to Waverly. "Listen," he said with his face less than an inch away from the prisoner's. "In a moment, Treavor Ashcroft is going to walk through that door," he said pointing. "When he does, you're going to laps into one of your religious trances, got it?" Before Waverly could respond, the door opened, and Ashcroft and three of his agents walked into the room. He quickly found Waverly in the chair.

"Why is this man handcuffed?" asked Ashcroft.

"It's prison policy to cuff inmates outside secured areas," intervened Duffy quickly.

"I think we can make an exception this time," responded Ashcroft.

Duffy was about to object but relented under the harsh glare of his superior.

Waverly smiled broadly at Duffy as the handcuffs were removed. Ashcroft was first to speak. "Do you know who I am, Mr. Waverly?"

"Top Narc," he replied without blinking.

"Waverly, I...," erupted Duffy only to be interrupted by Ashcroft.

"Right," smiled Ashcroft amused by the expression. "Well," he said, "I thought it was time that the Top Narc, as you put it, meets the Top Pusher."

Waverly laughed. "If you think that, you must be snorting the stuff yourself."

Ashcroft laughed himself. "All right, let's not bullshit each other. I'll concede that you may not be number one, but you're weighing in pretty heavy."

"I made a living."

"A pretty nice one, I'd say. In fact, we just tracked down a couple of your bank accounts in Nassau, about two million dollars they tell me. Can't wait to get my hands on that money."

"Damn," moaned Waverly.

"And then there's your yacht. You know, the one you registered in your cousin's name. A real beauty! My brother-in-law is planning to put a bid on it when it goes to auction."

Again Waverly moaned in obscenities.

Ashcroft moved in closer to Waverly. "But that's not what we really want, not your money."

"No?"

"No," echoed Ashcroft. "We want to stop the flow of narcotics in this country. To do that, we need your help. We need names and supply routes. You have that information, Mr. Waverly. You could help us."

"Why should I?"

Ashcroft's expression turned suddenly pensive. It was an expression that took Waverly by surprise. "Because it's the right thing to do."

"The right thing?" questioned Waverly, his head nodding in disbelief as he repeated the words slowly back to Ashcroft.

"Yes," counseled Ashcroft, coaxing the inmate along. "Sure, greed got the best of you. But you're not all bad. A lot of people are hurting because of this drug thing. And then there's the future of the country; the drug trade is killing America."

With that Waverly burst into laughter. Ashcroft sat patiently by until Waverly regained control of himself.

"Does my sense of patriotism offend you?" he asked the inmate.

"No, no," he replied, wiping his eyes in open defiance. "Someone's gotta shine the Cadillac. It just might as well be you."

"I don't believe that you're that callous."

"And I don't believe you're that stupid!" replied Waverly harshly.

No sooner had the last word slid off his tongue than he felt a sharp blow to the back of his head. Recoiling in his chair, he threw his arms about his head in anticipation of another blow. It didn't come. Ashcroft leaped out of his chair screaming. "I will have none of this," he demanded. "The next man to lay a hand on this inmate will have to answer to me personally, is that understood?" With that the guards backed away, and Ashcroft attempted to resume his questioning. "Now, where were we, Mr. Waverly?"

"You were fertilizing the warden's carpet with some bullshit about America being a great country."

"Obviously you take exception to patriotism. Is that right?"

"You politicians are all alike," moaned Waverly. "You've been talkin' that shit so long, you actually believe it!"

"You don't?"

"Hell no!"

"Really," replied Ashcroft, thumping the end of a pencil in the palm of his hand. "Okay," he finally said, "let's have it. Why not?"

"Why?" cried Waverly. "Are you blind, too? Just look at the junkies and pushers doing the time."

"Meaning?"

"I mean, they're black, brown and dirt poor!"

"They have also broken the law or they wouldn't be here," Ashcroft replied in a demur tone.

"Sure, but so have a lot of your basic white middle and upper class American types too. And don't tell me I don't know what I'm talkin' about. I sold the drugs, and my clients weren't the poor. They were the dudes with the fat wallets. I didn't get rich off the poor. So where are your neighbors?"

"Maybe they were lucky enough not to get caught."

"Bullshit!" shot back Waverly. "The cops target the ghetto, not the suburbs. The street kids get hassled, not the fraternities and sororities. The street kids end up in here. And if some poor sucker from the suburbs did get caught, he'd always buy his way out by paying a fine and running off to a rehab center. So the long and the short of it pal is that you've got a war going on but it's not against drugs as much as it is against the people in the streets. So don't expect my help, got that!"

"That's it," interrupted Duffy, looking at Waverly. "You just bought yourself a new roommate!"

Waverly laughed. His eyes were fixed not on Duffy but Ashcroft. "No, I don't think so. I want to talk with Mr. Top Narc alone. I've got information he needs to hear."

"You've got nothing," quipped Duffy. "It's moving day for you."

"Wait," interrupted Ashcroft whose attention had been caught by Waverly's air of confidence. "I'm here. I just might as well hear what he has to say. Leave us."

"But sir, you...," pleaded Duffy.

"Not to worry, Warden. You'll be right outside. What can happen?"

Realizing Ashcroft was not to be deterred, Duffy signaled for his men to leave. The federal agents followed suit, leaving the two men alone. Standing twenty feet from the door, the group of officials waited.

A few moments past before the silence was shattered by the strained voice of Ashcroft. Duffy was first to move, but, before he reached the door, it opened with Ashcroft racing out. He pushed Duffy up against the wall with such force that the warden's head banged against the hard plaster. Ashcroft was within inches of Duffy's face. "Waverly is to be taken back to his cell. He is not to be moved nor is anyone else to be placed in his cell. Do you understand, Warden?"

"Yes, sir," stammered Duffy obviously shaken.

Ashcroft turned and raced down the corridor leading to the front of the prison. His agents followed in hurried steps. Outside, Ashcroft motioned to Watkins. She moved closer. Ashcroft pulled her even closer. Looking around so as to be sure no one would be able to overhear their conversation, he spoke, "We've known each other a long time. Do you trust me?"

"Completely," the woman replied.

"Do I have your absolute confidence?"

The woman nodded.

"Then, I am going to give you a special assignment. Do not use any agents or contacts known to the department. Report only to me. Understand?"

Again the woman nodded.

Ashcroft removed a pad and pen from his vest pocket and scribble two names on it. He placed the paper in the woman's hand and held it there as he spoke, "I need all the information you can find. I need it immediately."

"It's done," replied Agent Watkins. "You can trust me, Sir."

"Good," he murmured, his lower lip trembling.

Once again, Waverly sat in the warden's office. It was exactly one week from his first visit. Outside the door, he could hear voices. They were soft, deliberately muffled so as to avoid attention. He waited patiently. He knew who his visitor was and why he had come. Hearing the handle of the door turn, he looked up to see Ashcroft enter. He moved slowly as he walked past Waverly to the window where he stood gazing out onto the courtyard below. His expression was haggard; the man looked utterly exhausted.

"Tough week?" opened Waverly.

Ashcroft turned. His eyes were ablaze with anger. "You son-of-a-bitch!" he cursed.

"Hey, don't blame me. I can't help it if your kid's a junkie."

"He's not a junkie!"

"Oh, excuse me," retorted Waverly. "For a moment I forgot. It's only street kids, ya know, gutter scum, that are junkies. Nice kids from neighborhoods like yours aren't junkies; they're substance abusers."

Ashcroft stood staring back at the man without comment. There was an element of truth in his words and, after all that had happened in the last week, he was beginning to realize it. Ashcroft fell into one of the chairs. "How did you know?" he asked.

"That your kid's a user?"

"Yeah."

"Hey, the joint is full of pushers. One of mine just happened to be your kid's source."

"Why didn't you use the information—to bargain with?"

Waverly laughed. "Man, you are naive. The information is too dangerous, ya know, all those nice, respectable people who are using or getting rich off of other people's habits. Think they'd let their names go public? I'd have been dead in a week."

"C'mom, who do you think you're dealing with. I don't put contracts out on people's lives."

Again Waverly laughed. "No, it wouldn't have been you. The system keeps people around for jobs like that. That someone would have paid another someone in the joint to do me. Anyway ya cut it, I'd be checking outta this place via the morgue exit."

"Then why now?"

"Duffy," answered Waverly. "He would have done it. He would have put me in the cell with that psycho Duboris, and the minute I would have closed my eyes, he would have ripped my throat out."

"It doesn't work like that."

"The hell it doesn't," shot back Waverly. "You know how many inmates die in prisons each year? Check it out for yourself and then come back and tell me it doesn't happen that way." The two men were silent for a moment. "So what did you do with the kid?" asked Waverly.

"I sent him to Havenhill Rehabilitation Center. It's the best."

Waverly nodded.

Ashcroft's mood turned even more intense. "Listen, Waverly," he pleaded, "you could help end this nightmare for us all."

"How?"

"Names and supply routes. We could bust the trade. I could protect you."

"Man," moaned Waverly disgustingly. "Haven't you learned anything? Have you talked to your kid?"

"Sure, but what's that got to do with it?"

"Everything," replied Waverly. "If you weren't so blinded by that damn Cadillac you've been shining all these years, you could see the answer."

Ashcroft looked puzzled.

"Okay," agreed Waverly finally. "I'll help. I'll give you what you need. But you're not going to like the answer."

"I don't care who we have to go after. No one is going to get off the hook just...."

"Wait," interrupted Waverly. "I'm not giving you any names."

"No?"

"Absolutely not. You can't end the drug problem in America by locking up pushers and users."

"I don't understand," admitted Ashcroft. "How are we going to end it?"

"By legalizing it—all of it."

"WHAT!" screamed Ashcroft. "Are you crazy?"

"No," defended Waverly. "I'm serious. It's the only way. Listen," he pleaded, "you'll never stop the flow of narcotics into this country. It's too big, and there's too much money to be made and too many cops and customs people willing to turn their heads for a buck. And, as far as pushers go, you'll never get rid of them. Every time you lock someone like me up, there's another guy out there laughing his ass off because it means he gets my territory. You can't stop it. There's too much money to be made. And who pays the price?—the public. Half of all crimes in this country are drug related. Someone's trying to get the money to support a habit. When I read in the paper that you guys just scored a big drug bust, I know what is going to happen—the price of the stuff is going to go sky high and that means more robberies, more assaults or more kids going hungry because mom's gotta dip into the grocery money."

"But people will still want drugs even if you legalize them."

"Sure," replied Waverly. "That's where the government would come in. They'd produce the stuff and give it away."

"Oh, God," moaned Ashcroft, "you can't be serious?"

"Of course. It costs next to nothing to produce the stuff. If the government gave it away free then who in his right mind would take the risk of mugging someone to buy it? That's the beauty of it. If there's no money in it, then there won't be the pushers walking the streets trying to hook people on their stuff just to make money."

Ashcroft was going through contortions with his face. "I don't know. I just don't know," he groaned.

"It's the only way. Think about the billions that you currently spend trying to stop the stuff. It hasn't worked. Take that money and put it into education and rehabilitation programs. You could put five drug counselors in every school in this country with the money you'd save. Drug abuse is a medical problem, not a legal problem."

"But the government giving drugs to its own people."

"C'mom, Ashcroft," taunted Waverly, "I see you shining that Cadillac again. Look," he said more seriously, "the government is already in the narcotics business. They subsidize tobacco, don't they?"

"Yes," admitted the man.

"And alcohol?"

"Not directly but there are tax deductions."

"Exactly!" cried Waverly. "Now think about it. How many people die from cigarettes and alcohol each year?"

Ashcroft shrugged.

"You know the figures as well as I do—over 300,000 a year from tobacco and over 100,000 from alcohol. All of the illegal drugs that you're trying to control, heron, coke, speed and all the others combined, killed less than 5,000 last year. That makes my drugs less dangerous than yours, right?"

Ashcroft was rubbing his forehead intently. "This whole conversation is pointless. Even if I agreed with you, it wouldn't make any difference. I'm just one man. I don't make the laws for the country."

"You're not just one man. You head the War on Drugs. People listen to you. The president listens to you. Just think what would happen if the nation's chief drug enforcement officer came out publicly on the side of legalization. You could start the ball rolling, don't you see? You have the power to do this."

"I don't know; I just don't know," moaned Ashcroft. "I'm going to have to think about this and talk with you later."

"No," replied Waverly with a knowing smile. "You're gonna have to carry the ball alone on this one. You won't be seeing me again."

"You won't meet again?"

Waverly laughed softly as he rose from his chair. "You still don't get it. I'm not going to be around in a week, by then I'll be dead."

"I can protect you," gasped Ashcroft.

"No, you can't. My fate is sealed. I suppose that's why I'm trying to help you," he laughed. "All my life I've bought my way out of trouble. I guess that's what I'm trying to do now, buy my way into heaven. Kinda like a payoff, ya know?"

"I can. I can protect you. It doesn't have to go down this way."

"No, you can't. I know about these things. Besides, you're going to have your hands full protecting yourself. A lot of powerful people in this country make millions off the drug business. If you do decide to take my advice and you're even remotely successful, they'll try to kill you."

"They can't touch me. I'm too insulated."

Waverly laughed. "No, you're not. They already have people inside your organization. It'll come from within."

"You're lying to me, Waverly. This whole spiel of yours has been nothing but a lie!"

"You think so. Then understand this. One week after you were nominated for your position, I sat in a room with twenty very powerful people—not your kind of people, if you get my drift," he added. "The discussion was who and how to place someone inside your organization." Waverly paused before continuing. "That person is in place."

"Who?" asked Ashcroft in a hushed nervous voice.

"Janet Watkins. She's connected."

"Liar!" screamed Ashcroft, grabbing Waverly by his prison shirt.

"It's true," stated Waverly as he removed Ashcroft's hands forcefully. "If you show any signs of success, she'll set you up for the hit or pull the trigger herself."

"That's impossible. Janet came to me by way of a confidential recommendation."

Waverly starred into Ashcroft's glare. "I know. It was James Holman. The big house, the car, the boat. All on a government salary? You probably thought he was just a shrewd investor, huh?"

Ashcroft's mouth hung open in disbelief. Waverly placed his hand on the man's shoulder. "It's a damn shame, isn't it?" Turning, he tapped lightly on the door. As it opened, Ashcroft caught sight of Duffy's fleshy face poking through the gap. Strange, he thought, how it now looked so malevolent, so very malevolent....

Name _____

Read each statement before coming to class. To the left check whether you agree or disagree with this statement. After discussing the statement with your group in class, record the total number of members agreeing and disagreeing in the boxes to the right and explain your position in a few sentences below.

A D   A D
☐ ☐   1. Once convicted, all drug pushers should be executed.   ☐ ☐

☐ ☐   2. You can't blame poor kids from joining gangs and selling drugs as long as the   ☐ ☐
           government fails to provide jobs and a decent education.

☐ ☐   3. Legalization will send a message to the kids of this nation that it is OK to use drugs.   ☐ ☐

☐ ☐   4. Waverly is right when he stated that the "war on drugs" is really a war on the   ☐ ☐
           minorities and the poor of this nation.

☐ ☐   5. Alcohol and tobacco should be banned along with all other illegal drugs.   ☐ ☐

Name _____

☐ ☐ 6. If you legalize drugs, you would have to allow minors to use them too. Otherwise, legalization wouldn't work. ☐ ☐

☐ ☐ 7. Jail will never serve as a deterrent to the sale or use of illegal drugs. ☐ ☐

☐ ☐ 8. Even if some people did die from using drugs under a legalization program, it would be better than all the crime and waste of tax dollars trying to control it. ☐ ☐

☐ ☐ 9. Subsidizing tobacco and giving corporate tax advantages to alcohol producers is no different than pushing drugs on the street. ☐ ☐

☐ ☐ 10. The real reason we can't control the drug problem in America is that too many politicians, judges, and cops are on the "take." ☐ ☐

Name _____

If you were Treavor Ashcroft, would you advocate legalization? Why?

_____

_____

_____

_____

_____

_____

_____

_____

_____

_____

_____

_____

_____

_____

_____

_____

_____

_____

_____

_____

_____

_____

_____

_____

_____

Name _____

Suppose that, in light of tobacco's harmful effects, third world countries requested that America stop producing and shipping it to other nations. Would you agree?

_____

_____

_____

_____

_____

_____

_____

_____

_____

_____

_____

_____

_____

_____

_____

_____

_____

_____

_____

_____

_____

_____

_____

_____

A Name by Any Other Name

The small child leaned back in the cushioned chair his feet dangling over the edge. His blue eyes were barely visible over the large walnut desk in front of him. To his left sat a tall thin woman meticulously dressed in a dark blue skirt and white jacket. On his right a short stubby-fingered man fumbled nervously through a stack of papers. Occasionally, when the man and woman conferred in soft whispers, as they often did, the young boy would steal a glance at the elderly couple seated at the table at his left. As the old man and woman caught sight of him, the boy would wave with all five fingers wiggling and, then, turn quickly away in a bashful giggle.

To Tommy, it was a wonderful game he played with the people he so dearly loved. To the others, his mother and his grandparents, today was neither wonderful nor a time for games. For today they were in court, billed as adversaries in a contest whose outcome would prove tragic for one and joyful to the other.

The stage was set, and the issue was well defined. The woman, Tommy's mother, wanted to change the name of her child. The parents of the child's late father were contesting. Supporters and well wishers for both sides crowded into the tiny courtroom. Those who could not find chairs simply stood. Pressed against the wall shoulder to shoulder in 90 degree heat, they waited. A young timid-looking woman dressed in overalls, a T-shirt, and loose-fitting sandals, offered paper fans to the spectators. Each fan bore the inscription: Justice for Sister Denise.

Denise was seated in the witness stand now. Her attorney, Harold Jameson, strolled leisurely toward her. In his hand was a legal folder. "Ms. Bernstein," he began, "you have recently changed your name. Is that correct?"

"Yes," she replied soberly.

"And the name you now possess is the name you obtained as a result of the action you initiated in this court less than a month ago, January 3rd, I believe it was. Is that correct?"

"Yes, this is correct," she repeated.

"Would you please look at this form?" Jameson said, handing her a piece of paper from the folder. "Would the court please note that the document Ms. Bernstein holds is change of name form, number 12974? Can you testify as to the validity of this document?"

"I can."

"Thank you," Jameson said while moving toward the bench. "Your Honor, the defense would like to enter this change of name form as exhibit #1." Withdrawing another document out of the legal folder, Jameson again approached Denise Bernstein. "Ms. Bernstein, would you be so kind as to look at this document? Let the court note that the document Ms. Bernstein now holds is change of name form, number 13997, dated September 5th of this year. Could you identify the document, Ms. Bernstein?"

"Yes, this is the change of name form I submitted on behalf of my son, Tommy. I wish to have his last name changed to Bernstein, the same as mine."

"Now, Ms. Bernstein, could you please tell the court your legal name prior to its change?"

"My name was Denise Jean Bennitti."

"How did you come by this name?"

"Through my marriage to Anthony Lee Bennitti."

"In your own words could you tell the court how you came to the decision to change your name and the name of your child from Bennitti to Bernstein and, in addition, why you feel this change is justifiable?"

For the moment Jameson's work was done. He would stand patiently by supporting Ms. Bernstein in her testimony, but, in the final analysis, it would be her and only her who could convince the court to grant the petition.

In words as clear and deliberate as the strokes an artist puts to canvas, Denise began. She told of her early years with her parents. Being raised in a small town by traditional Jewish parents, she was all too soon made aware of her position in society, that of a woman. It wasn't always that way she recalled. As a young child, she played baseball with her brother, Joey, and his friends, wrestled with the neighborhood bullies, and tramped the creeks and back alleys with the rest of the gang. But on her twelfth birthday it all ended. Her father took her into the house and explained that things must change. It would no longer be possible for her to play in the streets as before. After all, he explained, little Denise was a woman now and had more important things to do with her time. Although the adjustment was difficult at first and she longed to join her friends on the baseball diamond, Denise slowly began to accept her new position in the world. Soon curls and lace replaced pigtails and baseball bats.

After graduation from high school, Denise enrolled in the small private college located in her hometown. At one time she entertained thoughts of attending a large public university downstate; however, after talking with her parents, she elected to remain in Clairmont. It wasn't the money. It was just that her mother thought it would be more convenient. Why leave the comforts of home, she reasoned, when there was a perfectly good college so near-by? It was at Clairmont College that Denise met Tony in her sophomore year. He was tall, athletic, and handsome. Also, for Denise there was something reassuring about Tony. For though he loved to play sports and party, never once did he neglect his course work. If there was work to be done, he worked first and played later. She often remarked that even at nineteen, Tony had the maturity to look down the road and see the importance of finishing school and getting a good start in business.

As for Tony's feelings for Denise, they were equally as attractive. Denise represented everything he ever envisioned in a woman. He loved everything about her: her tenderness, her easiness, and her ability to understand him like no one else in the world. For the next three years of their college life, they were inseparable. In fact, the senior class in their college yearbook bestowed upon them the most amiable title of "couple most likely to succeed."

The only difficulty Denise and Tony encountered was over the issue of religion. Denise was Jewish; Tony was Catholic. But this they overcame with the help and consideration of their parents. Tony once remarked that their religious conflict was more a blessing than a curse because it allowed each the opportunity to appreciate the other's parents more, thus, resolving any future in-law difficulties. In fact, each lovingly referred to the other's parents as "Mom" and "Pop."

After graduation Tony found work in a nearby metropolitan community. Starting out on the lower rung of a huge corporate ladder, he found it necessary to work long and hard hours. At first, Denise paid little attention to the time Tony devoted to his work. The urban community presented many career opportunities for her, too. For the first five years of their marriage, Denise and Tony pursued their own careers, and their life together prospered. Denise enjoyed her work as a fashion designer, and Tony propelled himself into the ranks of mid-level management. Initially, Denise was pleased with Tony's success. It meant more money, and money meant more opportunities. However, as she was soon to discover, success also calls for sacrifices. Within a month after accepting a new management position with his company, Tony was transferred to a branch office in New York. Although the transfer would surely bring new opportunities, it also meant that Denise would be forced to leave her career behind. Tony and Denise discussed their options at length, weighing the alternatives. Denise was reluctant to abandon her career, but any other alternative was equally distasteful. For in order for Denise to remain at her present position, Tony would have to leave his present job and seek work elsewhere. But with the economy in a tailspin, the prospect of finding comparable employment was slim. If he were unable to find work, it would surely mean financial disaster. Another possible solution would be for Tony to travel to New York alone, see Denise on weekends and holidays, and hope that eventually the company transferred him back to the main office. This they rejected. So, in the end it would be Denise who would be forced to leave her work. Although disappointed, Denise decided to make the best out of the move. Denise and Tony wanted children. Therefore, given the situation, it seemed logical to begin now.

In one way the very thought of children excited Denise for in the ultimate sense it would symbolize the total expression of her own womanhood. It was as if all of life's preparation had suddenly focused, giving meaning and purpose to her own existence. And, of course, there was Tony always vigilant throughout her pregnancy. At nights he would return home from work exhausted but never too tired to help Denise in her preparations for delivery. Together they would exercise and practice breathing drills.

All the apprehension and fear Denise and Tony had about the intrusion of another human being into their lives suddenly disappeared with the baby's arrival. Much to the delight of Tony, it was a strong healthy boy. In fact, Denise recalled she could still see Tony hopping around the delivery room, slapping everyone on the back, shouting gleefully over and over, "It's a boy! It's a boy!" It took ten minutes to calm him down. What chaos she remembered. With Tony hopping up and down, the baby crying, the doctor stitching and the nurses trying to quiet Tony, it was a mad house. But then it was a mad house filled with joy. Never would she forget the moment she first gazed into the eyes of her newly born infant or the look on Tony's face when the nurse first handed him their child. He held the baby so lovingly, so carefully. The tenderness of the moment touched her deeply.

For a time everything seemed to be going their way. Tony received another promotion and appeared destined for upper-level management. His salary increased, as did their standard of living. And as for Tommy, no child could have been healthier or more well adjusted. He was truly a joy in their lives. In fact, he was such a joy that Denise and Tony decided to have yet another child. It was then that they learned of the tragic event about to befall them. Unable to conceive a second time, Denise and Tony sought medical help. In the course of a routine examination it was discovered that Tony was ill: cancer. It was terminal; nothing could be done. For a year and a half they struggled with the foreknowledge of Tony's impending death. There were agonizing moments, and there were loving moments. There were frightful moments, and there were insightful moments. There were moments when Tony vowed to fight off death with every ounce of strength left in him, and there were moments when he willfully submitted to the reality of his own demise. But through it all, there were revealing moments, difficult as they were, in which two human beings bare their inner most feelings and thoughts before the final parting.

In spite of Tony's long illness, Denise found the adjustment to her loss a difficult one. One of Denise's friends suggested, to help ease the pain, that she attend the weekly meeting of a local woman's group. Many of the women who belonged to the group had experienced similar losses. Besides, as her friend had said, the purpose of the group was to share experiences and knowledge of the problems facing women in today's society, and this, after all, was one common problem faced by many women—what to do after your husband dies. Although somewhat reluctant to attend at first, she finally relented, and, much to her surprise, she found it nothing like she imagined, a small group of frightened old women that banded together more out of loneliness than anything else. On the contrary, they were bright, talented, self-assured women of all ages from all walks of life with a definitive purpose to their meeting. Through the love and comfort of other women, Denise came to an understanding and acceptance of her own tragic loss.

Denise continued to attend the group's meetings long after her own personal needs had been fulfilled. In a way she felt drawn to the group. Through her interaction with other women, she began to understand her own position in the world, a position filled with prejudice, discrimination, and blocked opportunities. Slowly she came to the realization of how she'd been cheated, denied the same opportunities to develop and pursue her own aspirations that males typically believe their inherent right. In time Denise began not only to attend the groups but also leading them as she assumed a position in the forefront of the women's rights movement.

"It was then that you decided to return to your maiden name?" Denise heard the voice of her attorney interrupt.

"Yes, that is correct," she answered calmly without bitterness. "I felt that it was only right, particularly in light of my beliefs. It's not that I hold any ill feelings for Tony or his family. It's just that now that he's dead, I believe it is my right to name my child and that name happens to be Bernstein. Also, as you know, in my faith it is the mother who carries the birthright of her children. Since I am Jewish, I think it is only proper that Tommy's name reflect this heritage."

"That's all the questions I have for Ms. Bernstein now, your Honor." Judge Hinderson watched Jameson walk confidently back to his desk. Looking toward Desch, the Bennitti's lawyer, he routinely inquired if there were questions to be asked.

Desch rose from his chair and approached the witness. "Ms. Bernstein," he began, "you indicate that you felt cheated in not being able to develop or pursue your own goals, is that correct?"

"Yes, it is correct."

"Do you feel your late husband played a major role in your own victimization?"

"Most definitely. All men victimize women in one way or another, and since Tony was my husband, it was only natural for him to do so in my case."

"In your husband's case do you feel that it was a conscious or an unconscious victimization?"

"Unconscious."

"I see," Desch said, thumping the railing in front of the witness stand with his fingers. "Ms. Bernstein, could you please tell us how you and your late husband arrived at family decisions, you know, those decisions which jointly affected both of you?"

"Well, I suspect we made decisions like most of the couples we knew. We talked about the decision, we considered out alternatives, the pro's and con's of each decision, and then agreed on a course of action."

"In other words, then, you're saying that your husband did not dictate decisions to you or force you in any way to obey decisions you did not agree with, is that correct?"

Jameson who had been patiently enduring Desch's questioning suddenly sprang from his chair. "I object, your Honor. I fail to see the relevancy of this line of questioning. After all, we're here today to determine if Ms. Bernstein has the right to change her son's name, not to explore her relationship with her deceased husband."

Desch was quick to challenge, "Your Honor, I would like to remind the defense that it was he who first brought up the relationship between Ms. Bernstein and her deceased husband, and, as such, we do have the right to continue that line of questioning."

"Objection overruled," Hinderson stated routinely. "The witness will answer the question."

Undisturbed with the quick flurry of tempers, Denise Bernstein's answer was direct and to the point, "No, Tony did not force his decisions upon me. But then he didn't have to; society had already conditioned me to accept any decision he might make. Any other action would have been totally unacceptable. That's why whenever my needs, desires or wants conflicted with his, it was always I who acquiesced."

"But were you unhappy?" questioned Desch.

"No, not at the time, but...."

"Thank you, Ms. Bernstein. Could we move on to a different subject? In comparison to other men you know, how would you rate your late husband as a father?"

"I would say he was probably better than most men I know."

"How would you rate him as a husband, Ms. Bernstein?"

"I would have to rate him average, even though I did love him."

"I'm sorry, Ms. Bernstein, but I must confess that I'm somewhat confused. On the one hand, you say that Tony Bennitti was a good father, but, on the other, you say he was only an average husband. Is there not some discrepancy in your answers?"

"No, I see no discrepancy. He was an excellent father because he loved Tommy, and when he was home, he spent a lot of time with him. However, since he did work long hours, there was little time left for our relationship as husband and wife. He was never willing to reduce the amount of time he spent working so that we would have more time together. I personally felt he could have and should have, but he didn't; therefore, our relationship suffered. So I would have to rate him as a husband, average."

"I see," Desch said as if in thought. Returning to his desk, he retrieved a folder and returned to the witness stand. Thumbing through it without looking up, he asked, "Ms. Bernstein, nowhere in either my notes or in any of the court's records do I find a reference to your present state of employment." Looking up now directly into her eyes, he asked, "Are you currently employed, Ms. Bernstein?"

"No," she answered.

"That strikes me rather odd, Ms. Bernstein. I mean you live in a beautiful house in an exclusive neighborhood, you drive a late model car, you've taken several nice vacations in the last two years, you buy expensive clothing, and yet you don't work. How is that possible, Ms. Bernstein?"

Denise's eyes tightened as she glared at the attorney. Not only did she consider the question irrelevant to her right to change the name of her child but also a violation of her right to privacy. Immediately Jameson objected attempting to block Desch's intrusion. Charges and counter charges were launched by both attorneys in either support or rejection of the line of questioning. Judge Hinderson considered their argument and again ruled in Desch's favor. After all, he reasoned, civil cases allow greater latitude in questioning, and Jameson would have his chance with Desch's witnesses later.

"Let me repeat the question, Ms. Bernstein. How is it that you are able to support yourself without employment?"

"I support myself through the money I receive from a trust fund established by my husband prior to his death."

"And Tommy?" questioned Desch.

"Each month a certain portion of the trust's money is set aside for Tommy. Some of it will be used for his education. The rest he'll receive when he turns twenty-five."

"Considering your lifestyle, the trust must be generous," commented Desch.

In a defiant tone Denise Bernstein added, "Tony always had an unusual talent for planning. That's the...."

"Thank you, Ms. Bernstein," interrupted Desch again. "That will be all." Desch turned and started for his desk. Suddenly, as in afterthought, he stopped. Turning back in the direction of the witness, he said, "Oh, by the way, Ms. Bernstein, I almost forgot to ask. When was the last time you attended synagogue?"

"I don't remember," she answered.

"Have you attended since Tommy's birth?"

"No."

"Thank you, Ms. Bernstein. That will be all." Desch returned to his desk, leaving Ms. Bernstein a little bewildered and greatly enraged.

Others would testify in behalf of her good character and sound judgment. Desch would pay little attention to their testimony, failing to cross-examine even one witness. To him the essence of the case was not whether Denise Bernstein was a good person or even a capable person but, rather, if she possessed the right to change the name of the child in question. On that point he was confident with his case.

In defense of the plaintiff's case Desch called but one witness, Mr. Anthony Bennitti, Sr., whose testimony touched the hearts of all who fell victim to his words. For though the words spoke of death, life sprang from each and every utterance. Gingerly, almost reluctantly at times, he surrendered to the court the precious recollections of a grieved father for his dead son. To the surprise of many, the testimony of Ms. Bernstein and Anthony Bennitti, Sr. differed little. Both saw Tony Bennitti as a responsible, hard working, and a caring man who loved his wife and child. Their difference was a matter of perspective.

His most vivid memory was the day of Tony's and Denise's first visit to their house after Tommy's birth.

"I can still see him walking up the sidewalk carrying his son into my house," he recalled. "He was so careful. I'd swear he thought that if he squeezed too hard the kid would shatter like glass into a million pieces. Why all day long, the only thing you could get him to talk about was Tommy. It was as if nothing else mattered." The old man paused for a moment. A tear slipped from his eye. "In a way it reminded me of how I felt when...I...er... when I...." Choking on the words, he was unable to finish. Wiping his eyes, now red and swollen, he apologized, "Please forgive me. As you can tell, I'm just a foolish old man who can't let go of the past. Now, as I was saying, he was proud, so proud of his new baby boy. That's why me and Mildred are contesting this change. Tony wouldn't have wanted it this way. I just know he wouldn't have."

"How do you know that to be true, Mr. Bennitti?" Desch asked.

"Because he as much as told me so."

"When was that, Mr. Bennitti? Do you recall the exact occasion?"

"Yes, I do. It was the same day Denise and Tony first brought Tommy over to the house. Mildred planned a big dinner for everyone to see the baby. Well, right in the middle of dinner Tony stands up and taps his glass, you know, to get everyone's attention. That's when he said it. I'll never forget those words."

"What were they, Mr. Bennitti?" asked Desch.

The old man raised his hand as if toasting and said, "Here's to Thomas William Bennitti. May he carry the name in honor."

"And you took that as an indication he wanted his child to bear his name?" questioned Desch again seeking clarification.

"Oh, most definitely. You see it was very important because Tony was the last male in our family. So when Tommy was born, it meant that the Bennitti name would be continued."

"Is that the only time your son spoke of this matter?" inquired Desch.

"Oh, no. He spoke of it often, mostly in jokes about how he had fulfilled his obligation."

"When was the last time your son mentioned his feelings about Tommy's name, Mr. Bennitti?"

The old man closed his eyes momentarily and swallowed hard in an attempt to summon up all his strength for the task that lay ahead. He began in a weak unsteady voice that barely traveled the length of the courtroom. "The last time Tony mentioned it was about two weeks before his death. I can still remember it because it was just before he went to the hospital for the last time. The weather was nice. It was clear and warm. Tony was feeling pretty good so we decided we'd walk across the street to the park. We were sitting on one of the park benches just talking and watching the children when he reached over and touched my arm and said, 'Thanks, Pop. In spite of the fact that it has to end like this, I just want to say thanks to you and Mom.' I tell you I couldn't stand anymore. I reached over and grabbed him and held on for as long as I could. Man, we must have been some sight," the old man said, wiping his eyes again, "sitting there on that bench hugging and kissing each other. I think that's the first time I kissed my boy in 20 years. Well, anyway, we talked a lot that day, and his feelings about Tommy were very clear. He said that with Tommy it was like he was leaving something behind, that in a way it would be like he was still here." The old man stopped and looked at Denise Bernstein. "That's why we don't want Tommy's name changed. We don't care about the religion. It doesn't matter where he goes to church or even if he goes to church. It's the name, don't you see?"

Mr. Bennitti's testimony was so moving that Judge Hinderson recessed court early for lunch. Promptly at 1:00 p. m. the gavel struck thus allowing Mr. Jameson his first opportunity to cross-examine.

"Mr. Bennitti," he said, "let me offer my condolences to you and your wife for your loss. I personally lost my oldest child in Viet Nam so I am familiar with the pain you must have experienced. However, there are a few questions I must ask you."

"Certainly, I understand," answered the old man.

"Could you tell the court your opinion of WE."

"WE?"

"Yes, WE," repeated Jameson. "Women for Equality, it's one of the women's groups that your daughter-in-law belongs to."

"Oh, that," responded the old man. "Is that what they call it? Well, I may be a bit old-fashioned, but I don't have much to do with that sort of thing."

"That we realize, Mr. Bennitti, but how do you honestly feel about Denise's membership in this organization?"

"Personally, I think it's kind of foolish."

"Foolish," exclaimed Jameson. "Don't you believe in equality?"

"Sure, but not the way I hear some of these women talk nowadays. I mean, you can't be totally equal. After all, God still makes men and women different, doesn't he?" A blushed smile crossed the old man's lips as the courtroom broke into laughter. Even Jameson broke his composure, laughing slightly. Regaining his concentration, he asked, "Mr. Bennitti, you are a member of the Clairmont school board. Is that correct?"

"Yes, I am. I have been a member for the better part of two decades," announced the old man proudly.

"Within the last 10 years three major drives have been launched in your community by various women's groups to allow capable female students the right to participate in sports presently dominated by males. I'm talking about sports such as swimming, basketball, baseball and tennis. How did you vote, Mr. Bennitti?"

"I voted no."

"On all three occasions?"

"Yes, I voted no on all three of the petitions," responded the old man. "It is my belief that women should be allowed to compete in sports but not with men. Therefore, I have supported a dual system of athletic competition in Clairmont, one for the boys and one for the girls. It's the best way, believe me."

"Tell me, Mr. Bennitti. Do you recall how much money the Clairmont school system spent on its dual athletic system while you were in office?"

"I'm not sure. I suppose I could figure it up if I had time to go back through the records."

"Well, then, perhaps you'd be able to tell us roughly what percentage of money was spent on women's athletics?"

"I'm not sure about that either without checking the records."

"Well, let's see," Jameson said while circling the witness stand. "Was it approximately the same?"

"The same?"

"Yes, the same. Did you spend as much on women's athletics as you did the men's?"

"No."

"Was it half as much?"

"No, I don't think so."

"How about a fourth? Would say a fourth be a realistic figure?"

"Yes, I'd say about 25 percent would be about right."

"Wouldn't you say that the allocation of athletic funds was a bit lopsided, Mr. Bennitti?" asked Jameson.

"Perhaps so, but then it has improved. I can remember when the girls didn't get one dime."

Jameson smiled. "Yes, I suspect times are changing, and Clairmont is in the forefront of the movement, right?"

"Well, I don't know about the front, but I...."

"Mr. Bennitti," interrupted Jameson, "correct me if I'm wrong, but you had two children, didn't you, a boy and a girl?"

"Yes, that's correct."

"Now you named your son after yourself. Is that also correct?"

"Yes, Tony was named after me."

"Could you please tell us the name of your daughter?"

"My daughter's name is Susan Jean. She's here with us today, right over there," he said, pointing to a young woman seated behind his wife.

Jameson looked at the woman and then turned back to the old man. "What is the name of your wife, Mr. Bennitti?"

"Mildred. Her name is Mildred Ann."

"That's odd," muttered Jameson as if contemplating the situation. "You named your son, Anthony William Bennitti, after yourself. Your daughter you named Susan Jean Bennitti. Doesn't that strike you a bit odd, Mr. Bennitti?"

The old man looked puzzled as he tried to follow Jameson's line of questioning. Finally he confessed, "I really don't think I understand."

Jameson was moving back to his table when he turned back to the old man and said, "Yes, we know, Mr. Bennitti, but then that's why we're here, isn't it?"

Name _____

Read each statement before coming to class. To the left check whether you agree or disagree with this statement. After discussing the statement with your group in class, record the total number of members agreeing and disagreeing in the boxes to the right and explain your position in a few sentences below.

A D   **A D**

☐ ☐   1. People like Mr. Bennitti Sr. are chauvinistic pigs but don't know it.   ☐ ☐

☐ ☐   2. Denise is living off Tony's trust; therefore, she owes it to him not change Tommy's name.   ☐ ☐

☐ ☐   3. All men victimize women.   ☐ ☐

☐ ☐   4. If a woman really loved a man, she wouldn't ask him to give up his name.   ☐ ☐

☐ ☐   5. Most men are too insecure to consider using their wife's name in marriage.   ☐ ☐

Name _____

☐☐   6. Allowing women to use their name in marriage would greatly reduce sex   ☐☐
discrimination our society.

☐☐   7. Most politicians and judges are too bias to fairly rule on issues of gender   ☐☐
discrimination.

☐☐   8. In this society it is easier and more acceptable to discriminate on gender than race.   ☐☐

☐☐   9. The trouble with women in this society is that they want all the rights and none of   ☐☐
the responsibilities.

☐☐   10. Women are not as upset about equality as the media makes them out to be.   ☐☐
Otherwise, they would have used their voting power to change the laws and
conditions of society.

Name _____

If you were the judge in this case, what would your decision be and why?

_____

_____

_____

_____

_____

_____

_____

_____

_____

_____

_____

_____

_____

_____

_____

_____

_____

_____

_____

_____

_____

_____

_____

The Prickly, Stickily Case
of
Little Billy Cowan

Justice Marie Vasquez-Rodquiez moved slowly about her office as she surveyed its rich and spacious surroundings. Her mood was introspective, almost brooding. Contemplating the weighty decision before her, she wondered about those who had occupied this office and the agony they had endured within the confines of its walls as they reached out for inspiration in cases that would impact the lives of their fellow citizens for years to come. Yes, she thought, if only walls could talk. Now it was her turn.

Moving over to the large, polished, cherry desk, she slumped into the comfort of the supple leather chair behind it. It was the only thing that seemed to provide some measure of comfort these days. Pushing all other thoughts from her mind, she tried to focus her concentration on the case before her. It would be her first decision, her first vote cast as the Supreme Court's newest member. Ordinarily the first decision by any Court member was viewed with great scrutiny since it would serve as a signpost for future decisions. In her case the decision was of monumental importance since the Court was deadlocked in a four to four split between conservatives and liberals. Not only would her vote shift the balance to one side or the other, but also it was sure to unleash a national political struggle. She laughed contemplating the irony of it all. Who would have imagined years ago that she, Marie Vasquez-Rodquiez, a scrawny Hispanic girl growing up in the poverty of near westside Chicago, would some day find herself at the center of a raging political storm between the congressional and executive branches of our national government. But it was true. In the spring of the year, the president had selected her to replace Justice Brandon Blackwell, the Court's only minority, who had succumbed to a long and dreadful illness. He had fought valiantly, hanging on not only for the sake of life itself but also, understanding the conservative views of the president, to preserve a narrow one vote margin of victory for liberals on the Court. But in the end, Justice Blackwell failed, and it was the president who would finally have his opportunity to make good on his campaign pledge to turn back the rising tide of judicial activism in the Court and restore it to its rightful place in our constitutional government—one that enforced the supreme law of the land and not, as he put it, one that distorted the Constitution for its own political whim. However, with Blackwell's death came a mounting cry from liberals and minorities to preserve the unwritten tradition of having, at least, one minority on the Court. This was particularly galling to the president who had his eye on William Hampton, a federal district court judge and staunch conservative from the South but who, unfortunately, happened to be white. The president lobbied hard for Hampton but in the end, after consulting with several moderate members from his own political party serving on the Senate Judiciary Committee and finding them sensitive to the race issue, as well as reports that the committee's liberal members were prepared to fight to the end on this appointment, he relented and selected Marie Vasquez-Rodquiez, a federal appellate judge from the seventh circuit court.

Rising from her chair, she crossed the room to the window where she stood looking out over a scenic view of the capitol building. Yes, it was no secret why she had been selected. In past rulings she had maintained the center. She was, as one columnist pointed out, a justice hard to categorize. Hence, with her nomination the president, at least, had hope, something lacking in all the other minorities who had been suggested as possible replacements for Blackwell's vacancy. The president was also attracted to the Vasquez-Rodquiez nomination by the fact that in placing a minority woman on the Court he could clear the way for his next two appointments that were sure to come from the approaching retirements of two liberal-minded justices. Justice Vasquez-Rodquiez considered the thought. No doubt, this too was true. And even more alarming was the fact that her decisions would factor into the equation. Should her decisions sway left, the president would have the perfect excuse to incite the rage of conservatives and hammer the moderates of his own party into submission, forcing them to support strict constructionists the next two times around. On the other hand, if her decisions were more balanced or even slightly conservative, it would lend impetus to the moderates and liberals and perhaps maintain a balance in future appointments.

She shook her head in disgust. In providing for life appointments to the federal courts, the architects of our government had hoped to shield the judiciary from political pressure. This would protect the integrity of their decision that, in turn, would protect the Constitution. It was a grand ideal in theory, and though it worked reasonably well in practice, politics still occasionally leaked through the cracks. Only yesterday in the *Washington Post* she had read of how the president had openly stated that he was particularly interested in how Justice Vasquez-Rodquiez would rule in this case. And it was not only the president. Columnists across the nation were speculating on how she might rule. One columnist even went as far as to suggest that her vote might well turn out to be the liberal's "Waterloo."

Returning to her desk, she castigated herself for allowing politics to creep into her thoughts. True, politics were very much present, but now it was time to consider the legal implications of the case. Sitting at her desk, she leafed through the briefs of the state and the defendant. Though steeped in constitutional arguments, she was very much aware there was also a human side to this case not reflected in the briefs. It was a story she was well familiar with. A story as fascinating on its human merits as well as its legal complications. In the stillness of her office she leaned into the soft cushioned back of her chair as images danced in her mind.

Little Billy Cowan stood backside against the wall leading to the school auditorium. With his hands stuck deep in his jeans pockets, he leaned ever so cautiously forward to peer down the seemingly endless line of anxious children waiting to be marshaled through two large, gray, steel doors. Suddenly the door on the right opened, sliding effortlessly and without noise on three huge hinges. A rotund lady in a heavily starched white uniform appeared carrying a clipboard under one arm. A large smile spread across her face as she leaned down to speak with his very best friend, Tommy Martin. He strained to hear the words but couldn't make out the muffled whispers. He tried to read the woman's lips but couldn't, even though he had been practicing ever since he had seen his hero, Captain Starmaster, on his favorite after-school television show intercept a secret message in the same way from the evil Overlord, Death Viper. As the woman talked, Tommy Martin's eyes searched the long line of children until he found Billy. The two boys stood staring at one another, their eyes locked in desperation, until the woman patted Tommy on the head and then, placing a fleshy hand on his shoulder, she gently coaxed him through the door. Billy watched as the large door closed. It was as if his best friend in the whole wide world had just been swallowed up by an ominous evil force that only Captain Starmaster could conquer. Billy landed back against the wall helplessly. It was hopeless. There would be no daring rescue. For this was the real world, a land forbidden to the likes and fantasy of Captain Starmaster. Resting his head against the wall, he waited resignedly. Each time the door opened, the line of children would break into an agonizing groan as names of new victims were passed along the line and then grudgingly each would shuffle one spot closer to his or her own fate.

"Hey, Billy," whispered Sammy Willis who was standing next to him.

"What?"

"Know what I think?"

"No, what?" answered Billy halfheartedly as if he really cared what Sammy thought, and he didn't. Sammy was weird. All the kids thought so. He was the kind of kid that would, out of the blue, say the dumbest things at the strangest times. And the funny part of it all was no one knew if he really meant the things he said or if he was doing it just to get attention. Personally, Billy had always thought it was the latter.

"I think something real strange is going on here," said Sammy with his hand cupped over his mouth so as to avoid detection.

"Yeah, what?"

"I'm not sure. I just have this strange feeling about this thing."

Billy sighed heavily. He was too depressed and nervous to deal with Sammy today.

"No, I mean it. I have this strange feeling about all this."

"You have strange feelings about everything, Sammy."

"Yeah, I know," replied Sammy wide-eyed. "But this time I really feel it!"

"Feel what?" groaned Billy. He was beginning to get irritated now.

"I have this feeling that anyone who goes in there ain't ever coming out again."

"What?" he said, turning to Sammy. "Are you crazy or something?"

"No," gasped Sammy as his nervous finger worked his long red hair into tight knots. "I mean it. Everyone goes in, but nobody comes out."

"So?"

"So, I was reading this book about the Nazis yesterday. That's the way they did it. They took 'em all into a big building and gassed 'em."

"What?"

"Yeah," whispered Sammy with buggy eyes and a half-crazed expression. "And know what? Once they got 'em inside the building, they made 'em take all their clothes off and stand around naked—boys and girls together."

Billy turned to Sammy in stunned disbelief. "You're weird, Sammy. Don't talk to me anymore today, OK."

"I'm telling ya. I feel strange about this."

Billy turned his back to Sammy. He would just ignore him. It was the only way to deal with Sammy. Still, thought Billy as he leaned out, stealing a peek down the hall, Sammy was right about one thing. Of all the kids that went in, none had come back out. What was going on in there? What was taking so long? Why hadn't Tommy come out? That darn Sammy, thought Billy to himself. Why did he have to go and say all that crazy stuff about Nazis anyway? And why did the teacher have to put Sammy in line next to him? It was going to be one of those days; he just knew it.

Suddenly the other door to the auditorium opened slightly and, much to Billy's relief, out emerged Tommy Martin. He walked slowly up the hall. His head was hung down as he passed the long line of children who pointed to him and whispered to themselves. Billy took a step out into the hall to get a better look. He had never seen Tommy move so slowly. He watched Tommy intently as he neared, attempting to judge his mood, but he couldn't see his friend's face. Then, as Tommy approached Billy, he stopped and lifted his face to look at his best friend. His eyes were red and swollen and his mouth distorted as if he was about to break into tears. In embarrassment the child turned away to hide his face and then trudged away.

"Tommy," called Billy after the boy. "Tommy," he repeated, but the boy walked on without looking back.

"Oh, my God," muttered Sammy with his mouth hanging open, tugging at Billy's shirt. "I knew it. I had this feeling. I told ya, didn't I?"

Billy yanked his arm out of the boy's grip. "You're a weirdo, Sammy. Know that? And don't ever talk to me ever again, not as long as you live, hear?" he said as he watched Tommy disappear into his fourth-grade class. That was it. His fate was sealed. He was a goner for sure. There was no way out for him. There were very few things in life he was afraid of, but this was too much for him to handle alone. Why couldn't Captain Starmaster be real? He was just about the only person who could save him now. Billy had been so preoccupied with his fantasy about how Captain Starmaster might storm the auditorium and rescue him from the evil doings within that he failed to notice that he had inched slowly forward until he was next in line to enter the auditorium. Startled disbelief flooded his mind as he looked up to find himself standing in front of the huge steel doors. His mind raced. He wanted to turn and run, but his knees were locked, frozen stiff, almost as if the murderous Death Viper had paralyzed him with some strange evil mind ray. Then suddenly the door opened...ever so slowly. Billy's eyes widened as the large, heavy-set nurse in her stiff white uniform edged out to loom ever so menacingly over him. Looking up at the mass of flesh before him, he couldn't help but think that all the dreadful forces of fantasy had finally pooled their evil powers into one so as to create such a ghastly creature that even Captain Starmaster could not conquer.

"And who might you be?" boomed the voice down at him.

"B...B...Billy," he stammered.

"I see," nodded the woman smiling. "Billy who?"

"Billy Cowan."

The woman ran her pencil down the list of names until she came upon Billy's. "Ah, ha!" she cried, thumping her pencil in a thunderous gesture on the appropriate spot. "Gotcha!"

"Oh, my God," moaned Sammy from behind. "It's curtains!"

Upon hearing the remark, the woman threw back her head and laughed so boisterously that the large rolls of flesh surrounding her belly shook so hard that the clipboard stuck up under her armpit dislodged and fell to the floor face up in front of Billy's feet. Glancing down, he saw the names of friends who had gone before him. A blood red line was drawn through each name as if they had been stricken from existence.

"Now, now, now," replied the nurse, trying to restrain her laughter as she wiped her eyes and retrieved the clipboard. "Let's not let our imagination carry us away. It's not all that bad, and it'll be over before you know it."

Billy Cowan stared up at the woman who was smiling back at him, not believing a word she had said. It might be true for his classmates and friends but not for him. For him, the deed would have a much different ending.

Patting him on the head as she did to every child, the woman leaned over and whispered, "You're a big, brave boy, aren't you, Billy?"

Billy nodded.

"You're not afraid, are you, Billy?"

Billy shook his head. He wanted to speak but couldn't find his voice. He wanted to tell her that he wasn't afraid, but for him this was different.

"Good," she said, opening the door and standing aside. "Why don't we just step inside?"

Yes, that's the way it had begun, Justice Vasquez-Rodquiez remembered leaning forward to examine some papers. Even before the trial had begun, before she was nominated to fill Justice Blackwell's position, she had followed the story of "Little Billy Cowan" with great interest. With eyes riveted to the television, she had watched the bewildered face of the small child as he stood before the glaring lights of television cameras and fumbled over questions he didn't understand. How could he understand? How was it possible for a child of ten years to begin even to grasp the ominous conflicting forces that were about to collide in his life? That such a collision would occur was inevitable. However, it was only by chance that they would find their juncture in the life of little Billy Cowan as he stepped through that door. Yes, how must that first step have felt? She wondered....

Billy stepped guardedly into the auditorium he had so often gone to with glee. Now it seemed alien, so unlike the delightful spacious place where he and his friends had laughed and romped about in playful games. Now, across the gym floor stood six long folding tables pushed end to end in a vertical arrangement to form a huge V. The point of the V funneled into an opening of a large triangular structure constructed of six-foot high paneled screens fabricated from shinny white cloth and metal tubing. Undoubtedly, thought Billy, he had finally arrived at the innermost sanctum of the Overlord's evil laboratory. The nurse guided Billy to the right and seated him at the table. Lining each table were seven seats with the children shuffling from chair to chair as their fellow classmates were picked off one by one and fed into the mouth of this abominable chamber. With each new casualty, the victims moved closer and closer to the fate awaiting them. Billy moved slowly forward thinking of the fiendish efficiency of mental torture that the evil Over-lord extracted from each of his victims before subjecting them to their ultimate fate. Even though he was five chairs away from the opening, he could hear the whimpering cries within from those who had been taken. It was then, at this lowest point, the absolute darkest moment in this human tragedy, when he was sure life could get no worse, he looked up and who should he see scurrying across the floor toward him in short slippery steps but weird Sammy Willis. He dropped his head in agony. Why him? Why did these last few precious moments have to be squandered by the likes of Sammy Willis? Had he really done something that bad in life so as to deserve this?

"Oh, God," exclaimed Sammy as he slid into the chair next to Billy. "Boy, am I ever glad you're still here."

"Uh, huh?" moaned Billy, compliantly realizing there was nothing he could do about it now.

"Oh, God," Sammy suddenly blurted out looking across the table. "I knew it! I just knew it!"

"What now?"

"It's that new red-headed girl."

"Susie?"

"Yeah, that's her."

"What about it?"

"I knew it. I just had this feeling that this was gonna happen."

"What?"

"Look," cried Sammy desperately. "She's sitting directly across from me."

"So what?"

"So what!" he cried. "Do you know what this means?"

"No, what?"

"It means we're going in together."

"So?"

"So!" he exclaimed wildly. "It means that when they strip all our clothes off, I'll be standing naked in front of the new girl."

Billy looked at Sammy in utter disbelief. How could they keep putting this kid next to him? Was there no decency in the world, no sense of fair play? Hadn't they already punished him enough?

"Billy Cowan," called the nurse at the end of the table.

Billy's head jerked up as he heard his name. Looking up, he saw her large lips moving rapidly around her puffy face, but he couldn't make out the words. What was she saying? What demented instructions was she imparting to him? Finally, she motioned for him to stand. He couldn't even if he had wanted. Rising from her own chair, the woman walked around the table to him and scooted his chair out from under the table before grabbing his hand and gently helping him up. "I can't go in there," he uttered in a cracked voice.

"Sure, you can, Honey," she replied.

"No, you don't understand. I'm not suppose to go in there."

The nurse smiled and patted him on the head. "It's going to be okay. Why, it'll be over before you know it," she said as she pulled him toward the opening. Billy turned back to glance at Sammy. A death stare was locked on the boy's face, and his eyes were bulging so from fright that he would have sworn they were gonna pop right out of their sockets and roll around on the floor. It was the only time in his life that he had ever seen weird Sammy in such a condition that he couldn't even open his mouth to speak. Perhaps that was life's last parting gift to him.

Justice Vasquez-Rodquiez smiled recalling that of all the questions put to Billy Cowan by reporters the one that amused her most was when asked what the most difficult part of the entire ordeal for him was. He responded: "sitting next to weird Sammy Willis." That statement clearly captured the essence of the problem from the eyes of a ten-year-old. Still a problem remained, a very serious problem and one in which there was no clear-cut easy answer. It might be interesting, she thought, that in the years ahead, long after the smoke had cleared from the legal battlefield, if Billy Cowan could appreciate the enormous questions raised by the action he took once he stepped through the small screen opening....

Still in hand by the nurse, Billy was led over to a small chair in one corner of the makeshift chamber. To his side stood a metal cabinet with small rubber wheels. All sorts of small bottles filled with clear liquid were arranged in a row across the top shelf. In front of the bottles lie about half a dozen syringes with small sharp needles encased in plastic containers. By the cabinet was a waste basket stuffed full of discarded syringes and bloody patches of cotton gauze. No doubt this was the site of the evil Overlord's hideous experiments, he thought. Looking up, Billy watched as a tall lanky man in a white lab coat approached. His thin balding hair was slicked back with a heavy pasty substance. Quickly he searched his surroundings in hopes of finding an escape route. There was none; he was cornered.

"Well, well," mused the man. "Billy Cowan, right?"

Billy nodded.

"Whatta say we just get this over with real quick, huh?"

Billy shook his head.

"Now, now," laughed the man. "It isn't that bad, and it really doesn't hurt that much. Believe me," he said in a toothy grin that stretched malevolently across his thin face.

Billy could feel the hot rancid breath of the man on his face. Again he shook his head.

"I think we need a little encouragement for Billy," called the man over his shoulder.

Billy's mind raced. What encouragement? What type of hideous methods did they have to make unwilling victims submit to their depraved intentions? Furthermore, he wondered who was going to administer this encouragement? Almost instantly he could hear footsteps to his left. Turning, he saw the figure silhouetted against the screen walking toward the opening. It was impossible to discern much about the shrouded figure through the screen, but of one thing he was sure—this creature was definitely not of this world. Although its body resembled a human form, being tall and slender with arms and legs, its head was large and distorted with strange sweeping points toward the rear. No, he surmised convincingly, it definitely was not human. He watched as the creature moved in slow determined steps toward the opening. His body began to shake uncontrollably. With each step the creature took, the eyes of the boy widened more until he held out his own hands in front of his face afraid that his eyes, like those of weird Sammy Willis, were going to pop. Things like that could happen. He had read about it in one of his comic books. He watched in horror as the monster took one final step, pivoted, and then entered the chamber. His mouth fell open in shock as he sat staring up at Ms. Nece, the young and lovely school nurse, with whom just about every boy from the fourth grade on was madly in love with. How could this be possible? How could it be that Ms. Nece was a party to these diabolical experiments? Surely he had underestimated the power of the evil Overlord.

"Billy, Billy," called nurse Nece as she moved toward him. "What's all this about? Of all the children, I didn't expect this from you. You're such a brave boy." Billy watched as she reached into her pocket. As the hand began to withdraw, he drew back away from her in fear at what horrid instrument she might pull from it. Much to his surprise a large cherry flavored sucker appeared. "You'd like this, wouldn't you, Dear?"

Billy nodded. He loved cherry flavored suckers. They were his very favorite.

Nurse Nece quickly put the sucker in his hand. "That's what I thought," she said smiling. "Now, we'll just roll up this sleeve, and the good doctor is going to give us something that will protect us from nasty ol' germs."

The small child could feel large pools of water collecting at the bottom of his eyes. Though his vision was blurred, he could see the doctor inserting the needle into the top of the clear jar of liquid in preparation for the injection. He had been duped. How could he have fallen for such a trick? For sure, it was hopeless now. Or was it, he wondered? If, in fact, this was the work of the evil Overlord then a secret passageway through the stars to the forbidden land had to exist. That same passageway could be used by his hero, Captain Starmaster, to enter this world and rescue him. It could happen; it was possible! Frantically he searched his surroundings before locking in on the skylights. Yes, he concluded. It would be the skylights. With tears streaming down his face he waited desperately for Captain Starmaster to come crashing through the roof to his rescue. From the corner of his eye he saw the doctor approaching with needle in hand. It was too late. For whatever reason, Captain Starmaster was not coming. He would have to save himself. In one hand was clenched the sucker. Nurse Nece held the other hand. How well they had planned his demise. But they had sorely underestimated him. For what they did not know was that he was a skilled soldier in Captain Starmaster's Legion of Justice sworn to protect the American way of life. He and his dad had read the code together and agreed that it was a good one. Perhaps that's why Captain Starmaster had not appeared, he suddenly thought. Perhaps this was a test. Yes, that was it. This was his test! As the doctor bent low over him, he waited until the last moment, the moment at which the needle was about to prick his small arm. It was then, at this precise moment, that he launched his counterattack. Using the large sucker as a weapon, he flung back his arm and struck hard at the side of the doctor's head.

The blow landed hard, finding its mark on the corner of the man's glasses, which, upon impact, flew across the floor to the opposite end of the chamber. The startled doctor reared back shrieking in pain as he grabbed his nose. Immediately, the boy jumped from his chair twisting and turning as he attempted to break Ms. Nece's vice-like grip on his hand. Wrenching free, he spun backward into the metal cabinet and, in a thunderous crash the boy, cabinet, and all its contents—serum bottles, needles, cotton swabs, and Band-Aids—went skidding across the floor in all directions. Struggling to his feet, the boy made a desperate dash for freedom, but just before reaching the opening of the enclosure, the doctor, who was still holding his bleeding nose, reached out with one hand and grasped the back of his thin cotton shirt to fling him back toward the chair. Catching the weight of the boy, the shirt ripped lengthwise and was torn from his body. Billy flew through the air, up over the chair, and crashed into one panel of the partitions separating them from the auditorium. The flimsy structure collapsed sending the half-naked body of little Billy Cowan rolling out onto the auditorium floor for all the other children to see.

Catching sight of Billy, weird Sammy Willis leaped from his chair and jumped onto the top of the table to scream, "It's the Nazis. They're gonna strip us naked. Run for your lives!" Almost instantly, the doctor and Ms. Nece were on top of Billy, picking him up by both arms and whisking him away from sight. As Billy was ushered from the auditorium, he could hear the crashing and banging of chairs and tables as the puffy-faced nurse chased Sammy about the auditorium, who was still shrieking his warning of Nazis at the top of his lungs.

Justice Vasquez-Rodquiez recalled reading the account of the ordeal in the newspaper. Likewise, she had read of the vaccination program. The disease of AIDS had reached epidemic proportions in the nation. After laboring for nearly twenty years, scientists had finally developed a vaccination that would protect humans against it. However, the vaccination worked only to prevent one from contracting the disease. It could not cure the disease once someone had been infected. Hence, the federal government had launched a major campaign to eradicate the disease through the inoculation of school children, reasoning that if all children were inoculated, the disease would be, for all practical purposes, eliminated from the nation within a generation or two. All seemed to be going very smoothly until the day little Billy Cowan was to be inoculated. Yes, she recalled, that's when things began to unravel....

Billy sat in one corner of the principal's office. His small legs dangled from the oversized chair. It was the thing he hated most about the world. Everything was made for the "big people." He had been sitting for nearly an hour occasionally whimpering as he waited for his father and mother to arrive. Mr. Fellows, the school principal, had tried to talk to Billy about his behavior, but he would say nothing. Captain Starmaster's code dictated that no information was to be passed to the enemy. Besides, what could he say? He had tried to explain, but nobody would listen to him. So he sat quietly by, looking down at his hands that were neatly folded in his lap, trying hard to hold back the tears that wanted to spill forth from his eyes. He heard the outer door to the reception room open and recognized the confident voice of his father. As they entered the office, his mother went to him and whispered a quick hello before joining his father, who said nothing to him but smiled reassuringly. Both sat in front of the principal's desk. Billy listened intently as Mr. Fellows detailed the charges against him. Not only had Billy created pandemonium among the other children but also there was considerable monetary damage done as well as the matter of personal injury inflicted upon the good doctor who was attempting to administer the vaccination.

Billy's father listened patiently to Mr. Fellows describe in vivid detail the behavior of his son. Then, after the principal had finished, Mr. Cowan walked over to his son and asked, "Is all this true, Son?"

"But, Dad."

"Billy," he said more forcefully. "Is it true what Mr. Fellows tells me?"

Without speaking the small child nodded his head in an affirmative gesture.

The man patted his son on the head lovingly. "Good," he uttered approvingly. "I'm proud of you, Son—very, very proud."

A stunned expression crossed Mr. Fellows' face. "I'm not sure that I heard you correctly, Mr. Cowan. Did you say that you were proud of what your son did?"

"Absolutely!"

"I'm afraid that I don't understand."

"Obviously not, Mr. Fellows," declared Billy's father. "In fact, not only am I proud of the action that my son took, I can't convey how unhappy I am that you attempted to vaccinate my son behind my back."

Mr. Fellows slumped back into his chair. "I'm at a complete loss."

"At the start of the school year," began the man, "when I first learned that these vaccinations were to be given, I called the school nurse and expressly conveyed to her that my son was not allowed to participate. In fact, I was under the impression that this whole business was to begin next week. Otherwise, I would have kept him out of school today just to make sure that there would be no bureaucratic foul-up."

"Well, that was true," stated the principal, "but the state moved the date up on us. We sent a letter to each parent by way of the children."

"Billy," asked the child's father, "did you get a letter to bring home?"

The boy nodded. "I lost it. Sorry."

"I see," he murmured, turning back to Mr. Fellows. "Nevertheless, my son was still not to be given the vaccination."

"Mr. Cowan," stated the principal, moving to the offense. "I'm afraid that you have no choice in this matter. The government has mandated by law that every child of school age must receive the vaccination. It's in their best interest that they receive the vaccination."

"Whose interest?" laughed Cowan. "And please spare me your humanistic concerns for my child. I think that I'm in a better position to judge just what is or is not in the interest of my own child. And this clearly is not in his interest or that of any God-fearing Christian family."

"Excuse me?" responded Mr. Fellows obviously confused by the man's reference to God.

"I mean, that you and the government are attempting to undermine religious values. This vaccination that you claim is in his best interest really promotes evil and corruption. Why do you think that we have these diseases anyway? Because," he continued without providing Fellows with an opportunity to respond, "we have lost our sense of religious values."

"Mr. Cowan, I fail to understand this...."

"Obviously," interrupted Cowan. "Let me spell it out for you. First, it's sex education classes. Then, when the kids start putting into practice the things you've taught them, you give them contraceptives, and when that doesn't work, you shuffle them off to an abortionist to kill their child. And what's really amazing about all this is you do it without so much as even telling the parent that his kid is in trouble. How is it possible to raise children with respectable values when the government and the school keep undermining the role of parents?"

"Mr. Cowan," explained Fellows, "we're only trying to assist the parent."

The man stood looking at the principal, shaking his head sadly. "Do you believe that? Can you honestly tell me that things are better now than they were before the government began meddling in the affairs of the family? Do we have fewer teen pregnancies today than before? Are fewer kids on drugs now than before? And what about these sexual diseases? Where did they come from, and what's to say that a new disease won't come along once your government scientists have this one cured? Have you ever considered that the only way to really prevent these disasters is to return to religious values?"

Realizing that it was hopeless, Fellows removed his glasses and placed them before him on the table. "Well," he finally said, "in education we would call this an academic question because the state has mandated that every child of school age must receive the vaccination. It's the law. It's just that simple."

"No, it's not that simple, Mr. Fellows. C'mom, Billy," he called, motioning for the child to follow him. "We'll see how simple this really is."

The words uttered by Mr. Cowan proved more prophetic than Fellows could ever have imagined. Within days newspapers and television stations across the country began to carry the story of "Little Billy Cowan." Religious denominations, especially those predisposed toward spiritual healing, along with conservatives, fed up with the activist tactics of the courts, rallied around the Cowan family in support. Nationwide fundraisers were organized, and soon money began pouring in to mount a judicial challenge to the government's inoculation program. For its part, the school stood by its insistence that Billy be inoculated as required by law. Since inoculations were no longer being given at the school, the Cowans were given four weeks in which to have Billy inoculated at a private facility or face expulsion for noncompliance. On the final day of the grace period, Billy was called to the office. He walked the long hall leading to the office where the principal and school nurse waited for him. Asked if he had been inoculated, little Billy shook his head. The principal explained to Billy that he had no choice but to phone his parents. Billy was taken back to the room by the school nurse to clean out his desk. The other children in the room watched silently as Billy placed his personal objects into a box given to him by Mr. Fellows. Tommy, his best friend, helped. An hour later his father appeared, and he and Billy walked out of the school into the onrush of cameras and reporters. Asked how he felt, little Billy shrugged and commented that he felt sad, but then, all the kids had been teasing him because Sammy Willis had been telling everyone that he had killer germs in his body. After the interview was over, Billy turned back to look at his schoolroom one last time. In the corner window was the face of his very best friend, Tommy Martin, pressed against the glass, his small finger waving a final good-bye. Again the two boys stood staring at each other. This time it was Billy who would turn and walk away.

Challenged first in the state courts, the case made its way rapidly up the judicial pyramid to the Supreme Court. Citing statistics on the mounting number of AIDS cases in the nation, the government attempted to demonstrate the importance of a national program to attack this killer virus that had claimed the lives of more men, women and children than the entire Viet Nam war. Statistics were also presented to show that this number would increase to several hundred thousand as those who were presently infected would die in the near future. If left unattended, this number would surely climb to astronomical proportions in the next decade. Although admitting that it was true that the majority of cases could be prevented through lifestyle changes, there was no clear evidence that the disease could not be passed by means of casual contact with infected people. There were, pointed out the government, several unexplained cases in which celibate, nondrug users were infected in ways that baffled medical experts. Likewise, scientists had pointed out that the prospect of the virus mutating so as to become more virulent was a real possibility. That would leave all those not inoculated at an even greater risk. While it might be feasible to allow adults to take this risk, was it fair to assume such a risk for their children? Following up on this point, the government maintained that it was absolutely impossible for a parent to be able to guarantee that their children would not engage in "at risk" behavior at some point in their lives, thus leaving them vulnerable to the disease. And finally, the government presented statistics showing the cost of each AIDS patient to the taxpayers to be several hundred thousand dollars. Was it fair for those who opposed the vaccination program to ask taxpayers to foot the bill later should they or their child become infected? The fact that this cost would be borne by the taxpayer was a matter of law and public record. Opponents of the program were equally convincing. Their argument revolved around the rights of parenthood and an increasingly intrusive government. While they conceded that similar programs against polio, measles, mumps, and other contagious diseases may be necessary, the case of AIDS was very different. AIDS was contracted through lifestyle habits—unsafe sexual practices and intravenous drug use. Likewise, since no clear scientific evidence existed suggesting that casual contact could spread the disease, was it right to deny to people their right to practice their religion, a constitutional guarantee, as well as thrust the government even deeper into the homes and private lives of its citizens? If allowed to interfere on such a flimsy excuse as this, what other areas would the government claim for itself?

Rising from her desk, Justice Vasquez-Rodquiez walked methodically to the window again where she stood contemplating the issue. In the eyes of a small child such as Billy Cowan, it must all seem so simple. Thinking about it, she laughed softly realizing that most people would share that simplistic view of the problem—the rights of the state versus the rights of the individual. Or, more specifically, does the state, acting on behalf of the individual and for the common good of the society, have the right to require parents to provide certain medical treatments that may conflict with their personal and religious values, or should the right of the parent be preserved? Certainly, the state had always intervened on behalf of the child in cases where a definite and immediate threat of life existed. Such intervention was, in her view, justifiable. But what of this case, and perhaps others like it, where deadly viruses were not spread indiscriminately, but, rather, contracted through lifestyle practices? Should the government still usurp the right of parenthood to protect innocent children who are unable to make intelligent decisions for themselves? At what point was preserving the rights of a nation more important than a single life?

Did her fellow colleagues on the bench understand the issues? Apparently the issue was not so complicated to them for they had little difficulty making up their minds. Four were prepared to uphold the right of the government to intervene; four were set to cast their votes on the side of the parent. Why was this so hard for her? Maybe it was because she would cast the final and deciding vote. Her vote, and her vote alone, would decide the fate of millions of Americans. And, it was not only this issue of the legal rights of parents and the extent to which the state was permitted to intervene in private lives. There also remained the national politics surrounding this issue. Her decision could well set off a series of political events that would have consequences for the next two decades. No, she concluded, this was not a simple issue. Greater issues were present in this case, looming in the distance like the large and threatening clouds that now dominated the city's horizon. She stood watching the clouds approach. Storms had been forecast, so she had heard. But then, how many times had the forecasters been wrong? How could anyone really know? Placing her fingertips against the window, she felt the cold sting of winter through the pane of glass. Yes, she thought, how could anyone really know....

Name _____

Read each statement before coming to class. To the left check whether you agree or disagree with this statement. After discussing the statement with your group in class, record the total number of members agreeing and disagreeing in the boxes to the right and explain your position in a few sentences below.

A D   A D

☐ ☐ 1. Because time and conditions have changed since the creation of this nation, the   ☐ ☐
government has justifiably assumed greater powers than originally intended by
those who wrote the Constitution.

☐ ☐ 2. The problem with the Court is that the president selects its members more on the   ☐ ☐
basis of politics than ability.

☐ ☐ 3. Justice Vasquez-Rodquiez has no business letting politics affect her decision in   ☐ ☐
this case.

☐ ☐ 4. The inoculation of Billy clearly violates the "free-exercise" clause of the First   ☐ ☐
Amendment.

☐ ☐ 5. Since AIDS is different in that it is transmitted by "life-style" choices, the   ☐ ☐
national government has no business mandating that individuals be inoculated
against their free choice.

Name _____

☐☐   6. If society is going to have to foot the bill to care for AIDS patients once they have contracted the disease, it is only right that it has the power to require everyone to submit to inoculation once a vaccine is available.   ☐☐

☐☐   7. The increase in sexually contracted diseases, as well as the number of teen pregnancies and abortions, is evidence that liberal governmental policies have failed this society.   ☐☐

☐☐   8. People don't always make rational decisions. Therefore, in spite of the fact they may disagree, it is the obligation of the government to protect them.   ☐☐

☐☐   9. The issue of privacy in this case is greater than that of the lives that might be lost if the AIDS inoculation program was defeated. Therefore, Justice Vasquez-Rodquiez should vote against it.   ☐☐

☐☐   10. The Court's acceptance of the AIDS inoculation program will only encourage the federal government to become more intrusive into the private affairs of its citizens.   ☐☐

Name _____

If you were Justice Marie Vasquez-Rodquiez, what would your decision be? Why?

_____

_____

_____

_____

_____

_____

_____

_____

_____

_____

_____

_____

_____

_____

_____

_____

_____

_____

_____

_____

_____

_____

_____

_____

Visitors

Johnny Latham lay in one of two beds that dominated the small square-like room. The bed next to Latham's was unoccupied, and, though sorely in need, it was decided to leave it as such until the man's current infection abated and he could be transferred back to his original ward. This was not at Latham's request but, rather, a decision exercised by the foresight of hospital administrators seeking to avoid a potentially embarrassing situation. In fact, it had long been a matter of institutional policy not to room paraplegic veterans with other hospital patients.

The young man lay alone now clutching a small plastic vial in his left hand. His head was tilted slightly to the right and tears streamed from the corners of his eyes dousing the white pillowcase below. The last of his four visitors that day had left only moments before. Each had arrived alone, stayed fifteen minutes precisely, and then left. Only his mother begged to stay longer, but this he refused. It had been agreed upon the day before—only fifteen minutes, not a second longer. The woman tried vainly to protest, but the tightness in her throat choked off the words, thus rendering her defenseless. Rising from her chair, she stroked her son's forehead gently, and, then, lovingly kissed his scarred cheek for the last time. The others, his father, his brother, and his lifelong friend, Thomas Letkie, having resolved themselves beforehand to the difficulty of the occasion, behaved somewhat more stoically. It was as Johnny wished.

It was late now. With the arrival of night, darkness began to crowd the room. Shortly, the entirety of the room would be enveloped in blackness. He turned his head to look at the clock sitting on the bedstand next to him. It was 6:15, thirty minutes before the nurse would be in to help turn him for the night. Like a ritual, it was performed every two hours to prevent bedsores—an affliction that plagued people like Latham. The timing was perfect, and for this he was grateful, for that which he was about to do could not be hurried. No, he thought silently but reassuringly to himself, these last minutes, few and precious as they were, now were his to spend as he pleased. It was time. Carefully holding the vial between his thumb and forefinger, as the others were missing from his hand, he raised it slowly. His arm twitched slightly, but his movements were deliberate nonetheless. Finding his lips, he quickly and without hesitation emptied its contents into his mouth. His arm fell haplessly to his side. It was done. Relief permeated his weary body.

Again, he checked the clock—6:20. He turned so that his head lay facing the wall. Its appearance was sterile, absent of any decor, save for the paint that clung loosely to its surface. Still the young man lay staring at it, until suddenly it sprang to life with the images of a thousand dreams projected from his mind onto its bare, lackluster finish. Oblivious to the world about him now, he lay perfectly still and fully aware...watching and contemplating...and waiting....

The patrol leader flipped the water from his steel cup. Looking across the makeshift camp area, he surveyed his men. There were seven of them all huddled together and resting. It was midday

"Hey, Latham," he barked, "get your ass up here, and don't take all day about it!"

The young man picked up his M-16, slung it across his shoulder, and moved quickly over to the patrol leader. "Yeah, Sarg?"

"Latham, you've got the point. We move in two minutes."

"Point!" protested Latham. "I just had point. It's Speath's turn."

"I know," replied the patrol leader with a cursory glance.

"Then put Spaeth on point!"

"Can't."

"Why?"

"Cause he's a junkie, that's why, and he'd get the whole lot of us blown to hell!"

"Then..."

"Hey, Latham," interrupted the sergeant, "I don't wanna hear anymore of your shit. Just get your ass out there on point. NOW!" he barked.

The young man cursed as he turned, making his way toward his newly acquired position. He was tall with broad athletic shoulders and strong muscular features. The members of his patrol tagged him with the nickname "Jock" because of his intent interest in sporting matters. In fact, if any disagreement arose in the company regarding a sporting matter, it was Latham who arbitrated the dispute. The other men, lethargic in their movements, fell in behind Latham. From the middle of the line Latham heard the patrol leader give the command to move out. He stepped forward, pushing the brush aside. It was dense, jungle-like, and the ground beneath soft and muddy. Perspiration saturated his uniform, and a pungent stench filled the air as the sun sucked the moisture from the ground. For two hours the men moved through the terrain without rest. Insects swarmed about their bodies, and they grew wearier with each step. Then, less than a mile from their destination, an outpost where they would rejoin their company, it happened. Latham's foot sank through the murky soil and stuck a metallic object. He froze. The adrenaline shot through his body with the sudden realization of what was about to happen. Instantly he lunged forward, screaming at the top of his lungs, "MINE!!!" There was a sudden brilliant flash, followed by an ear-shattering explosion. A sensation of weightlessness engulfed him as he was hurled through the air and an intense pain, as none he had ever experienced, flashed across his skin as he felt his flesh being burned away from his body. He opened his mouth to scream but heard nothing. Then, as suddenly as it had happened, it was over. He lay face down in the mud, dazed, in a state of semi-consciousness. He could hear nothing, nor see nothing. Death was at the forefront of his mind, for he was sure of its approach. Then he saw it—an onrushing mass of blackness that swallowed him up whole—body and soul.

When Latham first regained consciousness, it was for a brief moment only. He could feel the wind moving rapidly across his face, and above he could hear a rhythmic pounding. Though half-delirious, he recognized the sounds as that of helicopter blades. The realization of survival surprised him. How could that be, he wondered? Mentally he searched his body and was surprised again for he felt no pain. Actually he was rather comfortable. Momentarily his thoughts turned toward his parents. He wondered how they'd feel when informed of his death. A strange feeling pervaded him now. For as he lay gazing into the light above, he could see in the back of his mind that same large mass of blackness rushing toward him again. He waited, paralyzed with inertia.

There was no sense of time, nor was Latham particularly concerned about it when he awoke for the second time. He was lying on his stomach this time, or so it seemed. His face was positioned down with his forehead resting on some sort of strap and below him littering the floor were rubber gloves, cotton balls soaked red with blood, and stained pieces of gauze. For a brief second the ringing in his head cleared, and he could hear the sounds of voices and footsteps rushing about. The best he could ascertain was that he was at a relay field hospital. He closed his eyes momentarily to rest and found himself back inside his mind. Suddenly he remembered. Turning, he quickly searched for the blackness that had twice before engulfed him. It wasn't there. He tried to open his eyes again but couldn't. He was trapped inside. He turned to the front again and panicked, for there in the distance it hung, omnipotent and foreboding in presence. He stood watching it as it began to move toward him, ever so slowly at first but steadily it gained in speed. It moved faster and faster and faster....

For ten days Latham lie unconscious, unaware of the doctors who labored over him. He awoke on Tuesday, the eleventh day. The ward nurse was first to discover him, lying in a dazed state. Immediately she rushed off to inform the doctors of her find.

"Johnny?"

Latham could hear his name echoing through his head as if he were standing at the mouth of a large canyon.

"Johnny, can you hear me?"

The blurred vision of Dr. Thompson began to clear as he focused his eyes directly above on the man's face. It was an old face, weathered with age. Had it not been for the kind empathic eyes, its appearance would have seemed stern and unrelenting.

"Johnny, pay attention to my voice. Do you hear me?"

"Yes," he muttered. "I hear you. Where am I?"

"You're back in the States. You're in a hospital, Johnny. You were wounded, but you're going to make it." Thompson's words were slow and distinct. "Do you understand?"

"Wounded?" replied Latham. "How bad?"

"We have plenty of time to talk about that later, Son. You just rest now."

"How bad?" demanded Latham. "I want to know!"

Thompson hesitated, fearful the truth would upset his patient.

"How bad!" repeated Latham.

"Okay, easy now, Johnny...I'll tell you."

"The truth!"

"Yes, the truth," Thompson paused for a minute. Then realizing Latham could see him, he looked directly into the man's eyes and said, "Johnny, you stepped on a mine. We had to amputate your legs, the right one just below the hip, the left one above the knee. Also you lost your right arm. But let me tell you," he said smiling, "you were one lucky boy to have even survived."

"I can't move...can't feel anything."

"I know, Johnny. There was some spinal damage. We don't know how much exactly yet."

"Paralyzed?"

"Yes, Johnny. I'm afraid so, but there's hope. There's always hope through therapy."

"Paralyzed?" he cried.

Dr. Thompson turned to the nurse, "50 milligrams of Demerol. Call me if anything should develop."

Johnny Latham recovered from his wounds, but the progress was slow and arduous. At first it was thought that the paralysis would affect only the lower portion of his body from his waist down. However, as later tests revealed, nerve damage was much more extensive than originally thought. Not only did Latham lose complete control of all lower body movements but also much of that in the upper portion of his body as well, particularly on his left side—the side of his only remaining limb. For all practical purposes Latham's paralysis was complete, and, shortly thereafter, his official classification was changed from paraplegia to quadriplegia. The realization of the seriousness of his condition sent Latham into a depression lasting for months. He was sullen and withdrawn, refusing to speak to anyone, even his parents. Days would pass and he wouldn't eat. His overall body weight dropped 30 percent and at one point it was thought that intravenous feedings would be necessary to sustain life. It was then that Paul Logan, another quadriplegic, rolled in on his automated wheelchair, parked next to Latham's bed, and spent the next two hours talking to the young man. Through his own example, Logan demonstrated to Latham that a quadriplegic was capable of living a useful and productive life.

Shortly after Logan's visit Latham's condition improved. He began eating, talking, and, more importantly, once he had regained his strength, he returned to therapy. For two years Latham worked to get out of bed and into a wheelchair like Logan's. It was his goal, and all his concentration was focused on it. At night he would dream of it and through all the lonely hospital hours. For once he had accomplished his goal, then and only then, could he leave the hospital and return home. On December 20 of his second year at the hospital, he left. It was a sight few would forget. Little more than a stump of a man, Latham was carefully fitted to the motorized wheelchair. His body was strapped to the back of the chair. Wires attached to a chest brace supported his head. And, by means of the lone rehabilitated arm that was tied to the control panel, he guided the chair down the hall, into the elevator, and out the front door to his father's waiting car.

Johnny's stay at the home of his parents lasted a little more than two years. During the days he filled his time reading, mostly about sporting events, and at nights he would watch television or exchange conversation with his parents. At first, some of his high school friends would come around to spend time with him, but soon that past and he was left only with the company of his family. Increasingly, Johnny turned more and more to past memories to occupy his time and with each passing month Mr. Latham's concern for his son's mental condition deepened. He was becoming sullen and withdrawn again, much like the period immediately following his injury. He would sit for hours at a time in his wheelchair by the front window, staring off into the distance. Then two years and three months to the day of his arrival home, complications developed. Johnny became deathly ill. He was taken back to the veteran's hospital where subsequent tests revealed massive kidney failure. All attempts to revive the organs and restore them to a useful function failed. And, a short time later, Latham was placed on dialysis. Once again Latham found himself trapped inside the hospital. To survive he needed three treatments weekly. Since his parents lived in a small rural community nearly a day's drive from the center, it necessitated that he move back into his ward at the hospital. Initially it was hoped that the arrangement would be temporary, lasting only until a donor kidney could be located and transplanted into his body. As Dr. Thompson emphatically pointed out to the Latham family, in Johnny's case a kidney transplant was imperative. Not only would it be required before he could return home, but also without it his chances for long-term survival were considerably reduced. For though a kidney machine could sustain life for years, without a transplant he would eventually die.

Johnny listened to Dr. Thompson's argument and then consented to the operation for it was his only hope of returning home again. In a matter of a few days his tissue was typed, and his name was placed on a waiting list. For two years Latham waited for word telling him of the availability of a kidney. Twice weekly his parents drove the distance to the hospital to visit their son, and with each visit Johnny grew more restless. Finally Dr. Thompson called the family together to inform them that the chances of a donor kidney being located for Johnny were almost nonexistent. As Dr. Thompson explained, the demand for kidneys far outnumbered their availability. And, in view of Johnny's condition—that being a quadriplegic—it was always decided to give the organ to someone else, one who could possibly lead a fuller life. Of course, this was not the official position of those responsible for making the decision, but, nevertheless, Johnny's condition weighed heavily on their minds.

It was now apparent that Johnny would not receive a kidney and, therefore, faced a lifetime of successive dialysis treatments. Of his family members, only his younger brother was capable of donating a kidney, and though it was offered, Johnny refused in spite of adamant protests to the contrary. The days passed slowly for Latham now, and though he had many friends among the other patients and staff members, his life grew lonely.

As Johnny Latham swooned in the darkness of his room, Mary Ellen Dubrowski pushed her way through the narrow hospital corridors which by this hour were cluttered with chairs, beds, and discarded trays. The young nurse's steps were quick and lively as she approached the elevator that would carry her up to her ninth floor station. Once on the elevator, she stood perfectly still in her freshly starched uniform watching the flickering numbers race up the panel. The elevator sped upward: 1-2-3-4-5- and then it slowed past the 6th floor and stopped.   The young woman cringed at the thought of stopping on floor seven—the burn ward. She glanced at the row of numbers above the door. There was no mistake. Seven was blinking. A soft bell rang, and the stainless steel doors slid open. An orderly, wheeling a patient about in a bed, stood waiting to enter.

"Coming on, please," he muttered as he pushed the bed gently forward.

Mary Ellen slowly edged backward, avoiding the bed, until she could feel the rear wall of the elevator against her back. She glanced down at the patient who was moaning softly. His head and neck were covered with gauze, as were his arms, and a thin sheet lay spread over the rest of his body making it difficult for her to ascertain exactly how serious the injury was or to what extent the rest of the man's body suffered from burns. She turned away and closed her eyes in an attempt to shut out the sight of the patient, but immediately the vision of a burning house leaped into her mind. The house, a two-story colonial with a brick face, was ablaze and fire shot out of the upper windows, lighting the night. She could see herself standing by the sidewalk watching it burn. The noise was deafening—the sirens, the equipment, the men shouting back and forth, and the screams from within the house. Yes, it was the screams of the girl inside, her younger sister, which now echoed through her mind the loudest. The smell of burnt flesh filled the elevator. She fell faint. Opening her eyes to regain the balance she felt slipping away from her, she found the orderly staring at her. Perspiration dripped from her forehead.

"You all right, ma'am?" asked the orderly politely.

"Yeah...sure," she said. "I'm fine—just fine."

"Good," he said as the door to the elevator slid back. "Then maybe you could help. I'm having trouble with this," he said, pointing to the wheel of the bed. "It seems to be sticking. If you could guide it while I push, it would be appreciated."

Mary Ellen hurriedly glanced at her wristwatch, frantically searching for an excuse. Looking back at the orderly, she pleaded her excuse, "I only have a minute to get to my station. Fact is," she said, checking her watch again, "I'm late now."

The orderly smiled as he held the elevator door. Nodding in the direction of the corridor in front of the elevator, he said, "It's just down the hall, 'bout half way is all."

She felt trapped. Under any other circumstances she would have refused, but with the needs of the patient at stake she felt obligated. It was only professional—she had to comply. Stepping over to the front side of the bed, she grasped the railing. The orderly smiled without speaking and then nudged the bed forward. Together the two of them wheeled the patient down the hall. Soon, thereafter, the cart slowed, and Mary Ellen, following the orderly's lead, eased her grasp.

"This is it," he said, again nodding, this time to the door.

Mary Ellen stopped and looked up. In front of her was the number 819. The blood drained from her face leaving it chalk white. It was the exact number of the room her sister occupied after the terrible accident. The orderly opened the door slightly, and in her mind she heard a thin almost inaudible voice calling out to her from within the room. She closed her eyes again, this time tighter than before hoping to hold back the memory.

"Mary Ellen...? Is that you, Mary Ellen?"

"Yes, Jenny. It's me," replied Mary Ellen softly from the opposite side of the room.

"Mary Ellen. Come closer." The voice of the young girl was strained, reflecting the intolerable burden of pain she struggled with beneath the bandages. Mary Ellen crossed the room and sat at the side of her sister's bed. She leaned forward, so as to ease her sister's fatigued voice.

"Mary Ellen?"

"Yes, Jenny?"

"It hurts...it hurts awful...."

"I know, Jenny...I know," answered Mary Ellen, tears streaming down her face.

"Mary Ellen, I need...," her voice trailed off.

"Yes, Jenny...anything. What can I do?"

"Come closer...."

Mary Ellen leaned closer to her sister's bandaged face.

"Mary Ellen?"

"Yes, Jenny. What do you want?"

"Your help!"

"Anything, Jenny. How can I help?"

With all the strength the young girl could summons she forced the anguished plea from her throat, "Kill me!"

Mary Ellen stood hovering over her sister's small burnt body, her vision blurred with tears. The young girl's bandaged arm moved toward her slowly as she reached out for help.

"Please, Mary Ellen, help me. I can't go on."

"No! I can't!" cried Mary Ellen as she buried her face in her hands. "I can't. It's wrong!"

The burden of the tragedy overwhelmed her. She felt faint once more. Her knees weakened under the weight of her body. She teetered and then fell backwards into the arms of the orderly, who had seen her distress and had come running to the rescue.

"Ma'am?" he asked frantically while directing her to a chair. "You okay? Maybe I should get someone...like a doctor...."

"No, no," she protested. "I'll be fine. Just let me sit here for a minute."

"Yeah, sure," he said, more relieved now. "Can I get you something...you know, like some water?"

"No. Go ahead and take care of your patient. I can wait."

"But...."

"Do as I say! Take care of your patient," she demanded.

"Okay," he said resignedly, "but I'll be right back. You just sit there until I get back, okay?"

Mary Ellen nodded indicating she would wait. As the orderly struggled to get the bed through the door, she took the opportunity of the solitude to clear her head. Her thoughts turned briefly back to her sister. At that stage in her life, it was impossible for her to honor her sister's request. She could still recall fleeing from the room, leaving her sister to struggle with her pain alone. Eleven agonizing days later Jenny died at the age of fifteen. It was five years later now, and the guilt still tormented her. She blotted the beads of perspiration on her forehead with a small, white handkerchief and for the first time in years allowed herself to contemplate Jenny's death. Perhaps her sister had been right. When brought to the emergency room, the doctors stated she had less than one chance out of a thousand for survival. Why then should Jenny have been forced to endure the agony of such a hideous death? How utterly terrified she must have been, and the pain, thought Mary Ellen, must have been beyond anything imaginable. And to think, she could have ended it all. It would have been so easy. But no, she couldn't. It wasn't the fear of being caught, of imprisonment, that prevented her from giving to her sister what she so desperately pleaded for that night. The deed could easily have been accomplished without anyone becoming suspicious. No, it wasn't fear—it was her own sense of morality. Her mind drifted back over those eleven days. How could she have been so sure then and, yet, so unsure now?

Mary Ellen felt stronger now, and not wanting to bother with the embarrassment of being doted over by the well-intentioned orderly, she decided to move on to her ninth floor station. She arrived ten minutes late and, after explaining her tardiness to the head nurse, she began her rounds. Hers was the night shift, and since the hospital was temporarily short of help, she would be the only nurse on duty for at least another two hours. Therefore, to simplify matters she decided to reverse her normal route by taking the rooms closest to the ward desk first. Such action would allow her to continue her work and still watch the hall desk. Her first stop was room 913, occupied by two elderly gentlemen, a Mr. Clutter and a

Mr. Mathews. Both were surprised at her early arrival. After attending to their needs, she moved quickly out the door to her next assignment—Johnny Latham. Though she had known Johnny for only a few days, she had, nevertheless, developed strong empathic feelings for him. To her he epitomized the horror and destructiveness of war. It was a view that even Johnny shared, or so she had been told when she had confessed to her supervisor her feelings about the man in room 915. She had been informed that Latham had unsuccessfully sought to be wheeled, bed, plasma bottles, and all, down the main avenue during the Veteran's Day parade last year. Since then, she had always felt something special for this man.

As she entered the room, she saw Latham lying on his back, his head was tilted toward her and she smiled. He did likewise. She walked over to his bed. His eyes appeared heavy.

"Sleepy, huh, Johnny?"

"Yeah," he replied lethargically. "You're early. Why?"

"There's no one else on duty so I'm taking the front rooms first so you get to see me early. Lucky you, huh?" she joked, stroking his head. "Need any medication?"

"No, just sleep."

"Fine," she said warmly. "Then we'll just turn you, and you can drift off to dreamland."

"No, please...I'm fine. Really I'm comfortable. Please leave me."

"Now wait one minute, Mr. Latham," she said sternly, as if trying to humor him. "The doctor's orders specifically state one turning and turn we must. Now be a good patient and help me," she said sliding her hands beneath his body. It was then that the plastic vial slipped from the bed and fell to the floor below. The sound of it bouncing across the hard tiles was magnified by the stillness of the room. Mary Ellen reached down and picked up the vial. She held it in her hands examining it and then turned to Johnny.

"What's this?"

Latham looked at the woman through drowsy eyes, searching for an answer. Finally he replied, "Holy water. The priest brought it to me this afternoon."

Mary Ellen stood staring at the man. His voice was dulled and the words he spoke slurred. She raised the vial to her nose and sniffed cautiously. Its odor was pernicious. She thought for a moment and then it came to her—suicide. Latham was trying to kill himself. Quickly she slid her hand under his head, propping it up close to her own.

"John, did you take this?"

Latham failed to respond. She slapped his cheek to gain his attention and asked again. Still no reply. Grabbing her flashlight, she pulled back the man's eyelids and shined the light directly into his eyes. The pupils were dilated and responded weakly to the light. She reached over Latham's body running her hand along side of the bed in search of the emergency cord. She found it, but Latham held it weakly in his left hand.

"Give it to me, John!" she demanded while attempting to pry it from his hand.

"No. Leave me alone," he muttered. "It's my life."

Latham began to choke on his own saliva. The coughing became violent, and Mary Ellen feared that she might lose him. Gently she held his face between her hands and attempted to calm him as she spoke.

"Relax, John. Everything is going to be just fine." The coughing subsided.

"Now," said Mary Ellen calmly, realizing that she had panicked and that there was still much time left, "before I call for help, I need to know what was in the vial. It'll help the doctor treat you."

"I don't want help...I want to die."

"John, think about it. The person who gave you this could get into a lot of trouble. You don't want that do you?"

"No. No one will ever know. They can't find out." The man's voice was weaker. Mary Ellen knew she had only a few seconds left before Latham would lose consciousness. She couldn't press the alarm for fear of exciting him. She had to be calm and convincing in order to get Latham to reveal the substance he had taken. She knew that if she could find out what he had taken it would increase his chances for living.

"John," she said, "this isn't right, and you know it. You're Catholic. Think of what the priest would say—it's a sin!"

"No. They're wrong. It's a sin to live this way."

"But John, you'll be dead...your life will be over."

The man smiled. His eyes opened slightly so he could see her blurred image silhouetted against the window. "No, Mary Ellen," he muttered softly. "That's not true. There is something after death. I know...just know there is. There's nothing left for me here. I want to go on." Even Latham could feel himself slipping away now. "Mary Ellen?"

"Yes, John."

"In a few minutes, I'll be there," he said ever so slowly. "Please, Mary Ellen, don't take it away from me."

The room was almost completely darkened now. Mary Ellen stood by Latham's bed. Outside she could hear the wind brushing against the window. Its sound was strange...eerie, like the voice of a small child calling to her from a distance.

"Mary Ellen...Mary Ellen," it seemed to say, *"come closer...come closer..."*

Name _____

Read each statement before coming to class. To the left check whether you agree or disagree with this statement. After discussing the statement with your group in class, record the total number of members agreeing and disagreeing in the boxes to the right and explain your position in a few sentences below.

A D   A D
☐☐   1. If we allow euthanasia for the terminally ill, next society will want to terminate the   ☐☐
        lives of the physically and mentally handicapped.

☐☐   **2.** The real reason the terminally ill are forced to suffer is because certain groups in   ☐☐
        our society have been able to politically force their religious beliefs onto others.

☐☐   3. Keeping patients like Mary Ellen's sister and Johnny Latham alive only serves to   ☐☐
        deny scarce medical care to others who could live more productive lives.

☐☐   4. Giving Johnny Latham an organ transplant and thereby denying it to someone else   ☐☐
        who might live a more productive life is morally wrong.

☐☐   5. The trouble with euthanasia is that it is impossible to establish proper safeguards   ☐☐
        and guidelines.

Name _____

☐☐ 6. If Mary Ellen had taken her sister's life and you were a juror at her trial, would you   ☐☐
vote for her conviction?

☐☐ 7. Only the family should have the right to say whether a terminally ill patient   ☐☐
should be allowed to end his/her life.

☐☐ 8. Jenny has more of a right to die than Johnny.   ☐☐

☐☐ 9. The medical knowledge we gain from attempting to keep hopelessly ill patients   ☐☐
alive will ultimately benefit others. This alone justifies preventing Johnny and
Jenny from taking their own lives.

☐☐ 10. Handing out prison sentences to people who have helped terminally ill loved ones to   ☐☐
die will not deter others from committing the same act. Therefore, the government
should stop prosecuting such crimes.

Name _____

Do you think that Mary Ellen should have assisted her sister in dying? Why?

_____

_____

_____

_____

_____

_____

_____

_____

_____

_____

_____

_____

_____

_____

_____

_____

_____

_____

_____

_____

_____

Name _____

If you were Mary Ellen, would you allow Johnny to kill himself? Why?

_____

_____

_____

_____

_____

_____

_____

_____

_____

_____

_____

_____

_____

_____

_____

_____

_____

_____

_____

_____

_____

_____

_____

_____

_____

Baby Talk

Judge Henry Witney quickly ushered the young couple and their attorneys into his chambers away from the chaotic confusion of the courtroom. Rarely did he feel it necessary to take such drastic action; however, the delicate nature of the topic necessitated the procedural change. After all, a public discussion of one's pregnancy would be a difficult task for even the most sophisticated woman, let alone for a woman like Marie. So, after listening to several minutes of stumbling, stammering, whispering, and choking on incomplete sentences, he opted for the sanctuary of inner chambers.

After seating everyone before his desk, Judge Witney walked over to the large wooden cabinet, withdrew a pitcher of ice water, and poured a small amount of it into a paper cup. The water went down smooth and easy, soothing the burning sensation in his tired throat. Returning to his seat, he slid his weary body into the softness of the chair. Speaking directly to the two attorneys, he said, "Now, I know you are both here to represent your clients, and I know you are being well paid to do so, but in this case I would like to dispense with formalities and have Miss Garolia and Mr. Robinson speak for themselves. Afterwards, you may add any comments you feel relevant to the case. Is that understood?"

Both attorneys nodded silently in agreement. It was never advisable to run counter to the wishes of a judge on his own turf; besides, since they did have the right to speak later, it made little difference.

Turning first to Marie, Judge Witney said, "Miss Garolia, since you are the plaintiff in this case, I would like to hear from you first. Why don't you begin by telling me exactly what it is that you wish from this court."

"I want only what should be mine!" she blurted out.

Judge Witney sank back into his chair. All day long it had been like this, he thought to himself. Sometimes he wondered if it was really possible to administer justice in the midst of such human confusion. Looking back up at the young woman staring at him through blurry eyes, her chin trembling, he commented, "I'm sure that you do want what you feel belongs to you, and, believe me, this court is interested in giving you exactly what you are entitled to; however, you have to be more succinct."

"Succinct?" she questioned.

Miss Garolia's attorney leaned over and whispered an explanation to her, but it was evident that even her attorney was having difficulty clearing up the misunderstanding. The two of them continued to confer back and forth until Judge Witney interrupted, "Excuse me, but perhaps I can help. Miss Garolia, why don't you just tell me your story in your own words. Then maybe we can get to the bottom of this case."

"Yes, your Honor, but of course. That is what I would like to do. I just didn't think you'd be interested."

"In a case like this, all information is helpful," responded Judge Witney. "Please continue."

The young woman appeared calmer now. Intently interested in conveying her story, she leaned forward, resting her elbows on the judge's desk. "Ya see, your Honor," she began, "it all began at Hoggie's, that's a little bar around the corner from where I live. I guess it's where I met Richard last June. Anyway, I was there sitting at my table alone when he walked over from the bar and started up this conversation with me. I liked him real well because we had lots in common, like work and pets. We had a great time. I mean, we joked and laughed all evening. And then, just before the place was ready to close, he asked me out, ya know, for a real date. Was I ever happy. I can't tell ya how good it made me feel. I mean, for a long time the only people asking me out were real creeps. But Richard, he was different." She closed her eyes as if reminiscing. "He had a good job, he was smart, and he was clean. I mean, he was really clean, about the cleanest guy that ever asked me out. When he came by to pick me up that weekend, I was really feeling good. He took me out for a pizza, and then we went to a movie. I really liked him, and I thought he liked me too because he asked me out again. After that, we started going out regularly, ya know, every Friday night. Then, all of a sudden, he was asking me out more often, about three times a week. I figured that he really cared for me. So when he asked me to spend the night with him, I did. I thought he loved me. I mean, I wouldn't have done it if I didn't think he loved me." Marie's voice was beginning to quiver under the strain. "I don't want ya to think I'm the kinda girl that sleeps around; I'm not. It's just that I thought that he loved me, ya know. That makes a difference, don't ya think?" The woman pleaded passionately for an answer.

Judge Witney said nothing, only nodding in agreement. It wasn't so much that he agreed or disagreed. It wasn't his position to judge moral conduct. He nodded only out of compassion for Marie. If his approval was important and could expedite matters, what difference would it make if he nodded?

"Well, anyway," she continued, "we spent the night together several times, and then I never saw him again, not once! The only time I ever heard from him was when he sent me a box of roses. One week later the roses died, and I found out I was pregnant. Your Honor, I need help! I can't make it by myself. I don't make enough money. There are the medical bells, and my landlord says I will have to move since they don't allow children where I live now. I only make four hundred dollars a month, and Richard," she said, pointing to the man on her left, "he makes over twenty-five thousand dollars a year. I know, because he told me so. It's not right that I should have to pay for everything." Marie's eyes were filling with tears again. She could hardly choke the words out. "It's his baby too; he should have to pay!"

Miss Garolia's attorney withdrew a packet of Kleenex from his briefcase and handed one to her.

Judge Witney dutifully scribbled a few notes on the pad before him, allowing the woman to regain her composure before he continued. Without looking up, he spoke to the man seated to the left of Miss Garolia, "Mr. Robinson, would you care to speak in your defense?"

"Yes, I would, your Honor."

Judge Witney waited for Robinson to speak—without results. The chamber was silent except for Marie's sobbing. Finally, Judge Witney looked up from his notes to find Robinson staring blankly back at him. "Mr. Robinson, if you do care to speak in your behalf, do so now."

"Oh, yes, excuse me, your Honor," he stammered. "Well, you see, your Honor, it is true that I am the father of Marie's baby—or, rather, the baby to be. Or should I say...."

"Please," moaned Judge Witney, interrupting Robinson. "We know what you are trying to say. Believe me, you needn't be concerned with exact wordage. You need only tell your account of Miss Garolia's pregnancy in your own words. Do I make myself clear?"

"Yes, sir, er I mean, your Honor!"

"Then try and do the same, OK?"

"Yes, by all means, your Honor. I will."

Silently, Judge Witney groaned to himself. Why couldn't people just open their mouths and tell what's on their minds, he thought. But, no, it never happened that way. Whenever they entered a courtroom, they felt compelled to speak with the ease of a Perry Mason. Of course, no one could do that very well, so what usually happened was that they became lost in endless retractions and qualifying statements.

"Well," began Robinson again, "it is true that Marie and I met at Hoggie's. I saw her sitting alone at the table so I went over and introduced myself. I do that a lot. There's nothing wrong in that. I mean, that's why everyone goes to a place like Hoggie's. Well, we talked awhile, and I found that I enjoyed her company so I asked her out. We dated some, and before long I noticed that I was developing vibes for her. I told Marie how I felt, and she said she felt the same way. Before you know, I was spending the night. I know it doesn't sound complicated, because it wasn't. It just happened. It happens a lot these days, you know. You meet a person. You find that you like them, so you have an affair. Then when it's over, everyone goes his/her own way. Well, in Marie's case it didn't turn out that way. About two weeks into the affair she begins talking marriage. I couldn't believe it! I mean, I didn't lie to her, tell her that I loved her or that I was looking for someone to settle down with. I told her that I enjoyed my freedom and wanted nothing more than to remain single. I laid it all out on the table that first night at Hoggie's. So, as far as I'm concerned, when we started spending the night together, it was strictly recreational. And, damn it all, she knew it too. In fact, I can't believe that she can actually sit there and say that she thought I cared when I specifically told her how I felt about marriage."

"People change," blurted Marie.

"Yeah, in soap operas but not in real life, Marie!"

"In real life too. I thought you changed when you asked to stay the night."

"Please, please," interrupted Judge Witney while rubbing his forehead. "If I wanted shouting, I could have let your attorneys argue the case. Now, Mr. Robinson, please continue, and, if possible, Miss Garolia, could you refrain from interrupting?"

Marie settled back in her chair, pressing the tissue to her face to muffle her sobs.

"Well, after about a week of being hammered by Marie with marriage, I left. Sure, I wanted to talk to her and tell her I was sorry for the way things turned out, but I couldn't bring myself to face her. It would only have stirred things up, don't you see? So, I sent the flowers. Anyway, about three weeks pass, and I get this call from her saying she is pregnant. Man, was I ever steamed. I couldn't believe it. I mean, before we did any messing around, I specifically asked her if it was safe. You know what—she laughed! Can you believe it? She just told me everything was fine and not to worry because she was using birth control." Robinson's voice was rising now. "Do you know what the birth control turned out to be—rhythm! Do you believe it?" shouted Robinson. "RHYTHM! Well, let me tell you, she had about as much rhythm as a deaf-mute saxophone player!"

Marie could contain herself no longer. "That's not true. I've used rhythm before, and everything was fine. But this time I was ill for a couple of days, and that messed everything up. My doctor said it was probably the medicine he gave me. How was I to know?"

"Miss Garolia," said Judge Witney, "need I remind you, it's Mr. Robinson's turn to tell the story?"

Again Marie sat back in her chair. Robinson continued, "Well, since there wasn't much we could do about the pregnancy then, I suggested an abortion. I offered to pay the complete cost, but, no, she wouldn't hear of it. She kept saying that it was murder, that it was against her religion, and she'd never be able to live with herself." Robinson scooted his chair closer to the judge's desk. Leaning forward, he pleaded his case. "Your Honor, I'm trying to be fair in this matter, but it's not right that I should have to financially ruin myself over this. I mean, it is true that I do make twenty-five thousand dollars a year, but surely you can appreciate that twenty-five grand isn't that much money. Besides, I work hard for my money. It doesn't come easy. Sometimes I have to drive my laundry truck twelve hours a day." Robinson scooted even closer now. "I mean, the Supreme Court said abortion is legal. So my position is that now that we have an alternative, she can get the abortion. We're talking about three hundred dollars versus something like a hundred thousand dollars. Now, I realize that Marie doesn't believe in abortion, but those are her beliefs, not mine. Why should I be penalized for her religious convictions? And, as for the money, her parents live three blocks from her. If she wants to keep the baby, let them help."

"My father won't help," Marie said, calmer this time. "He says it's your baby, not his."

"That's great, really great. He tells you not to have the abortion because it's against his religious beliefs, but he wants me to pay for it. Next he'll want me to put money in the collection plate for him!"

He was desperate now. Eye to eye with Judge Witney, Robinson's last words pleaded his case, "Don't men have any rights?"

It was now time for the attorneys to polish their clients' cases. Each would speak eloquently, spewing forth legalistic doctrines. Judge Witney would pay little attention. The attorneys' voices faded like early morning haze into the distance as he contemplated the testimony.

Name _____

> Read each statement before coming to class. To the left check whether you agree or disagree with this statement. After discussing the statement with your group in class, record the total number of members agreeing and disagreeing in the boxes to the right and explain your position in a few sentences below.

A D   **A D**
☐☐   1. The only way people will behave in a socially responsible manner is if you make   ☐☐
          them financially liable for their actions.

☐☐   2. After having two welfare babies, a woman should either be forced to be sterilized or ☐☐
          lose her welfare payments.

☐☐   3. If women can force the father of their child to pay paternity, then men should be   ☐☐
          able to prevent them from aborting their unborn children.

☐☐   4. Marie was just trying to trap Richard into marriage.   ☐☐

☐☐   5. If Marie can't afford the baby and the court rules in favor of Richard, then the child ☐☐
          should be put up for adoption.

Name _____

☐ ☐   6. Like most men, Richard's only interest is taking advantage of women.   ☐ ☐

☐ ☐   7. Women have all the rights when it comes to abortion and children; men have all the responsibilities.   ☐ ☐

☐ ☐   8. Now that the government has instituted affirmative action for women in our society, it's time to abandon old concepts like child support and alimony.   ☐ ☐

☐ ☐   9. Our welfare system has created a situation where many women get pregnant just so they don't have to work.   ☐ ☐

☐ ☐   10. Contrary to what Richard would like to think, he failed to take any responsibility in his relationship with Marie.   ☐ ☐

Name _____

If you were Judge Witney, what would your decision be and why?

_____

_____

_____

_____

_____

_____

_____

_____

_____

_____

_____

_____

_____

_____

_____

_____

_____

_____

_____

_____

_____

_____

Name _____

In the space below, list some ways the government can help avoid situations like that in *Baby Talk*.

_____

_____

_____

_____

_____

_____

_____

_____

_____

_____

_____

_____

_____

_____

_____

_____

_____

_____

_____

_____

_____

_____

_____

_____

Gramps

Bradley Helton and his wife, Marla, were seated at the dining room table sipping their coffee. It was late, nearly bedtime. The woman set her cup down. Looking to her husband with a determined expression, she spoke, "Brad, what are we going to do about Gramps? We have to make a decision. It's been almost two months since Grandma died."

Bradley quickly raised a finger to his lips silencing his wife. His eyes darted past her pointing to the steps leading to the bedrooms. The woman turned quickly to see an old man slowly, almost painfully, making his way down the steps. The couple sat quietly as the old man edged past them heading for the kitchen. His only acknowledgment of their presence was a simple nod accompanied by a muffled grunt.

"You'd better go see what he's up to, Brad," said the woman.

The man pushed his chair back and made his way to the kitchen. When he entered, he found the old man searching through the cabinets. "Whatcha need Pop?"

"A drink, Son, a nice cool drink. But I can't find a dadburn glass!"

"There on the top shelf."

The old man reached up and opened the cupboard door exposing the glasses. "Oh, yeah, now there they are," he said, reaching to get one. "You know, I never did see a woman who moved things around as much as Marla does."

"Pop," responded the man, "Marla has kept the glasses in the same spot since we moved here fifteen years ago."

"Sure, Son?"

"Yeah, I'm sure, Pop."

"That's funny," mumbled the old man as he moved to the sink to get a drink. "I could've swore that she had them somewhere else."

The younger man watched as the old man refreshed himself. "Pop?" he called.

"Yeah?"

"Aren't you forgetting something?"

The old man stared back puzzled.

"Your pill, Pop. It's time for your medicine."

66

The old man screwed up his face a bit, distorting his expression. "Do you really suppose I need them pills, Son?"

"Pop, we've been through this a dozen times. If you don't take your medicine, you're going to start forgetting things again."

"But I still forget things even when I do take them pills," he retorted.

"Pop!"

"OK, Son. If it'll make you happy." The old man took the pills, placed them in his mouth and returned to the sink for water. "There," he muttered. "At least them pills seem to help one of us." The old man turned, limped past his son, and headed back to his bedroom.

Marla joined her husband in the kitchen.

"I swear," he said, "that man has got to be half mule."

"That's what I mean. I really think we ought to consider a nursing home."

"No! Definitely not," said Brad, flaring to anger. "Not for Pop. It's out of the question."

"Why?" exclaimed Marla. "Bill Campbell put his father in a nursing home, and you thought that was fine."

"I know, but Pop's case is different."

"How?"

"It's just different, that's all. It's different!"

"How?" she repeated.

"I don't want to go into it, Marla. Just take my word for it, will you?" he said adamantly.

"All right," replied Marla, capitulating. "No use fighting about it tonight." The woman stepped into the dining room and began picking up. A short moment later Brad walked up behind her and put his arms about her.

"Sorry, Honey," he apologized. "I guess this is difficult for you, too."

Marla returned her husband's affection. "I know. Maybe we can talk about it later, huh?"

"Sure," he said. "By the way, you still taking Pop for his check-up tomorrow?"

"Yeah, at eleven."

"Any trouble getting out of the office at that time?"

"No, I've arranged to switch lunch hours with one of the other girls."

"If you can find the time, call me afterwards. I'll be in the office all day."

Brad and Marla turned off the lights and headed up the stairs to their bedroom. Outside, in the hall, Brad paused briefly by the old man's door to listen. He nodded to his wife indicating that Pop was asleep.

It was 1:15, and Brad had just returned from lunch when his office phone rang.

"Hi, Honey."

"Oh, hi. How did Pop's check-up go?"

"Well, good and bad," replied Marla.

"Meaning?"

"In some ways he's getting along fine and in others, not so fine. The doctor thought he was adjusting really well to Grandma's death. You know, I listened to the doctor talk to him about it, and he really has a good concept of life, death and living. So psychologically the doctor says he's in remarkable shape."

"So what's wrong?"

"Well, he's not taking his medication regularly. I guess when we're there to badger him about it, he'll take it. But when we're not there, he either refuses to take it or simply forgets about it."

"What did Dr. Gardner have to say about it?"

"Well, he made it quite clear that if Gramps doesn't take his medication regularly, he'll be completely senile in less than a year."

"No doubt about it, huh?"

"None whatsoever."

"It's amazing he's done so well up until now."

"You can thank your mother for that. Dr. Gardner said she was the one who kept him on schedule. But now someone else is going to have to make sure he gets his medication." There was a pause of silence between the two. "Brad?"

"Yeah?"

"We're going to have to talk about this tonight. You do understand that, don't you?"

"Yeah," came a sigh from the man. "I tell you what. After dinner tonight, we'll talk."

"How? Pop will be there. You know, we can't go anywhere in the house alone. If we go in the kitchen, he'll show up. If we move to the dining room, he'll follow. He just likes company. I'm not complaining. I'm just saying we can't talk."

"Well, after dishes we'll go for a nice long walk. That way we can talk, OK?"

"OK, that should give us time, that is, unless Pop decides he needs a walk."

"He won't. He likes to rest after eating. It's a long-standing habit of his."

"OK then, I'll see you tonight."

"See ya tonight, bye."

It was after dinner that night when the table was cleared and dishes done that Marla turned to Brad and said, "I think it's time we had that walk now."

Brad shrugged, "I suppose so. Let's go."

Marla grabbed a shawl and wrapped it about her shoulders. Brad wore a light jacket as the autumn air was slightly chilled now. As they passed through the living room along the way to the front door, they found the old man resting comfortably in a cushioned chair.

"Going out?" he inquired.

"Yeah, Pop, thought we'd get some air," said Brad.

"That sounds good. I could use a little stretching myself. Mind if I join you?"

"I don't know, Pop," said Brad hesitantly. "It's kind of chilly out. Maybe it'd be better if you stayed in tonight."

A sly smile crossed the old man's face. "Oh, I get it now," he chuckled. "You two love birds want to be alone, huh? That's what it's all about, right?"

"Well, sorta, Pop."

"Well, why didn't you just come out and say so? I'm not that old, ya know. Your ma and me used to walk pretty near every evening 'bout this time of night, too." The old man waved his hand at the two as he settled back into the chair. "Now go on—get along."

Brad and Marla stepped out onto the porch and started down the sidewalk. The woman gently slid her hand into her husband's. The early evening air was crisp, and the scent of autumn was everywhere. Brad was searching the heavens. "Look," said Marla, pointing to the moon. "Isn't it beautiful tonight—so bright, so full?"

"Yeah," he replied. "I was just looking at it." He squeezed her hand, laughing slightly.

"What's so funny?"

"Oh, nothing."

"Come on. Tell me. I want to know."

"It's ridiculous."

"Tell me anyway."

"Oh, I was just thinking about the first time I remember seeing a moon like that one."

"You can actually remember?"

"Yeah, I was about six. Pop and I were walking along on an evening much like this one. Anyway, I looked up and all of a sudden there it was—so big, so bright. Man, was I excited. When I asked about it,

Pop told me it was just the moon. Of course, I knew it was the moon, but nobody had ever taken the time to explain what a moon was. So my next question was 'what's a moon?' You know what the old codger told me?"

"What?"

"He told me the moon was God's window and that he put it in the sky so he could look down and see his people." The man laughed again. "You know, I spent half my childhood looking up at the moon expecting to see God watching me." The man was silent for a moment and then said, "You know, even now, sometimes I look up and catch myself...."

"Brad," interrupted Marla. "This isn't going to make it any easier."

"Yeah, I know. Guess I was just thinking out loud, you know."

"Uh huh—I know," muttered the woman softly. "Brad?"

"What?"

"Dr. Gardner said that Pop's condition is going to require a little more supervision than we expected."

"Meaning?"

"Meaning that someone is going to have to be with him most of the time to see that he takes his medicine, eats his meals, and gets his rest."

"Well, maybe we could work something out so that someone could be home."

"How?" asked Marla, stopping suddenly. "I work eight hours a day. Half the time you're on the road traveling, and the kids are in school."

"Well, maybe we could get by on less money. You know, you could reduce your hours and..."

"Brad, that's not fair. For fifteen years I stayed home. Now I have a chance for a promotion and a career. But I won't if I only work part time."

"All right, all right. What about the kids? Maybe they could help? Jenny and Paul could alternate coming home to check on Pop. We could all help. Even days when I'm not on the road, I could...."

"Brad, that's not the only problem. It's more than just a scheduling problem."

"I don't understand."

"I know. I hadn't told you yet because I know how much pressure you've been under with the Lockland contract."

"OK, let's have it, Marla."

"It's the kids, Jenny and Paul. They're pretty upset with having Pop in the house."

"Why?"

"Well, Paul resents having to give up his room to Pop. He didn't say anything at first because he thought it was temporary. Now that it looks as if it'll be permanent, he's awfully unhappy about having to sleep in the basement. In fact, he's now decided not to live at home next year and attend Harper College. He's been mailing applications to other resident schools in the state. I really had hoped he would attend Harper, at least for the first couple of years anyway, especially with the cost of attending a resident college and all the problems they have in those dormitories. And there's Jenny."

"What about Jenny?"

"Well, you know girls her age are finding boyfriends now. All ninth graders are, and Jenny's no exception. Anyway, I guess she and Larry, that's her latest, were sitting on the couch after school yesterday kissing when Pop walked in and caught them. From the way Jenny describes it, Pop made quite a scene. I guess the poor boy is so scared now he won't come near the house."

"Was he the one with the long, dark, curly hair?" asked Brad.

"Yeah, that's the boy."

"Well, I saw him, and, from the looks of it, Jenny's not losing much."

"That's not the point. The point is that she was embarrassed. I could hardly get her to go to school today." Marla was silent for a moment as they continued walking. Finally she said, "Then there's us."

"Us? What's wrong with us?" replied Brad, stopping now.

"Haven't you noticed? We have no privacy anymore. Every time we go into the bedroom, we lock the door. Can you imagine that!" exclaimed the woman. "We lock the bedroom door in our own house!"

"Well, you know Pop," said Brad half-apologizing. "Sometimes he forgets."

"That's the whole point," said the woman, searching her husband's eyes. "I honestly feel he would be better off in a nursing home."

"I can't do that to Pop, Marla."

"Why? Lots of people go to nursing homes."

"Pop's case is different."

"I don't see how."

"Marla, I told you last night that I don't want to talk about it. Just take my word for it. Pop's case is different."

"How can I understand if you won't tell me how it's different?"

"Marla? Have I ever lied to you before?"

"No."

"Haven't I always been open with you on everything else?"

"Yes."

"Then please let it be. Just trust me when I tell you Pop's case is different, OK?"

"OK," replied Marla resignedly. "But I still don't understand. Maybe he'd like it in a nursing home."

"Not, Pop!"

"How do you know? Have you asked him?" confronted Marla.

"No."

"Then how can you be so sure, Brad," said the woman desperately. "You have to ask him. It's only fair to us."

"OK, I'll ask him."

"When?"

"Tomorrow," replied Brad. "I'll ask him tomorrow. In fact, he's wanted to visit a friend of his in one of the nursing homes. Maybe I'll take him out, and when we're there, I can get him to sit down with one of the administrators and talk about their facilities and programs. Does that sound fair?" said Brad, emphasizing the word fair.

"Don't talk that way, Brad," said Marla as they approached the house. "He may surprise you and like it."

As they opened the door and entered, they found the house in chaos. Paul was scurrying down the stairs with two buckets filled with water. Jenny was headed upstairs with the mop and towels. Both kids were screaming at each other as they passed.

"What's wrong?" Brad quickly shouted over the confusion.

"It's Grandpa!" screamed Jenny. "He forgot and left the water running in the bathtub."

"Brad," protested Marla.

"Tomorrow," said the man, racing upstairs. "I'll talk to him tomorrow."

It was late the following evening when Marla returned home from work.

"Sorry, Dear," she said while joining her husband in the kitchen. "We had to finish the annual reports for the board meeting tomorrow."

Brad was sitting quietly at the table.

"Where's Pop?" she asked.

"Asleep," he replied.

"How did it go today?"

"Fine until he realized why we were there."

"Bad, huh?"

"You should have seen him when they began explaining their program. He was so pathetic. He didn't say a word. He just sat there looking straight at the counselor, tears streaming down his cheeks. I could hardly stand it myself. Then on the way home he was very stoic about it. You know how proud Pop is. He said living was like going to the amusement park. It's exciting at first, but after you've ridden all the rides two or three times you're ready to go home. He said that's how he felt now—he was ready to go home. The only thing though was that he had hoped he could ride home with us," Brad's lip quivered. He stopped to regain his composure. Then he continued, "In his own way he was pleading with me, don't you see? He wants to die here in our home."

"I know how difficult it must be, Brad, but you must consider us, too."

"Maybe there's another way. Perhaps we could get a nurse to come in."

"Where would we get the money for a nurse? You know how expensive that would be? Why we have a tough time making ends meet now."

"If we can't afford a nurse, how can we afford a nursing home?"

"I've thought about that, too," confessed Marla. "I think he'd have to go on welfare."

"WELFARE!" shouted Brad, jumping out of his chair. "Not Pop—he's too proud. It'd kill him."

"Brad, in the last twenty-five years we've saved $15,000. But there's the kids' educations coming up, and then we have to start thinking about our own retirement. Besides, lots of people in nursing homes are on welfare. It's no big disgrace."

"For Pop it would be a disgrace. He wouldn't want to do it."

"Well, life can't always be the way we want it. Sometimes we have to do things we don't like."

"I told you. Pop's case is different."

"I'm sick of it!" said Marla almost shouting now. "Do you hear me—I'm sick of hearing about how Pop's case is different from everybody else's. It isn't. It's all in your head, that's all."

Brad sat at the table, shaking his head. "I guess I'll have to tell you," he said. "There's no other way I can possibly make you understand." Brad slid out of his chair, opened the basement door, and disappeared. A few moments later he returned carrying a faded manila envelope, creased and limp from years of use. Marla watched intently as her husband opened the envelope and spilled its contents across the tabletop.

"What's this?" asked Marla as she shuffled through the pile of old letters, pictures, and documents.

"It's Pop's. I found it about five years ago when I helped Pop clean up his basement, you remember, when he finally decided to throw away all the junk he'd been saving for years."

"Yeah, I remember. It took you and Pop two days to finish the job."

"Well, that's when I found the envelope. Whenever Pop would pitch something, I'd sneak over and double check. You know how careless he can get sometimes. Anyway, after he had gone upstairs, I found this sealed envelope so I opened it up just to make sure it wasn't anything important."

"And?" questioned Marla.

"Let me show you," said Brad, searching through the papers. "Here it is," he said, handing her a wedding certificate. "Of course, you know that my natural mother died when I was five years old. This is their wedding certificate. Read the date."

"August 13, 1933."

"Right," he said, handing her another document. "Now look at my birth certificate. Read the date."

"February 9, 1934." The woman paused to reflect on what she had just read. Suddenly it struck her. "Brad, that's not your birthday. Yours is April 20th."

"Well, that's what Pop always said. But actually it's not."

"So that's why he always told you your birth certificate was lost. But what about the hospital's copy."

"Destroyed in a fire," answered Brad. "Convenient, huh?"

"Can you imagine that, Pop trying to hide the fact that you were conceived out of wedlock?"

"Well, not exactly. At first that's what I thought he was trying to hide, too, but then I found this," he said, handing Marla a picture.

"This is your natural mother and Pop at an amusement park."

"Exactly," he replied. "Now turn it over and read the inscription."

Marla turned the picture over, reading from the hand-written note, "It says—first date—August 2, 1933." The woman paused looking up at her husband. "So?" she asked finally.

"Count!"

The woman began counting silently to herself. Suddenly her expression changed to surprise. "Oh, my God!" she exclaimed.

"Exactly," he said calmly. "Pop is not my real father. Listen to me, Marla," the man said softly. "When I found out, I couldn't believe it myself. I went and talked to my stepmother. I guess I was so upset that she figured she had to tell me everything, but she did so only after making me promise not to tell anyone until after Pop's death. I'm going to break that promise now, but I think she would understand."

"I'm sure she would," replied Marla, listening intently.

Brad got up from his seat and paced the kitchen while telling the story. "From what I understand, my mother was kinda wild and irresponsible. Pop met her while on a two-week leave from the army and fell head over heels for her not knowing she was pregnant at the time. Anyway, he married her on the last day of his leave. Can you imagine that? Talk about a whirlwind romance! Anyway, after they were married, he returned to the army for a tour of duty in Europe. He was in Europe when I was born and obviously had to know I wasn't his child. But I guess he was able to sort things out for himself and decided it didn't matter. When he returned to the states, he was stationed at Fort Dix. He sent for my mother and me, and we lived there for about three years. When I was about four, my mother decided army life wasn't for her, and she picked up one night when Pop was on duty and left."

"She deserted him?"

"Yeah, without even a word. I guess Pop found her in Chicago with another man." The man paused briefly and then confessed, "You know, for the life of me I can't remember that. It was all too confusing. From what I understand, Pop tried to get her to come back with him, but she wouldn't. Six months later she was accidentally killed in a barroom fight."

Brad looked to his wife and saw the disbelief on her face. "It's true, all of it. After Mom told me, I checked out all the records, army and hospital records both."

"It's so hard to believe."

"I know, but let me finish. The rest of it I can remember. In fact, I remember when this strange lady with a stern voice came to the apartment. I guess the landlady let her in. Of course, Mom didn't return that night, and I was alone. The woman told me that my mother had left and would not be back and that I was to go with her to an orphanage. I was about five then. It was there that I was told that my mother had died, and this was to be my new home. You can't believe how I cried. I must have cried for two months straight. I hated that place. It was so sterile, so empty of any love or affection."

"But what about Pop?" questioned Marla unable to contain herself any longer.

"I'm getting to that. Anyway, I guess one of Pop's old army buddies was living in Chicago, saw the newspaper piece on my mother's death, and sent it to him." The man stood gazing across the room, tears were swelling up in his eyes. "I remember so well the day Pop came for me," he said, his voice cracking. "I was sitting by myself on the steps. I was alone, lost and scared half outta my mind by a world I didn't understand. All of a sudden, I looked down the walk to the gateway and saw a man walking toward me, presents stuck under both arms, and a smile strung clear across his face." He paused momentarily. "Marla," said Brad finally, "you can't possibly believe the joy I felt when I first recognized Pop's face. I don't even think my feet touched the ground as I raced into his arms. I wouldn't even let him put me down to pick up the presents," he said, wiping his eyes. "To this day I still can't remember what he brought me. I don't even recall opening them. The only thing that mattered was that Pop was there. That was the real gift—someone who cared for me." Brad paused again. "Don't you see, Marla? That's what makes Pop's case so different. He didn't have to come. I wasn't even his own kid, but he came anyway. He was there because he knew I needed him. How can I, his only child, abandon him now—when he needs me?"

Marla was silent as Brad explained his feelings. When he finished, he sat beside her staring into his coffee cup.

"I see," said the woman finally. "But what about us, Brad—your family? What about my chances for a promotion and a career? What about the kids? Paul is going to leave home, and Jenny's upset."

"We could talk to the kids, make them understand."

"How? Paul won't change his mind, and Pop will never change his views about Jenny's behavior. Why those two will be fighting until he dies or she leaves home. And there's more to consider."

"What's that?" asked Brad.

"Us. What about our privacy? For the first time in years we have a little money and freedom to really live again. Are we going to let that slip away from us? It may be our last chance."

"But, Marla," protested Brad. "I owe Pop."

The two of them sat silently, each alone with their own thoughts. Finally Brad spoke. "Marla?" he asked. "What are we going to do?"

"Brad," she answered, "you have to decide. It's your decision. You're the one that is going to have to live with it." She reached over and touched her husband's arm lovingly and said, "I just want you to know that whatever you decide, I'll stand by you."

Name _____

Read each statement before coming to class. To the left check whether you agree or disagree with this statement. After discussing the statement with your group in class, record the total number of members agreeing and disagreeing in the boxes to the right and explain your position in a few sentences below.

A D   A D
☐ ☐   1. Parents who truly love their children wouldn't ask to move into their homes.   ☐ ☐

☐ ☐   2. Parents who do not save for their retirement have to expect to spend their final   ☐ ☐
            days in a welfare home.

☐ ☐   3. Having an older parent in the home is bound to create a lot of problems.   ☐ ☐

☐ ☐   4. No parent really wants to leave his loved ones to live in a nursing home.   ☐ ☐

☐ ☐   5. Nursing homes are dumping grounds for the elderly in our society.   ☐ ☐

Name _____

☐☐ 6. Parents have a right to live with their children when they get too old to care for themselves. ☐☐

☐☐ 7. If Brad's father stays, Marla will suffer the most. ☐☐

☐☐ 8. If Brad wants Gramps to stay, he should quit his job to care for his father and let Marla go to work. ☐☐

☐☐ 9. Parents who are sent to nursing homes intuitively understand they are not loved. ☐☐

☐☐ 10. In this case Brad has more responsibility to Gramps since he was not his natural father. ☐☐

Name _____

If you were Brad, what would your decision be and why?

_____

_____

_____

_____

_____

_____

_____

_____

_____

_____

_____

_____

_____

_____

_____

_____

_____

_____

_____

_____

_____

_____

_____

Name _____

In the space below, list some ways the government can help families cope with the growing problem of elderly parents.

_____

_____

_____

_____

_____

_____

_____

_____

_____

_____

_____

_____

_____

_____

_____

_____

_____

_____

_____

_____

_____

_____

Fence Walking

Rachael Wilson stared aimlessly out the window of her congressional office, looking but not seeing. It was fall now, and everywhere there were the signs of change: from the brisk autumn winds to the few remaining leaves clinging desperately to barren branches. Soon the bitter northern winds would descend and nature would succumb.

A faint smile crossed her frail lips. It was ironic, almost symbolic, she thought, that this same wind that played troubadour to the changing season carried with it this year a special message for her. But then in the back of her mind she had known this day would eventually come, a day in which she would be forced to choose between her personal moral convictions and political expediency—but why now? Why did the issue have to be the National Health Care Plan? After all, she had co-authored several major portions of the bill and, in addition, felt strongly that the time had come when all Americans should be afforded a better quality of health care. Silently, in almost poetic reflection, she recounted past memories.

As a small child, Rachael Wilson had watched helplessly as her father slid into the despair of bankruptcy while desperately trying to prolong the life of her cancer-stricken mother. No one knew better than she did the relationship between "hard cash" and disease. And no one was more aware of the chain of events in the struggle to get that money. First, the home was sacrificed, then the automobile. Next came personal items such as life insurance, paintings, musical instruments, and other items the family could survive without. And finally, yes finally, she remembered those huge bank loans requiring a lifetime of her father's work to repay.

As she walked back to her desk, she wondered how many Americans were aware of the broken lives and hardships endured by tens of thousands of their fellow citizens each year. Even if they were, would they be willing to support a national health program, she wondered. Or would they be content to take their chances in life? If only there were room for compromise, she thought, but the sponsors of the bill had already made several major compromises. To compromise again would destroy the bill's purpose, making it of little value to anyone. No, she would have to decide to vote for or against the bill as it stood.

In spite of her moral convictions, she knew that she couldn't afford the luxury of making decisions solely on the basis of her personal beliefs. No politician could. She would have to weigh all factors carefully, political and moral, and come to a decision. Rachael Wilson was at the crossroads of her political career. This just might be the most crucial decision in her entire life.

One year ago Rachael Wilson had won one of the most contested congressional elections in the entire nation. Having lost in the Republican primary, she decided to run as an independent candidate and, in a surprise to everyone, won. Although her election to Congress might have been a fluke to many, it was not to Rachael Wilson. The congressional district in which she ran was an unusual mixture of people in terms of race, religion, and occupation. Of the 500,000 people she represented, thirty percent could be classified as poverty-stricken. This figure included a high proportion of African Americans and Mexican Americans. Sixty percent of the people were blue-collar urban workers with a high school education or less. The remainder represented a scattered mixture of professionals, white-collar employees, and farmers. In terms of religion, forty percent were Catholic, fifty-five percent Protestant, and five percent Jewish. Although one would expect that such a mixture would produce a Democratic district, the lack of a solid organization between the African Americans and Mexican Americans usually produced a slight majority for the Republican candidates. Rachael's election was considered by many professional politicians as a matter of unusual circumstances. For the first time in the history of the district a solid coalition was established among the African Americans, Mexican Americans and urban poor to defeat the Republican incumbent. Many expected the Democratic candidate, Thomas Johnson, to be the main benefactor of the newly formed coalition. He took seriously ill three days prior to the election, withdrew from the race, and threw his support to Rachael. With support from both sides, Rachael was able to edge out her opponent by a slight margin. During her campaign she vigorously urged for the redevelopment of the city's ghetto, for provisions for better health-care facilities for the urban poor, and the creation of a federally financed commission to deal with the problems of unemployment in the district. In order to pacify the influential members of the community, she promised to seek new industries that would establish themselves in the district. This, in turn, would create more jobs and provide new sources of revenue for the city. The promise of economic growth lured many liberal Republicans into her camp.

In spite of the fact that many Republicans felt that Rachael was a bit too liberal in some of her views, she was, after all, a Republican and deserved their support—at least until she proved otherwise. Therefore, she was welcomed into the fold and assigned by the party a seat on the Education and Labor Committee. It was an assignment that pleased her, for usually junior members of Congress are banished to obscure, less prestigious committees, totally unrelated to the needs of their constituents.

During her first year in office Rachael continued to maintain close contact with community leaders of both political parties in her district while promoting strong friendships within the Republican Party in Congress. She was so successful in walking the fence that a reporter in one of the local papers back home referred to her as "The Fence Walker." In fact, there was a rumor circulating locally that the Democrats were considering slating her on their ticket in the next election. Although the Democratic leadership had not yet approached Wilson, the rumor was not without its appeal. A young, wealthy Republican, Roy Adams, was building support in the local organization and announced that he would oppose her in the party primary. In the event that Adams gained too much support before the primary, she could always fall back on the Democratic ticket. Certainly she was sympathetic to many Democratic views and could fit easily into their party structure. Nevertheless, she preferred to remain with the Republicans—at least for the time being.

The National Health Care Plan placed her in a precarious situation. Even though she made several contributions to the bill, there was little question that the Democrats considered it their legislation. In fact, several key Democratic leaders proposed, wrote, and sponsored the legislation. The Speaker of the House carefully guided it to the Education and Labor Committee so that it would be in the friendly hands of the committee chairman, Frank Carlson.

Early predictions of a party fight over the legislation proved correct. As soon as the legislation was brought before the committee, members of Congress began lining up behind their respective parties. Debate over the bill was long and heated. Lobbyists from the AMA, insurance companies, and pharmaceutical firms testified before the committee that the bill would be disastrous to the medical profession and the entire country. In support of their case they outlined a convincing argument stating that America had the most advanced medical technology and care in the world. To provide everyone with unlimited health insurance, paid and controlled by the government, would, in essence, substitute quantity for quality. The AMA maintained that it was aware of the problems and was taking steps to correct them. However, they insisted, the federal government must allow them more time to resolve the difficulties.

After the various groups opposing the bill had presented their case, a number of independent organizations spoke in support of the pending legislation. The major thrust of their argument pointed to the fact that health care in America was basically elitist in nature and seriously deficient in serving the rural community and urban poor. This, they stated, was by design and not the result of any accident. As long as the AMA controlled the medical care in the country, the public was at its mercy. At the present time, health care was regarded a privilege with services going to those who could afford them. However, if the community as a whole was taxed to support medical schools for the purpose of training medical personnel, the advocates of the bill maintained that everyone should be entitled to health services regardless of their ability to pay. According to the organizations supporting the legislation, the medical profession was incapable of solving the problems because of their vested interest in maintaining lucrative fees for themselves. Therefore, the federal government should intervene.

During the testimony, to the displeasure of many of her Republican colleagues, Rachael appeared ambivalent. Occasionally she would ask a simple academic question, but always in such a manner that her intentions could not be ascertained. It appeared, in fact, that she was the only neutral member of Congress on the committee. Each time she was approached by the party leaders of either side as to her position on the bill, she would simply say that there were a few things that she wanted to clarify before committing himself. Although this did little to satisfy anyone, it provided her with valuable time.

On the morning of November 15, Rachael had arrived at her office promptly at nine. Her first order of business was to check with her aid regarding the mail from her constituents. She was surprised to find a great number of letters urging her to support the National Health Care Plan. In talking to her aid, she learned that letters were pouring in throughout the entire time that the committee was holding hearings on the legislation and that most of the responses were from the poor areas of her district. She was also informed that several very influential constituents had written strong letters opposing the bill. Rachael pondered the responses for a moment and then decided to let the issue slide for more pressing matters. She was preparing the final draft on her Urban Renewal Bill, and the deadline for completion was only four days off. This was the first piece of legislation that she would sponsor, and she wanted to ensure its success. Rachael felt that she had to demonstrate to her constituents that she was doing something for them in Washington.

Early that afternoon Rachael received a call from the Republican Party whip, Carl Hanson, informing her that, according to his survey, the National Health Care Plan was locked in a tie. She was the only member undecided and, therefore, would determine its fate. Hanson said he wanted to speak with her personally and would be down in a few minutes.

Ten minutes later Hanson appeared in the lobby of Rachael's office. After exchanging cordial greetings, the two got down to the business at hand. Hanson moved to the offensive quickly, "Look, Rachael, I know that you have strong feelings about this bill, even though you kept them to yourself in the committee. Believe me, we appreciate that, but it looks like you are going to have to make your move now. I don't have to tell you that many of our people are going to be very interested in your decision. You have a very promising future in our party, so don't blow it now."

"I don't know. I just don't know," Rachael muttered. "I'd like to help the party out, but I promised the people back home that I was going to help them get better health care. I still have constituents that have babies in unheated bedrooms because they can't afford to go to the hospital! Do you know what the disease and death rate is like in my district? The only hope they have is this bill."

"You're new here, Rachael," Hanson replied. "You have to learn that you can't solve all the problems at once. Besides, if the AMA doesn't support the plan, it's not going to work no matter how much money we pump into the program. The federal government just can't go around taking over everyone's life."

"That seems like a pretty callous attitude to me," she said.

"Look, I'm going to be honest with you, Rachael," Hanson continued. "Individual effort doesn't accomplish much in Congress. To pass legislation around here requires team effort. That may not sound very idealistic, but that's the way it is, like it or not! Let's take the Urban Renewal Bill that you plan to sponsor. That bill isn't going to pass on its own merit. If it's going to pass, it's because it has a team behind it." Looking earnestly at Rachael, Hanson said, "Listen, Rachael, you're going to have to make up your mind on what team you want to play ball. And believe me, I, for one, want you on our side."

For the rest of the meeting, which lasted two hours, Hanson and Rachael discussed the pros and cons of the bill. Throughout the conversation Rachael had the uneasy feeling that the discussion was strictly academic. The real issue had already been covered.

That night, while relaxing at home, Rachael received a phone call from Paul Longdale, a leading Democrat on the Education and Labor Committee. Rachael was surprised to find that Longdale was extremely well versed about local matters in her district. In fact, Longdale had spoken to Thomas Johnson at length on the matter and was quick to point out that the majority of Rachael's constituents were favorable to the plan— at least a majority of the people who were responsible for her election. He also hinted at the possibility of Democratic support for her Urban Renewal Bill. Since the Democrats were in control of the House of Representatives, their support was not to be taken lightly. Longdale also stated that it was unfair to expect a member of Congress to follow strict party lines on every issue. Instead, he argued that Rachael should take into consideration the wishes of her constituents. After all, he reminded her, she was elected to serve the people in her district, not the Republican Party. Before hanging up, Longdale assured Rachael that the rumor of her being asked to run on the Democratic slate was more than just hearsay. However, Longdale also made it clear that if Rachael decided to remain with the Republicans and vote against the Health Care Plan, the Democrats had a couple of proven "vote-getters" standing in the wings of the party, both of whom would be more than pleased to carry the party's banner in the next election against her.

"Come now, Paul," she interrupted, "is that a threat?" On the other end of the line, she could hear the faint sound of laughter.

"A threat?" said Longdale finally. "Good heavens, no," he chuckled. "Let's just call it a little realistic talk between two very practical politicians, huh?"

Rachael ended the conversation on a positive note by promising Longdale she would give the matter serious consideration.

While working at her desk the next day, Rachael was startled to hear her secretary announce the arrival of Terry Dean. Dean was considered by many to be one of the president's closest assistants. As Dean entered her office, he extended a friendly handshake and sat down in one of the plush leather chairs in front of Rachael's desk. Dean opened the conversation by saying, "I suppose you know why I'm here today?"

"The National Health Care Plan, right?" smiled Rachael knowingly.

Dean nodded as he stood and walked to the window. He stared out for a few moments as if in deep thought and then suddenly turned to Rachael and said, "Damn it, Rachael, there's just too much riding on this legislation. If it passes, it's going to blow the top right off the president's budget. And I don't have to tell you what that means to the economy. But you can settle the matter right in the committee. You have the power to kill it." Pointing to Rachael, Dean said, "The president wants you to settle it—he wants you to kill it!"

"But I was under the impression that the president supported better health care for the country. He campaigned on the issue, didn't he?" questioned Rachael.

"Listen, Rachael, as far as the president is concerned, this is a party matter. He's made that perfectly clear. I can't tell you how many times he has expressed his opposition to this bill to the leadership of the party."

"But health care was a major issue in his campaign," moaned Rachael.

"Yeah, it was. But that was before the economy took a turn for the worse. When we moved into the White House, things looked hopeful, but now with everything that has happened, it looks pretty bleak. Have you seen the latest economic indicators? We've got a tough couple of years coming up. That's why this bill can't pass. Man, if you think the economy is bad now, wait until the government starts shelling out $100 billion for a health-care plan. It'll kill any attempt to control the budget for the next ten years. Besides, this isn't a matter for the federal government, at least at this time. We already have too many federally financed programs. It is a matter for the states to handle in their own way."

"The trouble is that the states can't handle it," Rachael shot back. "The national government has cut federal grants to the bone. The states don't have the money to fund their own programs let alone come up with additional funds for increased health-care services."

"Listen, Rachael, you just can't change the world overnight," Dean said. "Be practical. Even if this bill does pass, we still won't have enough doctors or hospitals to cover everyone's needs, anyway. The AMA realizes the problem, and they're trying to correct it. It takes time. Give them a chance!"

The two sat staring at one another. Finally, Dean, realizing everything had been said, slipped out of his chair and concluded by saying, "Think it over. Rachael, we need you on our side this time."

With that Dean picked up his briefcase and walked to the door. Just before opening it, he turned to Rachael and said, "Oh, incidentally, I understand that the Democrats are planning a major drive to unseat you in the next election. I have already talked with the president about coming into your district to campaign for your reelection. Tentatively he agreed, but then," Dean said, grinning, "you never can tell what might come up at the last minute. If something did come up, he'd have to cancel out—get my drift?" With that Dean opened the door and left.

For the rest of the morning Rachael Wilson sat alone in her office contemplating the situation. Certainly, she would like to support the bill, but could she do so without damaging her political career? If the Republicans disowned her, she could always switch over to the Democrats. If she did switch, what would her chances be for reelection? The district had the make-up of a Democratic majority, and a coalition was established among the African Americans, Mexican Americans, and economically poor; however, it was a shaky alliance. Rachael knew that the courts were presently considering integrating the schools in her district and that might break the coalition. Even if the coalition weathered the storm of integration, would they come out and vote in the next election? On the other hand, if she voted against the bill, what chance would her Urban Renewal Bill have in the House of Representatives?

"Ms. Wilson." The voice of her secretary over the intercom suddenly broke her train of thought. "It's time for your committee meeting."

Name _____

When voting on a bill, a legislator must carefully weigh all relevant issues. The National Health Care Plan is no exception. Below list all political, economic and ethical issues that would influence Rachael to either vote for the bill or against it.

Issues supporting the bill	Issues opposing the bill

Name _____

If you were Rachael Wilson, how would you vote on the National Health Care Plan? Why?

_____

_____

_____

_____

_____

_____

_____

_____

_____

_____

_____

_____

_____

_____

_____

_____

_____

_____

_____

_____

_____

_____

_____

_____

_____

The Promised Land of Jackie (Moses) Witkowski

Mary Washington, a large, middle-aged, African-American woman, sat anxiously in the front seat of the bus opposite the driver. Like radar, her head swiveled in a continuous, almost mechanical, motion about broad shoulders as she scanned both sides of the street. The liter and abandoned storefronts that she had so often campaigned against dominated her view but that was not her principle concern at the moment. Now a more pressing problem occupied her thoughts.

From the corner of his eye the bus driver watched the woman. "My, my, my," he drawled in a knowing voice. "Don't have to be no psychologist to know that trouble's brewin'."

"Don't you go messin' with me, Bill Stokes," she snapped without taking her eyes off the street.

"Naw," he replied, pulling hard on the wheel to cut a sharp turn onto Second Street. "I ain't messin' with nobody! I was just thinking how easy life would be for you with a man around the house, know?"

"Don't even be thinking of it. I done throw'd one man outta my house."

"Yeah," he moaned. "But that was a long time ago."

"Might be," replied the woman determinedly, "but as long as this woman's breathin', it won't be long enough. Now you just shut your mouth 'bout all this foolishness and drive this here bus. That's what the city pays you for, not giving advice to folk who don't need it!" Suddenly the woman's eyes locked on a small figure darting into one of the abandoned buildings. "I know'd it; I just know'd it!" she murmured, leaping from her seat to grab the cord running along the length of the bus. "Stop," she blared at the driver. "Stop, the bus, you fool! Can't you see I need off?"

"Easy," he snapped back. "Can't stop a vehicle like this on a dime."

The woman had already moved out into the aisle of the bus and was standing at the door impatiently. As the door opened, she turned back to the driver. "Can you wait on me, Bill?"

The driver's expression turned sympathetic. "You know, I can't be waitin' on my riders. It's my job. I could get myself fired."

The woman nodded. "I'll be fine."

"This is my last go around today. You know that."

Again the woman nodded. "Then I'll be walking."

"It's three miles!" he exclaimed concerned.

"Won't be the first time this ol' gal's used her feet!" she replied, stepping off the bus. The woman quickly crossed the street carefully avoiding the garbage. The streetlights, those that were still in working order, were beginning to come on as dusk settled in upon the city. She approached the building where she had seen the small figure enter. Switching her purse to her left hand, she pounded hard on the door and waited for a response. There was none. Taking her hand, she wiped the dirt from the glass of the door and attempted to search the interior of the building, but the darkness within shielded everything from view. Again she pounded on the door, and yelled, "C'mom on boy. I know you're in there. You open this door now, ya hear, right now!" Still there was no reply. "All right, if that's the way ya want it," she yelled. With the full weight of her body she slammed up against the door, hip first. Giving way with little resistance, the door flew open, and the woman tumbled inside onto the floor. Getting up, she brushed herself off and stomped hurriedly to a lighted back room of the building to find a group of young boys sitting around on dilapidated sofas and cushioned chairs. Slogans and symbols were painted across the walls. The boys stared up at the woman standing in the doorway. "Nathan," she said sternly to her twelve-year-old son who was standing to the side of the room, "you get yourself over here right this minute!" The boy stood his ground. The woman's eyes narrowed to indiscernible slits. "I ain't saying it but one more time, Nathan. You get yourself over here, right now!" The boy started to move but, after glancing at one of the others who raised his hand, he stopped. The jaw of the woman tightened into a hard mass of muscle and bone as anger swept across her face. Quickly she scanned the interior of the room. On her left was a splintered board, four foot in length and one inch thick. Moving faster than one might think possible for a woman her size, she flung her purse out into the hall and grabbed the board with both hands, and racing over to Nathan, she smacked the boy hard across his back sending him rolling head over heels to the doorway. Racing after him, she swung the board again catching him this time on the back of the thighs. The boy screamed in pain and curled his legs and arms about his body for protection as the woman lifted the board over her head again. Instantly, the boy who had raised his hand and ordered Nathan to stop leaped from the couch. Catching the movement out of the corner of her eye, the woman pivoted to confront the boy with board in hand and eyes blazing. "You wanna be next?"

The boy grinned. Reaching into his pocket, he withdrew a switchblade. A long length of shinny steel sprang from its handle. "Not unless ya want a little of this," he said, waving the blade up in front of the woman's face.

"Why you little hooligan," cried the woman, shaking in rage at the threat. Before the boy could react, the woman had jerked the board high overhead and with one swift motion sent it crashing down on his head. The knife dropped from his hand as he spun backward. Seizing the moment, the woman charged and swatted the boy several more times unmercifully across his head and body. The other boys leaped out of the way and, to assure that none of them would join the fight, the woman whipped the board wildly around the center of the room cursing and screaming like a mental patient gone bezerk. When she stopped, the boy who had pulled the knife lie on the floor before her with blood streaming down his forehead. The others were pressed against the wall and into the corners of the room. "Don't you ever pull a knife on me again, boy, or next time I'll beat you so hard your momma won't even recognize you." Throwing the board down, the woman clamped a firm hand on her son's arm, retrieved her purse and headed for the door. Stepping outside, she was relieved to find the bus waiting for her. "Thank the Lord," she muttered as she pushed the child across the street to the open door of the vehicle. "Thought you couldn't wait for your riders?"

"Can't," he said without looking at the woman who was putting her clothes back in order. "I just had me some engine trouble. Everything's OK now, though." The engine roared as the bus started up. "Lord sure works in mysterious ways, don't He," commented the driver as he pulled away from the curb.

"Sorry, Momma," said the boy softly.

The woman looked down at her son. His large dark eyes were filled with tears.

"It's just that...."

"You don't have to explain, Nathan. I understand. Ain't easy saying no when all your friends be in gangs or starting 'em up. I know there's pressure on you to join up. But your momma didn't raise her son to be a street gang member and spend half his life in jail or, worse yet, get his fool head shot off. No, you're gonna make something outta of your life. God gave you the ability to do something special with your life, and that's what you're gonna do. Hear, boy?"

"But maybe," he stammered, "maybe the guys are right, that it ain't gonna matter with us."

The woman turned on her son. "Now don't you start up with me, Nathan. You know how I feel 'bout that discrimination nonsense. Everybody has problems, not just black folk. You telling me you ain't never seen no black lawyers or doctors? Sure you have and if they can make it, so can you." The woman was quiet as she picked splinters from her bleeding hand. "Now, you know I feel real bad 'bout hitting you so hard, but you shouldn't have made me so mad," she finally said, putting her arm around the boy and pulling him closer.

"Sorry, Momma."

"Yeah, I know," she replied, smiling down at the boy. "How about tomorrow, say after school, we go down and get those fancy sneakers you want."

"Momma, you don't have the money. You told me that yesterday."

"You just let me worry 'bout the money, ya hear."

Up in the distance, the woman could see the Robert Johnson building. Unlike the other projects, this one was unique in that it was a single building, twenty stories high, and isolated by the railyards on the east, the expressway on the south, and a solid row of abandoned industrial buildings to the west. With only one entryway into the complex, it was, virtually, an island unto itself. Though some residents complained about the lack of access, others, like Mary Washington, argued that it was a blessing since the residents were better able to monitor those entering or leaving the complex. This fact, in conjunction with a strong building organization headed by herself, provided a drug-free and gang-free environment in which to raise children. It was for this reason that Mary Washington was quick to criticize those complaining about the conditions of life at Robert Johnson. To her, an impoverished mother of four small children, it was far better than some of the other projects in which she had resided. Robert Johnson, at least, afforded hope that some day her children would escape project living and move across the row of industrial buildings into the neighborhood of small single family homes she could see from her bedroom window. She had expressed this hope openly in meetings among the residents and was angered when some laughed, claiming that the neighborhood she spoke of was white ethnics who opposed integration. Her children would never be welcomed in such a community, they scoffed. With fire in her eyes she stood up and chastised them for their pessimism. Was this how they were going to raise their children—without hope—without a vision for their own future? Not her children, she boomed. America was changing, and her children were going to be part of that change. They were moving out of Robert Johnson into a world filled with opportunity and dreams.

Seeing the building ahead, she reached into her pocketbook and carefully separated a dollar from the few remaining bills. She held it in her hand waiting for the bus to stop.

"Hear 'bout ol' Tom Blake?" asked the bus driver, looking back at the woman in his rear view mirror.

"No, don't even know the man," she replied.

"Yeah," he drawled. "Too bad 'bout ol' Tom."

"What happened to him?" she curiously asked after a moment of silence.

"Took some money from one of his riders."

"Stole it?"

"Nope," he said, shaking his head, "a tip. It's against the rules."

The woman opened her purse and put the dollar away.

A few miles away in a spacious high rise condominium overlooking the lake another drama was unfolding that ultimately would have a profound influence on Mary Washington's life. Real estate developer, Joseph Witkowski, and his wife, Jacqueline, who was coordinator for the distribution of federal education funds for the region, were celebrating. Earlier that day, Joseph had received city approval for the development of New Haven, an ambitious project that would redevelop eight square blocks of abandoned industrial buildings into an affordable residential community complete with schools and shopping facilities. Conceived and developed by Joseph Witkowski, the development's sole purpose was to lure middle income families back to the city. Witkowski's idea was centered on the fact that the children of many of the old, white, ethnic groups who had grown up in the city had left because of the lack of adequate schools and affordable housing. The mayor and the city council enthusiastically endorsed the project as the beginning for a new wave of migration back to the city. Although some areas of the city were being renovated and there was a small influx of suburbanites back into the city, the numbers were minimal and were drawn from predominately upper income professionals with no children. New Haven was designed to reverse that trend and, as such, was perceived as a means to breathe new life back into the city.

"Here's to New Haven," beamed Joseph Witkowski as he handed a glass of champagne to his wife while looking over a scale model of the project.

"To New Haven," replied Jackie, clinking her glass. "It's beautiful, truly a remarkable piece of work. You should be proud, Joseph."

"Well," he drawled, "a lot of people deserve credit."

"Maybe," she conceded, "but when I see the city politicians jumping in front of the line to grab the credit, it makes me mad as hell. Where were they the last five years when you were working night and day on this project? Now they're talking as if they invented it."

"That's politics, Jackie. The important thing is that they support the project now. Without that support New Haven would end up a dusty dream on an obscure shelf. Besides, we're going to make a pretty penny on this."

"I know, but I also know you well enough to know that New Haven is more than a financial venture."

"Yeah," he admitted, beaming even more than before. "It's a dream. A second chance for this city. And," he added, waving his arm in a wide sweep, "just wait until other cities see what's happening here. I can see New Havens springing up all over America." He paused to study his scaled model of New Haven and then asked, "What's the status of New Haven's federal school support proposal?"

"Would you relax, Joseph. It's not going to be a problem. This is exactly what the department is looking for—an alternative approach to forced busing. Rather than busing kids back and forth, this plan would plant the seeds of integration at the level where it is needed—housing. Selling this idea was the easiest job I've ever had to do since becoming regional coordinator. Besides," she added with a humorous twitch of her eyebrows, "as your friends in city hall would say, I'm the man in this city when it comes to school finance! If I support it, the department will support it. That's why they pay me."

Three weeks had passed. It was Saturday. Joseph was away on business, and Jacqueline had elected to go to the office in an attempt to reduce the mountain of paper piling up on her desk. Exiting the elevator, she turned and walked briskly down the long deserted hallway to her office. Inserting the plastic key card into the automatic lock, she opened the door to the reception area and crossed the room to her office. An uneasy feeling, almost a premonition, overcame her. She laughed as she quickly dismissed the feeling. She was a highly educated woman who took little stock in such notions. Opening the door, she threw her coat on the couch and, as she turned, she caught sight of a large figure in the shadows of the room. Startled, she screamed. The figure reeled in her direction as if to attack. Leaping for the door in an attempt to escape, she tripped and fell to the floor. Scooting up against the wall, she watched as the figure approached. She wanted to scream again but fear blocked her voice.

"Mrs. Witkowski," called Mary Washington softly.

Relaxing immediately as she heard a woman's voice, she put her hands to her face. "Oh, my God," she said embarrassed. "I thought...."

"Sorry, Mrs. Witkowski," apologized the woman, rushing over to help her up. "I should've said something before you done walked in on me."

"No, no," she offered graciously. "It's not all your fault. I should have expected that maintenance people would be around on Saturday."

"Who?" asked the large lady confused.

"Maintenance."

"Oh," she exclaimed as if it suddenly dawned on her. "You mean the cleaning lady."

The woman nodded embarrassedly.

"Yeah," she drawled. "There's so many names for us these days that I can't keep track of 'em all." Walking back to her equipment, she offered, "I could come back later."

"No, it's all right," Jackie replied, walking over to her desk and sitting down. "You keep right on with your work. It's not going to disturb me in the least." Mary Washington smiled and went back to her dusting. Although Jackie was buried in her own work, she could not help but notice that the lady was spending an inordinate amount of time around the conference table where she appeared to be trying to size-up a large chart spread across it. Rising from her desk, she walked over to her and remarked, "Are you interested in the New Haven development?"

Mary Washington looked up startled by the confrontation. "I didn't mean to...."

"It's all right," interrupted Jacqueline as she pulled a chair away from the table to invite the woman in for a closer look. "It's my husband's project."

"Yeah, I already knew that," replied the woman, leaning over to study the chart.

"You knew it was my husband's work?" inquired Jacqueline somewhat surprised at the revelation.

"Uh huh. I live right here," she said, pointing to the Robert Johnson building on the chart.

Jacqueline edged in closer for a better view. "So that's why you're so interested in New Haven. Are you thinking of buying a home in Joseph's development?"

With that, Mary Washington threw back her head and laughed boisterously. Her deep rich voice resonated throughout the room. Finally, after she had regained her composure, she wiped her eyes and quietly replied, "No, Honey, not's on a cleanin' lady's pay. It'd take me twenty years just to collect the money down, then I couldn't pay the bank its monthly due. No," she explained, pointing to a spot on the chart, "this here is my interest."

Jackie looked at the chart. Mary Washington had pointed to a plot of land designated for a school complex. It bore the name of the city's current and first African-American mayor, Clayton L. Williams.

"This be it," Mary Washington said pleasingly, "This'll be where my boys will go to school. Yeah," she uttered in a hushed reflective voice, "finally they'll get to go to a real good school."

Jacqueline moved even closer. Leaning over the table, she studied the area surrounding New Haven. "Where do your boys go to school now?"

"Here," she said, pointing to Matthew, a school fifteen blocks beyond the boundary lines of New Haven.

Again Jacqueline studied the chart. "Why not here?" she inquired, pointing to Linden, a school four blocks to the south of her complex.

"The expressway. Ain't no road cross it, and it's seventeen blocks around. But that good 'cause Linden even worst than Matthew. Lots of gang problems."

"You're right," she admitted after a few minutes of contemplation. "How could I have missed seeing this. The children of Robert Johnson will fall into the boundary lines of Clifton L. Williams. I can't believe it," she said after a brief pause. "Everytime I turn around something good is coming from New Haven. I don't even think that Joseph is aware of this. This only proves what he's been saying all along. The key to school integration is not busing, it's housing!" The two women stood looking upon the map. Finally Jacqueline looked at the other woman and embarrassedly admitted, "I'm sorry. How rude of me. Here we've been talking, and I don't even know your name."

"Mary Washington," she said, extending her hand.

"Well, I'm pleased to meet you Mary. You sure did open my eyes to something new this morning, and if there is ever anything that I can do in return, just ask." Jacqueline stood looking at Mary Washington. The woman's eyes lit up, and a big smile spread across her broad face. "Oh, oh," smiled Jacqueline, "you're going to take me up on that offer, aren't you?"

Mary Washington nodded. Her smile broadened.

"OK, let's have it."

"There is one thing. Maybe I shouldn't be asking and you don't have to do it, but I'm the head of the Robert Johnson Parent Organization and we're having a pot luck supper meeting this evening. I've been telling my members this here school was gonna happen, but you know how project people are. They just don't believe nothing good is gonna happen to 'em. Now, if you could come to the meeting, it sure would be a eye popper for 'em." Mary Washington studied the woman's eyes. "Now," she quickly added. "If you're worrying 'bout the neighborhood, I could call a friend of mine to pick you up and bring you down."

Jacqueline laughed. "Are you a mind reader, too, Mary Washington?" she asked amusingly to cover her own embarrassment. "I'll tell you what. What time do you get off work, and what time is the meeting?"

"I get off at five, and the meeting starts at six. The bus gets me home in plenty of time."

"What do you say to skipping the bus today, and I'll drive us to the meeting."

"Ya comin'?" exclaimed Mary Washington, clapping her hands together in excitement.

"The title on the door says I'm the Regional Coordinator for Education in this area. I guess it's time to meet some of the people I work for."

On the way over the two women chatted amicably. Mary Washington spoke proudly of what had been accomplished at Robert Johnson, about the various committees established to protect and maintain the building. There was a hallway cleaning committee, a grounds committee, a painting committee, a lighting committee, a parking committee, and a half dozen more committees all designed to provide a safe and livable environment for the residents and their children. Each member of the building served on a least two committees, and the residents did all the work. Mary Washington explained that was the key to the success of Robert Johnson, getting the residents involved. People tend to support and protect what they work hard to create. In all the other projects in which she had lived, the residents relied upon the city to keep things running and hence didn't care about the vandalism. When she came to Robert Johnson and was elected president of the building, she instituted project "Self-Help" as she termed it. It wasn't easy getting the people to work at first she explained, but slowly the work ethic took hold and the residents began volunteering for more committees. In fact, she maintained, the committee system bonded the residents together not only in work but provided a social and crisis network in which they could establish friendships and seek help from others in emergencies.

Jackie pulled into the one and only street leading to the Robert Johnson development. Looking up the stretch of road ahead, she braked slowly so as to better negotiate her car around the potholes. "Can't understand why the city don't get themselves out to fix this here road," apologized Mary Washington. "I made the call myself 'bout a dozen times. You'd think citizens could get some action." Turning into the lot, the woman directed her guest to a convenient spot next to the door. "This is the spot we reserved for guests. Not that it's unsafe to park elsewhere. We have the men out every night," she said, pointing to the corner of the building where two large middle-aged men were patrolling. "It just in case of rain or the snow in the winter, ya know?" Jackie nodded agreeably. Looking at the size of the two men, she couldn't help but think that this could well be the safest place in the city. By the time she climbed out of her car, Mary Washington was already at the door holding it open.

As she entered the building, she was surprised at the cleanliness of the halls. Certainly the building was old and in desperate need of some repairs, but its overall appearance was neat and cheerful. The walls were freshly painted in bright colors and pictures, which she correctly guessed to be the artwork of the residents, hung in abundance throughout. Stopping occasionally to view some of the pictures, Mary Washington provided a short biography of each artist and a personalized commentary on the piece. One didn't have to look hard to understand that something very special was working at Robert Johnson, thought Jackie as she and the woman walked down the basement steps to where the residents had set aside space for a meeting place. As they opened the door, the aroma of freshly baked foods greeted them. In traditional fashion the women circled about the table stirring and arranging the food while the men busied themselves setting up tables and chairs around the darting children for the meal that would follow the meeting. No sooner had Mary and Jacqueline entered than they were surrounded by a group of curious greeters. With a broad smug smile, Mary introduced her guest and immediately Jacqueline was bombarded by warm greetings, friendly handshakes, and a barrage of questions. After a few harried minutes, Mary rose to her rescue when she picked up a large school bell from the head table and, shaking it hard over her head, she shouted, "MEET-ING TIME!" With that, everyone moved to the rows of seats set up in front of the speaker's table. Follow-ing the others' lead, Jacqueline quickly took a seat to the side in the first row. But, no sooner had she sat down than Mary raced over and took her by the arm and escorted her to a chair next to herself at the head table. Mary took the bell and shook it with such force that the clanging nearly ruptured Jacqueline's ear-drums. "Sorry 'bout that," she apologized. "I've learned that if you're gonna lead round here, you've got to be the loudest." Mary began the meeting. In line with the agenda, she called for the reading of last month's minutes and then proceeded to a report of the committees.

In the midst of the reports Jacqueline leaned over to a man sitting next to her and asked, "What happened to all the children? Don't they attend the meetings?"

"Only twice a year," he explained in a whisper. "Rest of the time they're off to study hall once the meeting starts."

"Study hall?"

"Uh huh," he replied again, keeping his voice low. "We take up a collection and pay some of the older kids, the good ones in school, to help the young ones with their lessons. It works good both ways. The older ones get some pocket money, and the little ones get some help and an example to look up to."

Thirty minutes later all the committee reports were completed. Mary rose and announced that it was time for Sharing. Jacqueline looked out on the group in front of her puzzled as to what this item on the agenda was all about. A petite, middle-aged woman rose to her feet. In her hands she clutched a piece of white cloth which she twisted and pulled at violently. Then, blotting her eyes, she confessed to losing control with her teenage daughter and slapping her several times across the face. She chastised herself for being a horrible mother, but, in the same breath, she spoke of her love for her child and how it was tearing her apart that the two of them were not speaking. The others in the group protested loudly when the woman berated herself. Several rose to tell how they too had lost control of themselves with their own children and reassured the woman that her daughter would soon forget her anger and come to her. Finally from the back of the room a larger woman rose and spoke in a booming voice, "Now ya all listen up. Wanda Moore ain't no child beater. She be a good Christian woman. I'se knows that for a fact. Trouble is she just has too many little ones to look after. Never do get no time to spend with her older girl. Now, no one here be a better cook than Wanda. Be I right or be I wrong?" In a revival like fashion everyone's voice rose to affirm the declaration. "Now, I be sick an tire of cookin' for a while, and I'd be willin' to watch after them babies of yours, if'n you and your girl would do my supper cookin' for the week. I'll gives ya the money for the food and takes your babies from four until nine. That'll give ya girl and yourself plenty of time to patch things up. Whata say, Wanda? We got ourselves a deal?"

The woman nodded her head and sat back down bawling into the cloth with the others in the room clapping and shouting, "Amen!" Another member of the group stood, this time a man. He spoke of his anger at work of constantly being made the target of racial jokes. He spoke of the rage building up inside of him and his fear that he would be unable to resist his urge to strike back in violence at those who tormented him. Immediately, several of the men in the audience began to counsel the man against violence. Instead, they offered alternative approaches, ways in which the man could turn the situation into a learning experience and teach those around him at work of the evils of racism and, in turn, impress upon his superiors that he was a wise and thoughtful man, one that could lead others and help his company. And so it went. Even Mary herself testified, telling of her own experience of rescuing her child from the gangs. She spoke of the importance of love and communication with children and too she spoke of the importance of following one's convictions, of how one person could make a difference. Jacqueline watched in awe of the woman. Her language could make an English teacher faint, but the fire in her eyes and warmth in her heart inspired the best in others. In the absolute truest sense, Mary Washington was a leader.

"And now," announced Mary Washington proudly, "to our guest tonight." Picking up the Bible, she turned to a page she had marked with a napkin and quoted,

And the Lord said to Moses, I have surely seen the affliction of my people which by reason of their taskmasters; for I know their sorrows; And I am come down to deliver them out of the hand of the Egyptians, and to bring them up out of that land unto a good spacious land...flowing with milk and honey....

Mary closed her Bible and set it aside. "Neighbors," she said, "you all know the story of Moses. In the midst of their despair, the good Lord gave his people a leader to lead 'em to the promised land. Tonight, I'm proud to present to you another Moses. One that I believe the good Lord has sent to help our children to the promised land. I'm proud to introduce the government's Regional Coordinator for Federal Funds, Mrs. Jacqueline Witkowski." With the introduction the meeting hall filled with a thunderous clapping of hands and shouts of MOSES, MOSES, MOSES!

Jackie rose and took the podium. She raised her hand to quiet the crowd and then slowly began to speak, "I thank you for the kind words. Although it is nice to be compared to such a great leader, I think the truth, from what I have seen, is that you don't need anyone to show you the way. You're already headed in the right direction." With that the crowd once again broke into applause and when it subsided, the woman launched into an explanation of New Haven and how the federal government and the city had joined forces to create one of the best school systems in the state not only for the residents of the new development but also for children of Robert Johnson. It was, she concluded, a grand experiment in urban redevelopment, racial harmony, and equal opportunity. By the time Jacqueline had ended her speech, the crowd was on its feet. Turning to Mary Washington, she saw tears streaming down the woman's face. Embarrassed by her show of emotion, the woman grabbed the bell again and swept it back and forth over her head freezing the room in silence.

"I don't know 'bout the rest of ya, but I've worked up a taste for some of that food over there." With that everyone was up out of their chairs and headed for the table. A moment later the children appeared, and the auditorium was filled with a roar of shouting and laughter as they darted in between the adults to fill their plates. During dinner, Jacqueline and Mary sat together. The talk was of New Haven and the future. Afterwards, as the two women walked to the door to depart, Mary called her son, Nathan, over. The boy stood by his mother looking at the woman through rich brown eyes. "Now, boy," she said, "I told you that you can't be judging people by the color of their skin. Next time one of your friends start bad mouthin' white people, I wants you to think of this here woman and everything she's gonna do for us, hear?"

The boy nodded and said, "Thank you. We heard that a new school was going to be built. We just didn't think that they'd let us attend, on account of us being African American, you know?"

"Now there you go again," snapped May, "always assuming the worst."

"It's OK," interrupted Jacqueline. "There's plenty of fault to go around on both sides. What we need to build is trust, and that's what New Haven is all about."

Three weeks had passed since Mary Washington and Jacqueline had last spoken. Occasionally, in the morning when she arrived for work, she would find fresh cut flowers carefully arranged in an old, but very beautiful, chipped vase left for her from Mary Washington the night before. The card would simply read, "From the Garden Committee." She was always amazed with the loveliness of each flower, so exquisite, so perfect in every detail. One would have thought that they had come from the shop of a fine florist. No one would ever have expected that they were grown on the grounds of a project building. Perhaps that was the irony of it all, that something so beautiful could spring from something so bleak and so despairing. All that was needed was hope. It was the lesson Mary Washington preached to those locked within the confines of Robert Johnson; it was the vision she carried for her children. Why had it taken her so long to understand what Mary Washington had intuitively known all along? Why was it so difficult for others to understand?

Jacqueline had arrived earlier than usual that morning as she had a dinner engagement with her supervisor, John Stuart, who was flying in from Washington, D.C. to finalize several projects in her region. It was now three in the afternoon, and she decided to leave the office in order to avoid rush hour traffic. It would give her plenty of time to review the recommendations she had prepared for John. It was a pleasant day, and the trip home presented little difficulty. All seemed to be going well until she arrived home. A note on the dining room table informed her that Joseph would be late tonight as he was meeting with the mayor. The news was actually welcomed as she needed the time to prepare for her own meeting. In an hour she had dressed and was going over the last of her reports. She was pleased with her work. She placed the reports in her leather valise and closed it. It was then that she noticed the diagram of New Haven on the table. She had looked at the chart a hundred times, but now it looked different, as if something didn't fit or had been altered. Leaning down, she studied the chart. "Damn," she muttered. "How could they?" She rolled the chart quickly into a tight roll, grabbed her valise, and headed for the door. Forty-five minutes later, she arrived at city hall. Once in the building, she raced to catch a crowded elevator to the ninth floor where the mayor and her husband were conferring. The elevator door slid open, and she walked into the reception room and informed the secretary that she would like to see the mayor immediately.

"The mayor is in a meeting. Do you have an appointment?" he asked.

"No, but the mayor's with my husband now, and I would like to speak with both of them."

"My instructions were no interruptions. I'm sure that they'll be finishing up soon. If you would like to wait, I could get you some coffee, some tea, some...."

"Look," Jacqueline replied, trying to maintain her composure. "I don't have time to play the game here, understand? The mayor is meeting with my husband, Joseph Witkowski. Right now they're sitting on a powder keg that's about to blow, and I'm holding the match. I want to see them now!" The man promptly rose from his chair and disappeared into the mayor's office. In only a matter of seconds the mayor appeared.

"Jacqueline," he announced, smiling from the doorway. "Come in, please," he said, pushing the large door back. "I'm sorry about the confusion. I did tell Tim no interruptions, but the door is always open to you. I'll straighten it out later with him."

Joseph was on his feet racing over to his wife. "Jackie," he said perplexed. "What brings you down here? Is something wrong?"

"I think you both know why I'm down here," she replied as she threw the chart on the table before the two men. "New Haven. You've altered the plans."

The mayor looked at Joseph Witkowski as if confused. "Changes? I'm not aware of any changes, are you Joseph?"

"Just a couple of minor changes," he replied. "Nothing of consequence."

"Nothing of consequence!" scoffed Jacqueline. "Listen to yourself, Joseph. You're beginning to sound like a politician."

The man turned to the mayor. "Could I have a few minutes with Jacqueline?"

"Sure, Joseph," he replied. "I need to go down to Donally's office anyway. We'll finish over dinner tonight, OK."

The door closed behind Joseph and Jacqueline. The woman glared at her husband. "What's the matter, afraid to let Clayton know that you've cut the project kids out of his school?"

The man laughed.

"Don't you even dare treat me this way, Joseph," bristled the woman.

"No, no," he quickly apologized. "It's not you that I find amusing. It's reality that I find amusing," he responded, shaking his head. "There is no way you could know this, but I didn't cut the project kids out. Clayton did."

"I don't believe it," she countered.

"It's true," he retorted. "Clayton called me in yesterday and handed me the revised plans. Apparently our financial backers went to Clayton and threatened to withdraw their support if the project kids were allowed to enter New Haven's school system. They're the ones who suggested building a bridge over the expressway and moving New Haven's school system to a different parcel of land within the development. That way the project kids would have to attend Linden because it would be one block closer than our system. Want to hear something really great?" he asked. "They even presented the mayor with a cost analysis showing the money the city would save by having them walk rather than being bussed. It's all one neat little package."

"Those damned racist!" screamed Jacqueline bitterly. "How could Clayton be so dumb as to sell out the project kids for nickels and dimes?"

"Always the idealist, huh, Jacqueline?"

"At least, I have ideals," she replied and then asked, "Do those people really believe that I'm going to let New Haven slide on this? Do they really think that I'm still going to recommend that federal funds be spent on the New Haven school system after this?"

Again he laughed, only this time more resignedly than before. "I'm afraid that you don't have much choice."

"Oh, no!" she retorted. "Maybe you don't have choices, but I do!"

"It isn't that easy. By not recommending funds for New Haven, you'll create a domino effect. Should Washington choose to look at this as discrimination, they'd start yanking federal funds all over the place. The entire educational system of this city will be in jeopardy. Clayton has already told me that he'll kill the entire development before he would let that happen."

Jacqueline threw her coat on the couch. "Should Washington choose to look at this as discrimination?" she questioned sarcastically, repeating the words back. "How else can you look at it?"

"There is another way of viewing this, Jacqueline. The developers are right in the fact that if the project kids attend the New Haven school system, nobody will move into it. That's one of the prime reasons they left the city in the first place, remember?"

"But these kids are not bad kids."

"Maybe, but do you think that you can convince white suburbanites of that? I doubt it," he said without allowing her to answer. "The key to New Haven's success is the schools. The people we hope to attract are not the rich who can afford costly private schools and, besides, they're not the type of people we're after. New Haven's mission is to get working class and middle class families back to the city. That's the only hope the city has to survive the future."

"But that's still discrimination."

"Only if you look at it in the immediate present. That's what I mean by how you look at discrimination. You can look at it as a plan for future integration. For over forty years the government has attempted to mandate an end to segregation through legal actions. What good has it done? This city is as segregated today as it was before the *Brown* case in 1954. Forced desegregation has failed miserably. Voluntary desegregation through economic incentives is the future, and New Haven is a beginning point. First, we have to get whites to move back to the city. When the people begin to move back, business and manufacturing will follow and with that will come jobs and economic prosperity, not only for whites but also for minorities. Listen, Jacqueline," he pleaded, "the only way minorities are going to break free of discrimination is if they have the economic power to buy their way out. New Haven brings it all together—kill it and you kill the dream."

"But what about Robert Johnson's kids?"

"Look at it this way. This is a war we're fighting, and in any war there are always casualties."

"Don't insult me."

"Seriously, Jackie," he pleaded. "It is a war, and the enemy we face here is tougher than any we've ever faced on a battlefield—racism. You've heard the expression: won the battle but lost the war?"

The woman nodded.

"That's what this is all about. No doubt, you have the power to win this battle over New Haven. But, believe me, Jackie, you'll lose the war."

The door to the office opened, and the mayor's head popped in. "Joseph, we need you down in Donally's office now. Can you come?"

"Gotta run, Jackie. I'm counting on you." With that he was gone. The woman stood contemplating her husband's arguments before remembering her own meeting. Looking at her watch, she realized the lateness of the hour.

Located on the 60th floor of the Hamilton building, the Skyview was one of the city's finest restaurants. Across from her sat John Stuart, a liberal who had championed the cause of forceful federal intervention in racial discrimination for over thirty years. He was a man of unwavering conviction, one who pursued each case of injustice as if he were the one who had been personally victimized. She wondered how he would have reacted to her husband's arguments. Not well, she supposed. Before her sat a glass of fine champagne, pure and pristine in color, its effervescent bubbles rising upward in an uncompromising spirit of expectation. Such was the spirit too of Mary Washington. She thought of the woman now. She recalled the speech in which Mary had referred to her as a Moses for Robert Johnson. Thinking of the new expresswalk across the interstate, she could not help but think of the analogy between it and the parting of the Red Sea. Only this time the parting would not lead to the promised land but to a sea of new problems as the gangs gained access to Robert Johnson. She could stop it. If New Haven were canceled, there would be no expresswalk.

John Stuart, who had been droning on about a variety of federal projects in the city, suddenly stopped and then asked, "By the way, Jackie, how is the New Haven development coming along?" Without looking up, the woman turned to look out into the blackness of the night but saw nothing but her own reflection staring back at her in the empty pane of glass. Who was this woman? She wondered....

Name _____

> Read each statement before coming to class. To the left check whether you agree or disagree with this statement. After discussing the statement with your group in class, record the total number of members agreeing and disagreeing in the boxes to the right and explain your position in a few sentences below.

A D   **A D**
☐☐   1. Mayor Williams can't be blamed for his actions; he has to do what is necessary to   ☐☐
          survive politically.

☐☐   2. Integration is the only way inner city schools will improve.   ☐☐

☐☐   3. State and local government officials are too vulnerable to community pressure.   ☐☐
          Therefore, integration and equal opportunity can only be achieved through federal
          intervention.

☐☐   4. Mayor Williams' capitulation to the developers is proof that he has sold out to the   ☐☐
          "white establishment."

☐☐   5. The rational of the developers is just another way of saying that they don't want   ☐☐
          minorities in their neighborhood.

Name _____

☐ ☐   6. Forced bussing is one of the main reasons for "white flight."   ☐ ☐

☐ ☐   7. Social and economic mobility of minorities can only be achieved through self-help programs, not through government coersion.   ☐ ☐

☐ ☐   8. The deterioration of American cities prove that forced integration does not work.   ☐ ☐

☐ ☐   9. American cities can only be revived when the federal government stops shoving all these social programs down the throats of the middle class.   ☐ ☐

☐ ☐   10. Revitalizing the cities will ultimately provide greater benefits for both minorities and whites, therefore, it is morally right to bend the present rules in order to achieve the ultimate goal.   ☐ ☐

Name _____

If you were Jackie Witkowski, what would your decision be? Why?

_____

_____

_____

_____

_____

_____

_____

_____

_____

_____

_____

_____

_____

_____

_____

_____

_____

_____

_____

_____

_____

_____

_____

_____

A Shade Off

The sun, streaming through the narrow openings of the stained-glass windows, cast its light on a strange scene. A short, stocky man wrapped in a brown tweed coat and baggy trousers sat isolated from the others at the end of a long oval table. Shifting nervously in the high-back leather chair, he carefully examined the contents of two manila folders. His stubby fingers quivered as they turned the pages. He tried to concentrate, but his mind drifted.

At the age of 32 and with impeccable credentials, Bill Streder had been bounced from one university to another across the nation. It wasn't that he was unqualified; it was just that there were so many others, just as qualified and just as bright, who wanted to teach at the college level. Indeed, there were so many that one almost needed an influential mentor to get a permanent position. Bill Streder had no such mentor and, therefore, was forced to live the life of an academic vagabond, drifting from one school to another, taking only one year assignments for tenured faculty on leave. This was his first tenure track position.

In his mind he recounted the events leading to his appointment. He had taken the assignment like the others, as a one-year appointment for a professor on sabbatical leave. Then, in the middle of the year the man died of a heart attack. In a way, he thought, the whole thing was an accident, a sudden turn of fate. And though he felt sorry for the man, he was happy for the opportunity to settle into the profession he loved. Now, three years later, he was up for tenure. The trustees of the university would decide his fate in less than three months.

Three other men and a woman peered relentlessly at Streder from the opposite end of the table. He could feel their contempt for him crowd the room as they waited for his decision. With the last candidate to be chosen and the vote deadlocked, it was his decision between two students: one white and one Mexican. He would decide the last name to be entered on the final roster for the medical class. It was an abominable position. With his wife pregnant and his tenure hearing approaching, the last thing he needed was to make enemies. Besides, it would make more sense for one of the others to decide. They were all doctors. He was an educator, an outsider, so why should he have to take the responsibility?

He tried to clear his mind, pushing the mounting pressure from his head so that he could concentrate. Now, more than ever, he would have to be sure of himself. Not only were the lives of two students at stake but, also, the future of the entire medical school. His decision could well constitute a precedent the entire university would be forced to live with for decades. He had to make a decision that he and the school could live with and, yet, at the same time ensure that each student was treated fairly.

Suddenly, the eluding sounds of stillness that filled the empty spaces of the small, sterile room ruptured with the coarse, heavy voice of Dr. James Bennett, "Mr. Streder, we are waiting for your decision."

Without looking up from the papers, Bill Streder slowly shook his head and confessed, "I have no decision. I need more time."

Once again silence engulfed the room. Expecting a decision and receiving nothing left the others with a hollow feeling of emptiness that comes from the unfulfilled need for direction. Dr. James Bennett sat in his chair noticeably disturbed. His large, fat cheeks and the huge cigar jammed between his thick swollen lips quivered with anger. Unable to contain his resentment any longer, Bennett sprang from the table, sending his chair sliding across the floor and crashing into the wall. "I knew it, damn it; I knew it!" he shouted while pointing to Streder in short, jabbing motions. "Didn't I tell everyone this would happen if we let some outsider try to tell us how to run our school?"

Startled by the apparent outbreak of Bennett's madness, Streder quickly defended his request for more time. "Look," he stated firmly. "It's not that I refuse to make a decision. It's just that I would like to have a little more information. That doesn't seem to be such an unreasonable request, does it?"

In three, quick, choppy steps Bennett leaped across the room and hovered over Streder. "More information? More information?" he shouted. "You have all the information you need in these reports," Bennett said, flipping through the pages. "You have some of the best scientific data available here in these tests. For God's sake, man, what more could you possibly want?"

Streder could feel Bennett's hot, stale breath on the back of his neck. "Listen," Streder said in a deliberate voice. "I understand that these tests are probably the best on the market, but they don't tell me everything I need to know about these two students. I need more information."

"Like what?" demanded Bennett.

"Like where they came from, who their parents were, how they feel about life, and things like that!" answered Streder.

"Oh, God," moaned Bennett as he crossed the room back to his chair. "Next he'll want to call everyone back and find out when they were toilet-trained!"

James Perison, a slight, middle-aged surgeon with thin cheekbones and a long narrow face, watched nervously as the confrontation between the two men intensified. He wanted to intervene yet was reluctant for fear of being caught in the middle, a spot he didn't like. However, the bickering between the two men finally exceeded his tolerance for conflict. He could stand no more. "Wait a minute," he shouted. "Let's calm down. After all, we are professionals, aren't we? So let's handle this in a professional manner. Perhaps, just perhaps," he offered, "we might not have to call the two students back. Perhaps someone here could change his/her mind. Let's review the two cases," he coached. "Dr. Lewenski, how about you? What are your feelings now?"

Dr. Lewenski looked over the rim of his glasses, resenting Perison's intrusion. "How many times do I have to repeat myself?" he inquired of Perison. "Of all the people in this room, I'm probably the last who would change my mind. After all these years of working with me, don't you know that?"

"Well, then perhaps you might be able to change someone else's mind," offered Perison apologetically.

"Very well, but I doubt if it will do much good," Dr. Lewenski stated. He crossed the room to where the students' folders lay. "To me, it's a matter of fact. Before us we have two students: Jamie Curtis and Carlos Rodriguez. On the one hand we have Curtis, a brilliant young man who attended UCLA and graduated with a 3.75 grade-point average. Believe me, anyone who could graduate from that school with these marks has something going for him. However, that's not all. His cumulative score on the medical entrance exam was in the seventy-third percentile." Looking around the room, Lewenski asked, "How many of you did as well?" Nodding his head approvingly, as if proud of himself for making his point so sequaciously, he continued, "On the other hand we have Carlos Rodriguez. Let's see here now. Carlos attended California State College at Palos Verdes. I don't know too much about the school other than the fact that it is a relatively new institution. It indicates here that Carlos' GPA is 3.4, and his cumulative medical entrance exam score is in the sixty-fourth percentile. The only other difference between the two is that Jamie Curtis completed his undergraduate work in four years, and Carlos Rodriguez took five years to complete a similar course of study." Dr. Lewenski replaced the folders on the table. "As far as I'm concerned, this isn't even a contest. Curtis is by far the superior candidate!"

"Well put," exclaimed Dr. Bennett. "I couldn't have done a better job of it myself!"

"Aren't you forgetting something?" Streder asked from the far side of the room.

"No, I don't believe so," stated Lewenski. "In fact, I think I was quite thorough."

"What about their backgrounds? You know their..."

"Their backgrounds?" interrupted Dr. Lewenski. "Of what concern are their backgrounds to me? Perhaps we ought to get one thing straight. As far as I'm concerned, this is a medical institution, not a welfare agency, and I am a doctor, not a social planner. As I see it, my job is to save lives, not reform them, and, to do that, I need the best minds I can get into this school. Sir, you're an educator, not a doctor, so you may have difficulty in appreciating our dilemma over here. If you select the wrong student in your department, it may cause an inconvenience to some people, but, surely, it's not going to cost anyone their life. Is it?" he demanded to know.

"No, I doubt that it would," admitted Streder.

"Well, let me tell you about our business over here. In no possible way could you ever, even in your wildest imagination, envision how it feels to send a student into an operating room for the first time. When he picks up the knife and makes his first cut into human flesh, something inside of you begins to turn. It's almost as if you can feel the scalpel, with its razor-sharp edge sliding along the top of your skin, cutting deeper and deeper." Lewenski was standing over Streder now, almost whispering into his ear. "Do you know what that feels like? Well, I'll tell you what it feels like. It feels like your stomach is on fire. Professor Streder, I have the same feeling 120 times each year, so don't try to make me feel like some unfeeling bastard. It's not that I'm against reform. Personally, I think a lot of things in this society could stand a little improvement. I just think this is a damn poor place to start. If you really want to revamp the system, start at the bottom in the elementary and secondary schools but not here. It's just too damn risky up here."

Dr. Janet Owens, a young woman with plain features and thick auburn hair, listened patiently until Lewenski had finished his discourse. Grinning, she said, "Aren't you overdramatizing our lives over here, Doctor? Not everything is a matter of life and death, you know."

"Perhaps that's true if you're just a GP," countered Lewenski.

"Oh, no," shouted Owens. "Here we go again. The God Almighty surgeon has spoken! When are you people going to wake up to the fact that there's more to medicine than just cutting flesh and sawing bones?"

"Wait, wait," intervened Perison. "Let's not start with that crap. We have a job to do here, and we'll never get it done if we continue to spend all of our time fighting one another." A surge of pride swelled up inside Perison. Normally, he was not as forceful, and even he was taken by surprise. "Let's try again. Dr. Owens, do you have anything new to add that might help us break this deadlock?"

"No," she said. "My position remains the same. My choice is Carlos Rodriguez."

"Excuse me, Dr. Owens?" asked Dr. Bennett in a tone inundated with contempt. "Could you be so kind as to tell us why you are voting for the less qualified candidate?"

"In my professional opinion he is not the less qualified candidate. I believe him to be the best qualified given the circumstances."

"What circumstances?" asked Dr. Bennett.

"Don't play so naive, Dr. Bennett. You know perfectly well what I'm talking about. As of now, we have selected 119 students for admission to our medical school. Out of those presently selected we have 109 white students, 2 women, and 8 minorities. As far as I'm concerned, Carlos Rodriguez is qualified; therefore, he is my choice and will remain so until the birds fly north for the winter."

"Nice, real nice," muttered Bennett as he slumped back down in his chair. "The way she feels, if God wanted in this medical school he'd have to have one hell of a suntan!"

"I resent that, Bennett," shouted Dr. Owens. "Not only have you slandered my professional character but, also, you have exhibited your true racist prejudice. I demand an apology!"

"I'll apologize when the birds fly north, you know, in the winter."

"Please, please," pleaded Perison. "Must we always get sidetracked like this? Could we get back to the decision at hand? Dr. Bennett, since you seem to want the floor so badly, perhaps you could offer something new to the committee."

"Huh!" muttered Bennett, taking the cigar out of his mouth. "The only thing new that could help this God-forsaken committee is a miracle that would give the Curtis boy a sudden craving for refried beans."

"Could you please spare us your racist comments, Dr. Bennett?" requested Dr. Perison emphatically.

"Racist? Who's racist?" demanded Bennett. "If you care to check, you'll find that I was the first to recommend and vote for all eight of the minority students thus far admitted by this committee. When I look at a student, I see only the test scores. It doesn't matter to me what color they are. If they're qualified, then I vote for them. It seems to me that of all the people on this committee, I'm the least racist! The only ones concerned about the color of a student's skin are you three," he said, pointing to Perison, Owens, and Streder. "The only reason you won't vote for Curtis is because he is white. Now, that's what I call racism!"

"That's not necessarily an accurate representation of Dr. Owens' and my position," replied Dr. Perison.

"Well, then tell me, what other possible explanation can you have for voting for Carlos Rodriguez? Unless I'm blind, Jamie Curtis has Rodriguez beat in every category."

"Test scores are not the only measure of what kind of a doctor an individual will make," replied Dr. Perison.

"The only thing I can say to that, my trusted colleague, is that if you don't have any more confidence in those test scores than that, we might just as well throw them all out and select our future doctors by tossing coins!"

"It's not that I don't have confidence in the tests," Perison said in an almost apologetic tone. "It's just that things are a little more complicated. We can't always do just what we want. Let's be realistic. We are already in trouble. Of the 119 students we've selected, only 10 can qualify as minorities. Do you know what the government is going to say about that? The same thing they said last year when they told us we should attempt to recruit more minorities in the next class. Well, here we are again—same damn situation! So the way I have it figured is that while one more minority will not put us up to quota, it sure couldn't hurt."

"My God, Perison, can't you even remember that this is a private institution, not a public university? All of the money used to support this institution comes from private sources—tuition, investments, endowments, and other private funds. Not one dime of the taxpayers' money is used to float our budget; therefore, the government can't tell us who to, or who not to, admit, right Perison?"

"Well, not entirely."

"What do you mean, not entirely?"

"Well," replied Perison sharply, "the government does channel a lot of federal dollars into the university in the form of research grants."

"I'll be damned. That's it, isn't it?" accused Bennett. "Here all this time you were filling me full of your crap about disadvantaged children, and in reality your chasing your own 'pork barrel'!"

"What does that mean?" demanded Perison.

"What does that mean?" repeated Bennett. "Oh, come on. You're not that stupid. You know perfectly well what I mean. But for the sake of clarity, just to make sure there is no misunderstanding among the others, perhaps you would like to inform the committee of your most recent job offer."

"I don't see what that has to do with the matter before us," replied Dr. Perison.

"You don't huh? Well, perhaps not, but I think the rest of the committee would like the opportunity to congratulate you on being offered the new position of Dean of the School of Research Medicine here at the university. The federal government sponsors most of the research around here, right Perison?"

"That has nothing to do with it," stated Perison emphatically. "I just felt it was my obligation to bring to the attention of this committee all aspects of this case. Besides, I haven't even decided whether to accept the appointment or not."

"Sure, Perison, sure," scoffed Bennett as he stuffed the cigar back into his mouth.

Dr. Owens removed the thick-framed glasses from the arch of her long pointed nose. "I guess that puts us right back where we started: two votes for each student. That is, unless, have you made a decision, Mr. Streder?"

"I can't," replied Streder. "The only information I have to go on is what's contained in these files and a short hurried-up interview in which nothing substantial was learned about the two individuals. I need more information. Don't you see? I have to be sure!"

It was evident to everyone now. Streder had finally gotten his point across.

Resignedly, Dr. Lewenski pulled the wristwatch out from under his sleeve. "May I suggest that we adjourn for the evening and try to finish this tomorrow afternoon. It is late, and I seriously doubt if we can get both students back here tonight for another interview. Besides, it may give everyone a chance to think things over. God only knows, this committee needs all the help it can get."

"I agree," announced Dr. Bennett. "But may I suggest the following afternoon. I have surgery scheduled for tomorrow."

With the others deferring to Dr. Bennett's schedule, Dr. Owens set the time for the meeting and arranged for the secretary to contact both students regarding their respective appointments.

The decision to postpone the meeting proved disastrous, for soon news of the deadlock spread rapidly throughout the community, like fire through kindling, igniting years of racial unrest. Although it was never learned how word leaked out, the newspapers were first to catch wind of it. Bold headlines announcing the committee's dilemma appeared in the morning edition of the city's leading paper. Following the headline was a lengthy account of the events and details surrounding the deadlock. Also, the same paper, only this time in its editorial section, carried a scathing attack on reverse discrimination. Similar reports were released from the Mexican community paper, *El Reportero*. Normally a weekly publication, it geared up for daily production. Soon the name of Carlos Rodriguez became a symbol for those in the community who regarded the Mexican people as an oppressed group. In essence, as the *Reportero* stated it, this would be a test case for all disenfranchised people in America.

The first scheduled meeting of the committee had to be postponed due to a demonstration by several groups supporting Carlos Rodriguez. Such demonstrations became common and, with each passing day, more violent. While trying to address one group of demonstrators, Dr. Bennett was slightly injured when a rock thrown by a demonstrator hit him in the head. Three stitches were required to close the wound, and, after a rather salacious display of language, the doctor publicly vowed never to serve on the committee again. Finally, after three meetings had been postponed, the committee decided to convene in hopes of ending hostilities.

Bill Streder was the last to arrive at the meeting. When he entered the room, he found the committee solemn and hostile. Quickly he took his chair and made his apologies for being late. However, the solemn faces revealed the committee less concerned with his tardiness than with the position he had put them in.

"I hope you're satisfied," chided Bennett.

"Satisfied?" questioned Streder.

"Yes, satisfied with this whole damn mess. If you had made your decision when you were suppose to, none of this would have happened. Now we have the Mexicans and the KKK rioting in the streets; the federal government is snooping all over the campus, playing big brother; and one group of backers of this institution is threatening to withhold the money they pledged to put toilets in the new wing of the cafeteria."

"Toilets?"

"Yes, toilets," replied Bennett. "It appears that James Bruet, the spokesman for the group, says any place succumbing to this sort of pressure has to be a cesspool, and, as he put it, everyone knows cesspools don't need toilets."

"Nasty," muttered Streder.

"Nasty isn't the word for it. Bruet could make King Herod look like a Montessori school marm!"

"I read about the riots," said Streder. "But I had no idea of...."

"Of course not," interrupted Dr. Owens. "These matters are handled very discreetly, and since you are an outsider, no one bothered to contact you. Obviously, they have no idea that it is your vote everyone is waiting on. I don't know if it will make any difference on your vote, but I think you are entitled to know everything that has transpired since our last meeting."

"Yeah, let's share some of the heat with good ol' Billy boy," taunted Bennett.

"Sharing the heat, as you put it, Dr. Bennett, is not the reason I think Mr. Streder should be informed," replied Dr. Owens.

"It's good enough for me," stated Bennett as he lit his cigar.

Dr. Owens sat on the edge of the table while briefing Streder in a calm tone. "It has been reported," she continued, "by a number of students and faculty that agents from H.E.W. have made unofficial inquiries regarding the recruiting practices and racial composition of the medical school."

"What does that mean?" asked Streder.

"Well, normally it wouldn't mean much since we are a private school. However, I do have close friends in the federal bureaucracy, and one of them called last night to inform me that the government is going to try and enforce nondiscriminatory standards on private schools by threatening to withhold federal grant and research moneys. Presently the medical school alone receives two million from the government each year. I suspect the total amount for the entire university is substantially greater."

"Damn Feds," muttered Bennett. "Always trying to run things they know nothing about."

Streder looked to Bennett but decided not to comment. Turning back to Owens, he asked, "Have you passed this information along to the administration?"

"No, I can't, because the information was given to me in strict confidence. It can never leave this room. The others have agreed to respect the confidentiality of my source, and I expect the same from you. Besides, if you do tell, I'll simply deny it."

"No, no," replied Streder, shaking his head. "You have nothing to worry about. I can understand your position. I will respect the confidence."

"Dr. Bennett will tell you the rest."

Owens walked around the table and stretched out in her chair. She looked exhausted but, then, so did the entire committee.

Without removing the cigar, Bennett began to speak. Spewing ashes everywhere, the large black cigar jerked back and forth as he relayed his information, "After the news of the deadlock hit the papers, I received a call from the president's office. At first it appeared that he only wanted to be informed of the situation, you know, so he could be on top of everything. I really didn't see any harm in that so I agreed to meet him for dinner that night. Well, right in the middle of this beautiful five-course meal he begins to lay all this heavy stuff on me, you know, like the financial realities of the university. Well, it seems that there is a family named Strongston who happens to own about five square miles of the richest oil land in Oklahoma. It also happens that the Strongstons have committed themselves to building a $2 million wing for cardiovascular research onto the hospital. The Strongstons are somewhat conservative in their political and social views. Needless to say, when they picked up their morning newspaper, they were not too pleased. I guess the president had the privilege of listening to the family story of how their once poor and destitute grandfather pulled himself up by his bootstraps and made over $10 million."

Bennett pulled on the cigar and released a cloud of smoke into the air. Smiling, he said, "The president says the story takes a whole afternoon to tell. Well, the Strongstons are not too keen on the idea of reverse discrimination. They feel if their grandfather could make it without favoritism, then, anyone else can, too. In fact, they feel so strongly about this they informed the president that if the Mexican student were selected, the school could forget the grant."

"I guess the president isn't too happy about that, is he?" inquired Streder.

"You guessed right," came the response. "Now, I want to make it clear that he didn't tell me whom we should select. But I got the message that he would be enormously pleased if the school didn't lose the grant."

Perison was listening intently as Bennett spoke. Finally he put the question to Streder, "By any chance, have you decided who you are going to vote for?"

"Not yet, not without talking to the students. After all, we have nothing to lose by interviewing them now, have we?"

"Not now, we haven't," answered Bennett as he frowned at Streder.

"Well, then," said Perison. "Shall we get on with it?"

With that, Perison pressed the square orange button on the intercom before him and requested the secretary to show Carlos Rodriguez into the room. The door opened halfway, and the young Mexican boy slid his slender body around it. He approached the table cautiously. Dr. Bennett was the first to speak, "Mr. Rodriguez, would you please be seated?"

The boy, almost a man now, sat nervously on the edge of his cushioned chair. His black hair, with each coarse strand pasted down with a grease-like substance, glistened beneath the fluorescent lights. In spite of all his efforts to appear poised, a slight quiver in the forced smile betrayed the tension in his body.

"As you are probably already aware, Mr. Rodriguez, we are in the process of finalizing our list of successful candidates," Bennett liked the expression, "successful candidates." It was a phrase he had picked up in the military where he had done his residency. "And since we are so close to the end, we thought perhaps we ought to take a closer look at yourself and another applicant. That way we can all get to know one another better. Mr. Streder, would you care to begin the questioning?"

"Thank you," replied Streder, taking charge. Bill Streder's first question was indicative of the information he sought. "Could you tell us a little about your parents' education, Mr. Rodriguez." From here Streder moved to other aspects of the young Mexican's life.

Carlos, open and relaxed with the man's apparent sincerity, spoke freely, revealing much about himself and his family. Although uncertain of his parents' education, he knew it was not beyond a fourth-grade equivalency. His father had entered the fields as a migrant worker at an early age. It was only later when the children reached school age that the family settled in the valley. Here his father picked seasonal crops and worked odd jobs in the off-season in order to support the family. The boy's description of his early years portrayed a hard life tempered with moments of gaiety and happiness. Though the family was hard-pressed and struggled from meal to meal, there was a sense of security and a feeling of togetherness that sprang from the basic solidarity of a loving family unit. In essence, Carlos' family was poor but proud, and the inflection in his voice, which rang smooth and clear when he spoke of his family, left little doubt in anyone's mind as to his family pride.

During most of the questioning, Bennett remained observant but quiet, almost sullen. His appearance displayed an attitude bordering on benign indifference. However, after nearly an hour of listening, he began to stir. The sudden change in his attitude caught the attention of the others.

"Would you care to ask something, Dr. Bennett?" Streder finally inquired, annoyed by Bennett's restlessness.

"Well, as a matter of fact, there is one little matter I would like to clear up," reported Bennett.

"Of course," replied Streder, "I'm sure Mr. Rodriguez would be happy to answer any question. Right?" he said, looking toward the student.

The student returned the nod, indicating his approval.

"Well then, Mr. Rodriguez, perhaps you could tell me how long your father has been in America?"

An abrupt silence seized the room, almost as if someone had suddenly snatched the life from it. Bennett's intent was as obvious as the question he asked. A despairing smile sketched in rows of crooked white teeth emerged from the student's thin brown lips. He shook his head slowly from side to side.

"I don't believe it. I just don't believe it."

"Believe what?" asked Bennett demandingly.

"That you asked that question," came the response.

"Why?"

"Because I had hoped that you people would be beyond such pettiness. But I guess I misjudged you," he said sadly. "You're no different than anyone else. So, since it's obvious I have nothing to lose, I'll be happy to tell you about my father."

The boy sat upright in his chair. "Yes, Dr. Bennett, your suspicions are right. My father is what people like yourself call a 'wetback'."

The word sprang off the young Mexican's tongue so defiantly that Bennett flushed with embarrassment.

"I'm sorry if I'm making you uncomfortable, Dr. Bennett," Rodriguez apologized. "But you needn't feel sorry for me. All my life I've been the son of a 'wetback' Mexican. The word doesn't anger me anymore. At first, when the kids in my school called my father a wetback, I didn't know what it meant, so I went running home and asked. My father didn't lie to me. He came right out and told me the truth without sparing one word. God, I'll never forget how I felt," the boy said, recalling the day. "It was a burning feeling that twists at your guts until your anger is so great you begin to feel yourself being consumed by it." The student paused, cupping his hands over his head. More composed, he continued, "That's the type of shame that destroys people, but my father saved me from it, and that's part of the reason why I'm here today. He taught me how to understand that all people have faults, that, you know, nobody's perfect. Isn't that funny? He taught me how to understand the same people who wouldn't think of wasting one spare minute of their time on the likes of a person like him. But, you know what's really funny? It's people like you. Here you sit judging a man you don't even know." His voice, slow and deliberate at first, gained in intensity as the anger within him swelled to indignation. "How could you possibly judge him? You have no conception of what life is really like for people like my father. Do you think he wanted to come to America to a land where he would be reduced to some kind of an animal just because he was a wetback Mexican? My God, do you think he has no pride? It would have been easy to stay in Mexico with his family and friends. Sure, he would have been poor, but he still would have been treated like a man—a human being! No, it wasn't easy for him. It was a decision he agonized over. You couldn't believe the doubt and uncertainty that tormented him. But, he did it, dammit!" the young man shouted as he slammed his fist against the table. "He did it for us. He sacrificed his life—the only one he had for his children and their children. Now, tell me," he said bluntly. "If the positions were reversed, could you do what my father did? Would you have the love and courage to give it all up for so little in return?" Carlos searched the eyes of those in the room. "No, I don't imagine so, but then few men would. So don't try to tell me about my father," he choked. "I know he's a wetback, but I also know he is one hell of a man!" The student sat back in his chair. His eyes were glassy. "I guess that pretty well takes care of my chances, doesn't it?" responded the boy.

"No, it doesn't," replied Streder while looking up and down the table at the others. "I think I can speak for the other members of the committee when I say we appreciate your candor. This isn't a popularity contest, Carlos, and we are not here to give an award for congeniality. We want to find out who would make the best doctor, and the only way we can accomplish the task is if people are honest with us, OK?"

Carlos nodded his head while wiping the moisture from his eyes. Reassured, Carlos relaxed, and the questioning continued. A short time later the committee was finished and dismissed the young Mexican with a promise to inform him of their decision as soon as possible. The student left as inconspicuously as he had entered.

When Bennett looked up from his papers, he found the others staring at him despairingly. "Perhaps that wasn't the best question I've ever asked in my life, so let me offer my apology to the committee. However, let us keep in mind that we have another student out there who deserves a just hearing, too. I would hope my indiscretion would not result in the selection of Carlos Rodriguez just because we felt sorry for him. Let's hear out the other student and then make a decision on the merit of both applicants."

"That's precisely what we intend to do, Dr. Bennett," replied Dr. Owens.

Still peering at Bennett contemptuously, she pressed the button once again, and Jamie Curtis was ushered in.

Curtis appeared relaxed and comfortable in the company of the doctors. Every question was answered honestly, sincerely, and in a straightforward manner. The young student appeared to be talented and very confident of his abilities. In pursuing much the same line of questioning, Streder found that the boy came from an upper-middle class background. His father was a successful architect who took time from his busy schedule to ensure that his children received the love and guidance they needed for survival in an often complex and technological world. Jamie had attended good schools at the elementary and secondary levels. In addition, Jamie's father had set aside money for each child in the family so that, when the time came, they could attend a prestigious university.

The questioning of Curtis went on for some time until the committee had satisfied their curiosity, exhausting all avenues that might help them understand the student better. Finally, as with Rodriguez, they dismissed Jamie Curtis with a promise to contact him as soon as possible. Jamie Curtis picked himself up out of the chair and moved slowly to the door. He turned around, as if to say something, but found himself unable to speak. His hand moved to the doorknob. The latch clicked as he pushed the handle down, but the door remained shut. The boy stood frozen in place, his hand clenching the cold, steel handle.

The others in the room watched and waited, anticipating something, yet, unsure of exactly what. Eventually the boy was able to recapture enough of his composure to speak. His voice drifted across the room in a shallow resigning tone, "I can't help it if my father is successful. I didn't choose it that way; it just worked out. Nor can I help it that the young man here before me might not have had the same opportunities my father was able to provide me. Personally, I don't even understand why we have racism, discrimination, and poverty in this country. If it were up to me, it wouldn't be that way. I'd just make all of the problems disappear. But again, I don't know why things are the way they are or how to make them better. The only thing I know is that I want to be a doctor. Ever since I was fourteen years old, I've wanted to be a doctor, and I've worked hard to get where I'm at. And now, after all that work, the only questions you ask me are: What does your father do for a living? How much money does he make? What kind of home do you live in?" A lone tear streaming down the boy's face witnessed his frustration. "Maybe you can help me understand. What has all this got to do with me being a doctor? My father isn't applying for medical school. I am!" The boy waited for the tightness in his throat to ease. "Am I suppose to be some sort of sacrificial lamb atoning for the sins of others? How is that going to help?" The boy searched the room wantingly, waiting for someone's support. "I just don't understand," he finally said. "The only thing I do understand is that I want to be a doctor, and if I'm not admitted here, my chances of getting into another medical school this late in the year are next to none."

The committee members stared blankly back at the young man, their frustration mirrored in the student's eyes. Pushing the latch down again, he opened the door and left as bewilderingly as he had entered.

For a few moments the committee sat, each with his own thoughts.

"Well," Bennett said, looking squarely at Streder as he nodded to the half-closed door, "his future is in your hands now."

Name _____

Read each statement before coming to class. To the left check whether you agree or disagree with this statement. After discussing the statement with your group in class, record the total number of members agreeing and disagreeing in the boxes to the right and explain your position in a few sentences below.

A D   **A D**

☐ ☐   1. Quotas are just another form of discrimination. The government should outlaw   ☐ ☐
          their use.

☐ ☐   2. Jamie Curtis had better academic scores and, therefore, would make a better doctor.   ☐ ☐

☐ ☐   3. The Strongston's threat to withhold money so as to influence the selection of Curtis   ☐ ☐
          is morally wrong.

☐ ☐   4. If this case would have involved a poor white male instead of a Mexican American,   ☐ ☐
          there is no doubt that Curtis would have been selected without any concern from
          the government.

☐ ☐   5. Regardless of race, creed, or religion, everyone in America has an equal opportunity   ☐ ☐
          to achieve their dreams.

Name _____

☐☐ 6. Private schools should not be subjected to any governmental efforts to eliminate inequality. ☐☐

☐☐ 7. Total equality can never be achieved. Therefore, the government should stop shoving all these social programs down the throats of the middle class. ☐☐

☐☐ 8. Academic scores are the only criteria that should be used to determine entrance into medical schools. ☐☐

☐☐ 9. America is rapidly solving its problem with racism. ☐☐

☐☐ 10. The educational system treats everyone the same regardless of their racial or social background. ☐☐

Name _____

If you were Streder, whom would you select? Why?

_____

_____

_____

_____

_____

_____

_____

_____

_____

_____

_____

_____

_____

_____

_____

_____

_____

_____

_____

_____

_____

_____

Judge Smith's Dilemma

"Hear ye, hear ye, the court of the Honorable Judge Alden Smith is now in session. Everyone please rise." As the bailiff announced the opening of court, Judge Alden Smith stepped from the inner chamber of his office and approached the bench.

Once seated, Judge Smith paused briefly to assure himself that everything was in order before proceeding. Satisfied, he took the gavel, struck it twice, and announced, "The next case on the docket is the State of Illinois, the plaintiff, versus Harold W. Johnson, Jr., the defendant. What says the State? Are you ready to go to trial?"

"The State is ready, your Honor," replied Russel Long, the prosecuting attorney.

Turning to the defense, Judge Smith asked, "What says the defendant? Are you ready to go to trial?"

Roger Barwick, a prominent and successful attorney, rose to his feet and answered, "The defense is ready, your Honor."

According to customary procedures, Judge Smith moved rapidly through the initial formalities with the ease and expertise that so well characterized his tenure on the bench. Having informed the defendant of his rights and the charges against him, Judge Smith proceeded to ask for the plea.

"My client pleads innocent, your Honor," responded Barwick confidently. Judge Smith was so stunned with the plea of innocent that he failed to notice the courtroom had erupted into sheer chaos—undoubtedly due to the plea of Johnson. Even the prosecuting attorney appeared shocked as he sat staring at Johnson in total disbelief. The reaction of the spectators in the courtroom was to be expected; however, the surprise that Smith and Long displayed was not. Judge Smith was under the impression that Barwick and Long had hammered out an agreement two weeks prior to the preliminary hearing, namely, that Johnson would plead guilty to a lesser offense in return for a light sentence. Apparently Johnson and Barwick had undergone a change of heart at the last minute. Recovering from the initial shock, Judge Smith picked up the gavel and quickly brought the courtroom to order.

Thus began the trial of Harold W. Johnson, Jr., a wealthy and influential businessman, who on the night of August 2, of that same year, struck and killed Mason Porter while driving under the influence of alcohol. Apprehended by the police two miles from the scene of the accident, Johnson was charged with driving while intoxicated, leaving the scene of an accident, and involuntary manslaughter. One of the arresting officers was reported to have commented that Johnson might never have been apprehended had he not passed out and crashed his car into a telephone pole. Although there were no witnesses to the accident, traces of Porter's blood and hair on Johnson's car provided all the evidence that the police needed to wrap up their case against Johnson.

The following day, local newspapers carried accounts of the accident in bold headlines: WEALTHY BUSINESSMAN CHARGED; FATHER OF FIVE DEAD. The response of the community was immediate. Phone calls flooded the mayor's and district attorney's offices. Hosts for local talk shows aired over the radio were confronted with angry callers demanding justice for several days after the incident.

Widowed Tammy Porter granted interviews with the press—complete with pictures of the family. In her interviews with newsmen, Mrs. Porter indicated that the family was having serious financial difficulties. Her husband had been unemployed for several months, and there was very little insurance money available after the funeral. Throughout the interview, Mrs. Porter repeatedly stated, "Someone has to pay for my husband's death, no matter how important they are." Although Mrs. Porter did not mention Johnson explicitly in her statements, the general public had little trouble filling in Johnson's name.

Rumors of political deals and payoffs began circulating throughout the community. The pressure became so great that District Attorney Anthony Marrettie found it necessary to reassure the public that justice would be served in this case. In a press release Marrettie stated, "Our office intends to prosecute this case to the fullest possible extent. It makes no difference how much money, influence, or power an individual possesses. No deals or payoffs have been made, nor ever will be made as long as I am district attorney."

An editorial in one of the leading papers suggested that Marrettie's statement was prompted more out of a desire to see himself re-elected than out of devotion to justice. After all, with the election only two months away it would be foolish to buck public sentiment.

The fact that Johnson's case was assigned to the Superior Court of Judge Alden Smith seemed to have more of a calming effect on the public than Marrettie's statements. Judge Smith was well known to the public and had an excellent reputation for being fair and impartial in his judgment. For several years Smith had been an outspoken critic of the judicial system. He had written several articles condemning the inequalities of the system in the treatment of the poor and the total lack of rehabilitative facilities of the prisons.

During the course of the trial, Barwick proved to be an extremely capable lawyer. What was thought to be an airtight case against Johnson evaporated as Barwick picked his way through the State's evidence. As Barwick was quick to point out, since there were no witnesses to the accident, how could one assume, beyond reasonable doubt, that it was Johnson's car that caused Mason Porter's death? The fact that Johnson's car struck Porter does not necessarily mean that it was the cause of death. Perhaps another car had struck and killed Porter and what Johnson hit was the dead body of Mason Porter. Naturally this would explain the traces of blood and hair on Johnson's car. The fact that Johnson had wrecked his car destroyed any chance of establishing the body's point of impact. Therefore, Barwick maintained, it was impossible for the police to determine whether Johnson's car hit Porter while he was standing or lying in the street.

"Even if Johnson did strike Porter in a standing position, it is difficult to determine the full extent of the circumstances surrounding the accident," stated Barwick. "The street on which the accident occurred was poorly lit, and a number of large trucks were parked along the side of the street. According to the testimony of a local bartender, Porter had been drinking very heavily on the night of the accident. Was it not possible that Porter stepped out between two of the large trucks into the path of Johnson's automobile? Even if Johnson had not been intoxicated, it might have been impossible to avoid the accident." In support of his position Barwick pointed to the testimony of the police that the accident occurred approximately one hundred feet from the nearest intersection.

To complicate matters further, the autopsy report revealed that Porter died of a massive head injury. Through the testimony of the local bartender, Barwick established the fact that Porter had in his possession a billfold containing several large bills. According to the police report, no billfold or money was found on Porter's body. Barwick now had the opportunity to construct a third possibility. Turning to the jury, Barwick stated, "It is possible that Porter was struck on the head with a blunt object, robbed, and left dead in the middle of the street. If this were the case, then Johnson could not be held legally responsible for the death of Porter."

As Judge Smith listened to Barwick skillfully pick apart the State's case, he wondered how much Johnson was paying Barwick. It had to be a mint, thought Smith. He couldn't help but wonder what Johnson's chances would be if he didn't have Barwick at his side. Undoubtedly he would have already been convicted and on his way to jail. Perhaps some of the radicals were right—you get just the amount of justice that you can afford to buy.

After implanting one doubt after another in the minds of the jury, Barwick turned to Johnson's personal life. One character witness after another testified to the strong moral convictions of Harold Johnson. A respected community leader testified that, in spite of his wealth, Harold Johnson always had time to give of himself and his money. He had contributed literally tens of thousands of dollars to local charitable organizations and served on the board of trustees for several of those organizations. In his business Johnson made it a practice to hire a number of people from the "hard-core unemployed." Throughout his entire life Johnson exercised total responsibility and the utmost concern for the well being of others. From the expressions on the faces of the jury, it was obvious that they were impressed.

Although the State's case against Johnson suffered an apparent setback, prosecuting attorney Long was quick to regain some of the lost yardage. The police officer who investigated the accident testified that while it was impossible to determine the exact instrument that produced the wound to Porter's head, it was in his opinion so massive that it was almost impossible to inflict with any weapon. Nor would it be possible to throw a victim to the ground with such force as to produce the wound. As for his missing wallet, this was not an uncommon event. Each year dozens of similar incidents are reported in the records of the police department. The usual explanation given is the body is discovered after the accident and robbed. In this particular case an anonymous caller notified the police that a body was lying in the street. As the police officer stated, "The caller who refused to identify himself probably robbed the body."

Barwick immediately jumped to his feet and shouted, "Objection, your Honor. The statement by the witness is pure conjecture."

Long turned to Judge Smith and candidly replied, "But, your Honor, surely the defense cannot object to conjecture; his entire case is built upon it!" Much to Judge Smith's displeasure, Long's statement brought a roar of laughter from the spectators.

Obviously disgruntled, Smith replied, "Objection sustained; the witness will refrain from offering his personal opinion. You may continue, Mr. Long." Although Smith instructed the jury to disregard the statement, it was evident that Long had made his point.

Throughout the trial Judge Smith occasionally glanced at the jury. His years of experience provided him with a unique ability to "read" juries. However, Barwick was so successful in the art of manipulation and confusion that it was impossible for Smith to determine exactly where the jury stood. As Smith contemplated their position, he realized for the first time that this case had all the earmarks of a hung jury.

The trial was well into its third week when Barwick asked permission to approach the bench. In a low whisper Barwick requested a meeting in Judge Smith's chambers with Russel Long and Judge Smith. The purpose of the proposed meeting would be to discuss a possible plea change. A change of plea, even in the middle of a trial, was well within the rights of the defendant. However, the meeting was entirely up to the prerogative of Judge Smith. Nevertheless, Judge Smith was curious as to why Johnson had suddenly changed his mind, particularly since Barwick was doing such an excellent job in defending him. When Judge Smith questioned Russel Long as to the acceptability of a meeting, he was surprised to find him so accommodating. Therefore, Smith agreed to the meeting and recessed court until the following day.

Barwick was first to arrive in the judge's chambers. Once seated, he immediately began to discuss his client's position. However, Smith interrupted, indicating he would prefer to wait until Long was present.

Not wanting to alienate Judge Smith, Barwick apologized, and the two of them sat quietly until Long arrived.

Hurriedly, Long took a seat next to Barwick and while removing his coat turned to Barwick and said, "Have you discussed the decision we reached last night?"

"No, I thought you might like to be here before we started," interjected Smith. "However, since I'm the only one who doesn't know what's going on, perhaps you'd better fill me in."

Barwick was first to reply. "I'm the one who negotiated this deal, so maybe I should explain."

"By all means, please do," replied Smith.

Barwick continued, "First, I think that it is important for both of you to understand that I personally feel we have a good chance of winning this case. I've communicated this to my client, and he has full confidence in my judgment. However, Mr. Johnson is very anxious about his situation and the position that Mrs. Porter finds herself in as a result of her husband's death. In fact, it was Mr. Johnson's concern for Mrs. Porter that prompted our action. To this day my client has no recollection of what happened the night of the accident. He was too intoxicated to be aware of anything. Nevertheless, even if there were the remotest possibility that he was responsible for the death of Mrs. Porter's husband, he feels a sense of obligation to the family. So, in the best interests of all concerned, my client is prepared to offer restitution to Mrs. Porter and the family if allowed to plead guilty to a lesser offense and to be placed on probation. I have spoken to Mr. Long, and we are in full agreement on this matter."

"I don't think that Mrs. Porter would be too pleased with placing Johnson on probation," replied Smith. "Have you talked to her about this, Russ?"

"I have, your Honor," answered Long. "She's very receptive to the idea."

Leaning over his desk with a puzzled expression, Smith stated, "I don't understand her sudden change of heart. From the statements in the newspapers and in court, it looked as if she wanted to nail Johnson to the wall."

"I understand, but I guess she decided that the welfare of her family was more important than revenge. After all, you have to admit that the family is in a pretty bad financial spot," replied Long.

"Yes, but she still can file a lawsuit against Johnson even if he is convicted," countered Smith.

"I know that, but a lawsuit of this proportion would take literally years to settle," stated Long. "Besides, Johnson's wife is in the process of divorcing him and that could really complicate matters. Mrs. Porter needs the money now. If she doesn't get it, the family will be forced to go on welfare, and those kids will never get an even break in life. Since Johnson was drunk, the insurance company won't give a penny to Mrs. Porter."

Barwick was sitting quietly in his chair, listening to Smith and Long. Instinctively he knew it was time for him to join the conversation. Rising from his chair, he stated, "Look, gentlemen, let us assume that Johnson was responsible for Porter's death. Every man is capable of making a mistake. Johnson's mistake was getting drunk and then attempting to drive home. But, God, the man isn't a criminal! Look at all the good things that he has done for this community. Is it going to help anyone by throwing him in jail? Is that going to help his family or the Porter kids? After all, you can't expect a man to support two families if he's locked up in jail, can you? Besides, Johnson doesn't need rehabilitation; and even if he did, he wouldn't get it in jail." Barwick could tell by Smith's expression that he was less than impressed. Something more definitive needed to be offered. Barwick sat down and leaned in closer to Smith's desk. "Look, with all due respect, your Honor, you've written several articles yourself on the brutality of our prison system. Putting Johnson in jail would be like throwing a cat into a cage with a bunch of pitbull dogs—he wouldn't stand a chance. They'll kill him! Is that fair to Johnson? Is that justice?"

Smith contemplated Barwick's arguments and then replied, "What you're proposing is giving Johnson special consideration because he's wealthy"

"I suppose you could look at it that way," said Barwick, shrugging. "However, the law and the sentence we impose on violators is flexible. I believe that it was designed that way to meet each individual case. I happen to believe that Johnson deserves special consideration."

"I can understand why you feel that way," replied Smith. "But what about all the people who can't buy their way out of mistakes?"

"Admittedly, the law is not perfect; but things won't improve just by throwing Johnson in jail," stated Barwick.

"I'll tell you what, Mr. Barwick," said Smith. "I'll give your proposal some serious thought and let you know this afternoon." As Judge Smith rose from his chair, Long and Barwick stood up and started for the door. Before Long could reach the door, Judge Smith said, "Russ, could I speak with you privately for a moment?" Russel Long returned and sat back down in one of the chairs facing Smith's desk.

"I suppose if I should decide to grant Barwick's request, Marrettie would back up the decision publicly?" said Smith.

"No, I don't think so; Marrettie has his back against the wall. You know how stirred up the public is over this case, and elections are just around the corner. The public would cut him to shreds if they thought for a moment that he favored letting Johnson off."

"Surely Marrettie is aware that he isn't the only one up for re-election—I'm on the ballot too, you know," replied Smith.

"I know, but judges seldom have trouble at the polls," said Long.

Judge Smith looked at Long sternly and replied, "You and I know that's not always true. Tell me. If I grant Johnson's probation and things get hot, will you support the decision?"

Long paused briefly, as if to collect his thoughts, and then said, "I doubt it—Marrettie is district attorney, and I work for him. I can't go over his head. If I do, my career in the department will be ended."

The voice of Russel Long drifted into the background as Judge Smith's mind turned to his impending decision. On the one hand, he knew that Johnson would only be destroyed by prison. Yet, was it fair to let Johnson off while thousands of others less fortunate were forced to serve time? And, of course, what if Johnson was found innocent? There was little question that the Porter family needed the help that Johnson was willing to provide. But this was a criminal trial, not a civil trial. Or was the line between the two so distinguishable? As Judge Smith weighed the options, his eyes were drawn to a small metal statue on his desk. It was the grand lady of American justice, blindfolded and with her scales perfectly balanced, a gift given to him by his father on the day of his graduation from law school. On the bottom of the statue were inscribed the words, "Equal Justice Under the Law." Such a simple ideal, yet so profound. But in the harsh reality of the decision before him, he contemplated its meaning. What was justice, he wondered....

Name _____

Read each statement before coming to class. To the left check whether you agree or disagree with this statement. After discussing the statement with your group in class, record the total number of members agreeing and disagreeing in the boxes to the right and explain your position in a few sentences below.

A D · **A D**

☐ ☐ 1. The fate of the Porter children should have no influence on Smith's decision. ☐ ☐

☐ ☐ 2. It is wrong for Mrs. Porter to support Johnson's deal just for the money. ☐ ☐

☐ ☐ 3. Greedy lawyers like Barwick who sell their legal skills to the highest bidder actually promote the inequalities in our judicial system. ☐ ☐

☐ ☐ 4. If society really understood how bad jails were they would demand that their legislators give them more money to improve conditions. ☐ ☐

☐ ☐ 5. "Equal Justice Under the Law" is only a myth in America because people like Johnson can buy their way out of trouble. ☐ ☐

Name _____

☐☐ 6. Throwing Johnson in jail would serve no useful purpose in society. ☐☐

☐☐ 7. Since Porter was drunk, Johnson wasn't totally to blame for his death. Therefore, Johnson should not be sent to jail if found guilty. ☐☐

☐☐ 8. Johnson isn't really concerned about Porter's kids—he's only trying to buy his way out. ☐☐

☐☐ 9. There is really little doubt that Johnson struck and killed Porter. ☐☐

☐☐ 10. Johnson is not getting a fair trial because of the publicity. ☐☐

Name _____

If you were Judge Smith, what would your decision be?

_____
_____
_____
_____
_____
_____
_____
_____
_____
_____
_____
_____
_____
_____
_____
_____
_____
_____
_____
_____
_____
_____
_____
_____

Cities, States, and the Feds

It was shortly after 12 noon. Wesley Garth, Congressional Representative of the 6th district in Hampton, Iowa, had just completed reviewing some material for a late-afternoon conference when his secretary broke in on the office intercom.

"Congressman Garth, I'm sorry to disturb you, but there's a gentleman here who would like to speak with you. He doesn't have an appointment, but he claims he's an old friend of yours. I specifically told him an appointment was necessary, but he said that...."

"Judy," interrupted Congressman Garth, "what is the gentleman's name?"

"Mr. Lanston. Mr. Paul Lanston, I believe."

"Good heavens—Paul 'Eagle-eye' Lanston!" The door to Garth's office burst open with the congressman all but leaping into the reception room. The two men stood staring at one another as if in disbelief. "Good God!" exclaimed Garth. "How long has it been?"

"Twenty-five years," replied the lanky man. A broad warm smile broke across Lanston's face as he extended his hand. Garth pushed the hand away and grabbed the man. For a brief moment the two men hugged and slapped each other on the back.

"Hey," said Garth, breaking away. "Let's go back into my office, OK?"

"Yeah, sure."

Turning back to his secretary, Garth requested that he not be disturbed. Once inside he led Lanston to a chair and then hurried to a cabinet where he withdrew two glasses and a bottle of fine red wine. "What this occasion needs is a little celebration drink, right!"

"Right," replied Lanston, smiling warmly again.

Garth poured the drinks, and the two men sat staring at one another, each recounting the past in their own minds.

"Twenty-five years," replied Garth again. "The last time I saw you we were standing on an airstrip waiting to board a plane."

"Yeah," laughed Lanston. "I was sure we'd never get out of Vietnam alive."

"I remember," shouted Garth almost gleefully. "You were certain the Viet Cong had mined the airfield. I can still see you tiptoeing out to the plane. God, did you ever look funny!" The two men sat laughing and sipping their wine while recalling memories of a past era.

"It has been a long time," replied Lanston, shaking his head.

"Too long," answered Garth.

"I know. I kept hoping I'd see you at one of the army reunions. But then, I suppose politics keep you pretty busy, huh?"

"Unfortunately, it's truer than you might think," replied Garth. "You don't know how many times I've made plans to attend. But every time it was the same old story. An emergency would come up, and I'd have to cancel out. But this time nothing is going to keep me away. I don't care if Washington is burning down; I'll be there."

"Good. It'll give us some time to catch up. God knows, twenty-five years is a long time."

"Say, I have a great idea. As long as you're here, why don't you take a few days and stay with me and the family? I could even...."

"Can't do it, Wes," interrupted Lanston. "Business, you know how it is."

"Come on. At least spend the night."

"Really, I'd like to, but I can't."

"What about dinner tonight? Just you and me. I know this great little place that serves the best Oriental food in the city. It'll be like old times."

Lanston smiled. "Maybe I can switch to a later flight."

"Great. I'll have my secretary arrange it for you, and I'll send a cab over to your hotel to pick you up at 8:00, OK?"

"Sure." Lanston's mood became more serious. "Listen, Wes," he said, "it's great to see you, but actually I'm here on business too. I hope you don't mind me taking advantage of our friendship to see you?"

"Of course not. Hundreds of people walk through that door every month on business. Why can't a friend do the same?"

"I was hoping you'd see it that way."

"What's on your mind, Paul?"

"House Bill 358."

"Oh, yeah. The New York City relief bill. I'm attending the conference on it this afternoon. In fact, I was just reviewing the file before you arrived."

"Any conclusions yet?"

"No, why?"

"Well, I represent a group back in Iowa known as the Iowan Development Committee. It's a new coalition of several statewide organizations who have pooled their efforts to improve state economic conditions."

"Excellent. I've always felt something like this was needed. But what has it got to do with the New York City bill?"

"A lot, Wes. We want you to vote against the bill. We feel that this bill is not in line with the best interest of our state."

"Why?"

"For a number of reasons. First, financial matters of cities in this country are no concern of the national government. It's strictly a matter for the states. That's what federalism is all about."

"I know that, Paul," replied Garth, "but I was talking with Bill Trivilla, one of the New York City Representatives, and he tells me things look pretty bad for the city—worse than the last crisis."

"No doubt about it. I checked into their fiscal problems myself. Presently New York City owes $20 billion to creditors. That's why they're asking for both a transfer payment and a multibillion dollar loan."

"Transfer payment?" questioned Garth as he began flipping through the pages of his report. "I don't recall seeing anything about a transfer payment."

"You won't find it there," Lanston finally offered. "They've decided to revise their original proposal so that $10 billion will be transferred to the federal debt. You'll hear about it this afternoon in the conference."

"Transfer payment," muttered Garth again. "I'll have to really think about that one. But still, it doesn't alter the fact that New York City is in serious financial shape."

"Of course not," replied Lanston. "Any city would be in serious financial shape if they managed themselves as poorly as New York City does. I'm sure you know how they got themselves into this mess."

"Well, not exactly, but that's why I'm attending this conference."

Lanston laughed slightly. Its tone was inundated with malice. "I'm sure they'll conveniently leave out some of the more relevant facts."

"Like what?" asked Garth.

"Like the fact that New York City spends more on public assistance than the entire gross national product of some medium-size countries in the world."

"You're kidding?"

"No. Anyone can get on relief in New York City. They have more cheaters than any five states combined. And the worst of it is that they have over 30,000 people employed in the welfare bureaucracy to supervise the payments—and still they can't effectively control it! Why, the welfare bureaucracy in New York City represents the largest municipal agency in the world."

"Hey, Paul, it's a big city. Maybe they need the people."

"Not all of them. It's a well-known fact the welfare department has been a dumping ground for political workers."

"Are you sure of that?"

"Of course. And it's just not the welfare bureaucracy. It's the entire city working force. New York City has close to 350,000 city employees. Within the last ten years New York City's work force increased by 50 percent while that in other cities grew by 37 percent. You know why?"

"Why?"

"Politics. Of the 900,000 people who show up for the Democratic primary, 500,000 are municipal-union workers or members of their families. The politicians are scared to death to buck the city-workers' union. That's why they keep hiring more workers and handing out lucrative contracts. In 1980, the city had to come up with $9 billion to pay their city workers. That alone represents over half of the entire city's budget. Do you know that city workers can retire after 20 years at half-salary? Tell me another city in this country that does the same for its city workers?"

"I don't know of one, do you?" asked Garth.

"No, and I'm sure that there isn't one. So the point is if we can't afford to offer our own workers such generous contracts, why should we help New York City do it for their employees? The same thing is true of education. In New York City, students attend college almost free. Virtually no tuition is charged at all."

"I'm aware of that," admitted Garth.

"OK. Then don't you think the people in Iowa are going to be a bit upset when they have to help foot the bill, especially when they have to pay thousands of dollars in tuition costs for their own children?"

"I suspect so."

"You're damn right. And that isn't all. It's the waste and corruption that makes a federal payoff so unjustified. Right now, current estimates show that $2 billion in real estate, water, and sewer taxes went uncollected last year in New York City. Why, even the New York City politicians admit themselves that anywhere from 10 to 15 percent of the city's budget is lost through waste and corruption. If the government bails New York City out by assuming its debts through a transfer scheme, it's just going to encourage more inefficiency, more waste, and more corruption. And it's not only New York. What's to keep Chicago, Los Angeles, Washington D.C., or any other city from pulling the same sham if they know Uncle Sam is standing by with his hand out?" Lanston paused for a moment as if to catch his breath. "Listen, Wes. This is serious. If you open the Treasury to New York City, it's going to start a stampede, believe me."

The two men talked at length. At about 2:30 p.m. Lanston looked at his watch. "Maybe we could talk more about this tonight at dinner," he said, pulling himself out of his chair. "Right now, I've got another appointment to keep."

"More lobbying?" asked Garth kiddingly.

"Not this time. Right now I'm heading for a meeting with some corporate executives who are considering establishing a business in Iowa. If it works out, it'll be a real boost for our economy."

"If there's anything I can do to help, let me know. You know, Paul," said Garth earnestly, "we're on the same team."

"Right," replied Lanston. "Just like in the old days, huh?"

"Yeah, like the old days," repeated Garth. "See you tonight, ole buddy."

Lanston turned and walked out.

Across the city yet another political confrontation was taking place. Thomas Roth, mayor of Washington D.C., was conferring with his Director of Revenue, Alfred Mason.

"What the hell do you mean, they don't want to pay their taxes?" yelled Roth. "Everybody has to pay taxes. Even the President of the United States pays taxes."

"Well, apparently officials of the McDrew Manufacturing Corporation feel that the tax is too high," answered Mason.

"Too high! Did you say too high?"

"Yes, that's what they claim."

"Were they assessed at the same rate as everyone else?"

"Yes, of course."

"Then you get over there and tell McDrew and the rest of his high-priced executives that if they don't pay the tax by tomorrow afternoon, they'll all be standing in a courtroom."

"I don't know if that would be too wise, Tom," offered Mason somewhat apologetically.

"Why?"

"Because once they know we'll haul them into court, they'll simply pay the tax and then carry out their threat."

"What threat?" inquired the mayor.

"Didn't you read my memo?"

"No, I haven't had time to read anything since yesterday. I've been tied up in budget hearings. What's the threat?"

"They're threatening to pick up their operation and move out of the city. According to them, they've been negotiating with a representative from Iowa." Mason reached into his briefcase and withdrew a memo pad. Flipping the pages, he finally came upon the one he wanted. "Yes, here it is. The representative's name is Paul Lanston. I believe he represents a group calling themselves the Iowan Development Committee. It's my understanding that they've promised McDrew preferential tax treatment both at the local and state levels if he'll relocate."

"I don't believe they'd really move. When you consider the total cost of moving an operation like that, even with the tax break, they still couldn't come out ahead."

"I wouldn't count on it, Tom," replied Mason. "It seems as if the company is at a stage where they are going to have to retool their basic operations, you know, make room for new equipment, redesign their assembly process. Anyway, they figure it would be just as easy to do it in another state as to bring it all here. And there's the labor cost. I'm sure it's lower in Iowa. They might make the move if we don't deal with them."

"What are we talking about in terms of jobs and revenue?"

Mason flipped back through the pages of his notebook. "McDrew hires about 800 workers. Their total volume of business is in the vicinity of $500 million, and last year they paid a total of $276,060 in city taxes."

"What kind of reduction are they requesting?"

"Somewhere in the vicinity of 50 percent," answered Mason.

"50 percent! Are they kidding?"

"Unfortunately not. They're quite serious."

"$276,060, huh? We could live without it, couldn't we?" said the mayor, leaning back in his chair.

"Sure," said Mason, "but I think it is important that we keep in mind what's happening here. Last year this city lost three major corporations and 1760 jobs. The year before it was five and the year before that four. What we're seeing in this city is a reoccurring nationwide pattern. Businesses are leaving the cities. Unless we do something to stop it, we are going to be facing serious problems in the future."

"I know that we're losing some major industry, but aren't we also gaining some each year?"

"Not as many as we are losing," answered Mason.

"But dealing on McDrew's terms might create more problems in the long run. Once the word gets out that we'll deal, every business in this city will be in here trying to blackmail us. And each time we reduce a corporation's tax bill, you know who is going to have to pick up the burden."

"Yeah, the taxpayer," responded Mason remorsefully.

"Is that fair?"

"Tom, I can't tell you what's fair. Believe me, I know the problem. If we reduce one, we'll run the risk of reducing them all. I don't know what to tell you." There was a pause between the two men. Finally Mason asked, "What are you going to do?"

"I'm not sure, but I'll tell you one thing I am going to do."

"What's that?"

"Make a phone call!"

"A call?" questioned Mason, obviously confused.

The chairperson of the conference struck the gavel promptly at 3:00 p.m. Wes Garth sat with approximately 30 other House members representing various states across the nation. In front and facing the members of the committee was Ms. Clare Williams, the official spokesperson for the city of New York. Surrounding her was an entourage of legal and financial experts. From the setting it was evident New York City was not taking the meeting lightly. They needed money, and they came prepared to convince Congress of the fact.

"Ms. Williams," began the chairperson, "perhaps you'd like to begin by summarizing some of the major areas in your proposal."

"As you wish," replied the woman agreeably. The rest of the committee members, including Garth, opened their copies to follow along. For the next 30 minutes the woman leafed casually through the proposal, highlighting important information. As revealed in the proposal's background material and further noted by Ms. Williams, the city's present debt was $20 billion. In order to reduce the amount to a manageable sum, and thereby guarantee the city's fiscal solvency, she advanced a twofold plan of action. First, it was recommended that $10 billion of the debt be transferred outright to the national debt, thus absolving the city of any responsibility for approximately one-half of the total debt. Second, in order to satisfy the city's present creditors, it was suggested that the transfer payments be backed up by a $5 billion low-interest federal loan upon which the city's first installment would be due when its overall borrowing for current expenditures could be reduced to approximately one-sixth of its operating budget. By her own calculations, Ms. Williams estimated that such payments to the national government would commence in ten years. However, the exact date was indeterminable due to the unpredictability of economic conditions.

For the remainder of the meeting Ms. Williams defended her proposal. As she so effectively argued, New York City was America's largest and most complex city. As such, the city was forced to contend with problems uncommon to any other city in the country. At one point a committee member from Kansas interrupted to ask why his constituents should be forced to pay for the operational and maintenance costs of a city in another state. Her answer was simple and to the point. "New York City is an integral part of American society—more so than any other city in the country. As such, all Americans have enjoyed her art, her business, her technology, and her international trade for decades. Now that the city is in trouble, all Americans should share the burden."

Garth listened to the woman's arguments, finding them quite persuasive. But Lanston's description of inefficiency, waste, and corruption crowded his mind. He had to settle the issue. "Ms. Williams," he called, gaining the attention of the woman.

"Yes, Congressman Garth," she acknowledged.

"Correct me if I'm wrong, but, according to information I have here, the city of New York employs over 30,000 people to supervise its public assistance program. Is that correct?"

"I'm not sure of the exact number, Congressman Garth, but I suspect your figure is reasonably close."

"Again, correct me if I'm wrong," Garth continued. "Is it true that currently the city has close to 350,000 city employees?"

The woman stared at Garth. The intent of his line of questioning was all too obvious. For a brief moment she debated with herself on how to handle it. Finally she replied, "Yes, Congressman Garth, that is correct."

Garth was about to continue when the woman seized the initiative. "And it is also true that the salaries, pension plans, and benefits of these employees are the highest in the nation. Perhaps that may surprise you, but it shouldn't. As I informed you earlier, New York City's problems are unique. Let's take your own example of our public assistance program. On the surface 30,000 employees might seem unusually high. However, when you compare it to the problem, it isn't. For decades New York City has been everyone's nirvana, especially the poor, the illiterate, and those handicapped by discrimination. From the South came almost 2 million uneducated African Americans. Puerto Rico added another million untrained Latinos. In both cases the major job skill these people brought with them was crop picking. Unfortunately, since there aren't any crops to be picked in New York City, most of these people ended up on welfare. But that's not the only problem. In addition to the problems I've just mentioned, recent studies suggest that perhaps as many as 2 million illegal aliens live either in the city or in the surrounding area. These people work and draw welfare, use the public schools, the city hospitals, and all other facilities and services the city offers. In return they pay either no or minimal taxes and send most of their money abroad." The woman paused to sip some water and then continued, "Now, the point I'm attempting to make here is that most of these people came to New York City from other states or areas the federal government is responsible for like Puerto Rico. This means that we in New York City have actually assumed much of the burden from other states. In light of this, is it too much to ask for a little help? Believe me," she pleaded to the committee, "it's not that New Yorkers are unwilling to help themselves. Right now our city residents pay more in taxes than any other city-dweller in the country. It's just that the burden is getting too heavy."

"Certainly I understand your welfare dilemma," replied Garth, "however, there's the matter of the salaries and pension plans of your city workers and also the waste and inefficiency."

"Congressman Garth," answered Ms. Williams, "New York City is a big place with big city politics and strong unions. We do what we have to in order to survive. And, in regards to the waste and inefficiency, all I can say is that every city contends with these problems. We're working on it, but, as you must keep in mind, New York City is three times as large as any other city, and, as I'm sure you're quite aware, the larger an organization, or bureaucracy, or city becomes, the more difficult it becomes to manage." The woman paused again, this time to search the eyes of the committee members. Finally she said, "I hate to be redundant, but I repeat—New York City's problems are unique!"

By the time Garth arrived back from the conference meeting, it was growing dark outside. He stepped into his office briefly to gather up a few papers he wanted to look over later that evening. It was then that he discovered the memo on his desk marked "URGENT." The message simply requested him to call Thomas Roth immediately. Garth checked his watch. It was late, and for a fleeting moment he entertained the notion of letting it slide until the next day. Then, at last, he picked up the phone and punched out the numbers.

"Good afternoon. Mayor Thomas Roth's office." The voice on the phone sounded alert and fresh, almost too refreshing for so late in the day, thought Garth.

"This is Congressman Garth. I have a message to call the mayor."

"One moment please."

"Hi, Wes. How are you?" answered Roth.

"Fine," replied Garth. "How about yourself?"

"Not so good. In fact, that's why I'm calling, Wes. It seems as if we have a little problem over here, and I thought you might be able to help us with it."

"Sure, if I can, I'd be happy to lend a hand. What's the trouble?"

"Now don't get me wrong, Wes. I'm not calling you because I think you're involved. It's just that we know each other, and this concerns your home state."

"Iowa?" said Garth, somewhat surprised. "What could Iowa possibly have to do with Washington D.C.'s municipal business?"

"Unfortunately, a lot. Have you heard of a group from your state calling themselves the Iowan Development Committee?"

"Yes. Fact of the matter one of their representatives was in to see me earlier this afternoon."

"Did he tell you what they've been up to?"

"Sure, just what their name implies, the development of Iowa."

"I suppose he didn't tell you exactly how they plan to accomplish their objective, did he?"

"Not in so many words. I mean, we didn't get into the particulars of the matter. Why, is there something wrong with their methods?"

"I'd say so. In fact, if I had to label their tactics, I'd have to call it pirating."

"Pirating!"

"Exactly. For the last two months this guy, Paul Lanston I believe his name is, has been writing letters to every major corporation in the city trying to get them to leave Washington D. C. and move to Iowa. He's even gone as far as to obtain tax records of each company so he could offer better deals. One company, the McDrew Corporation, was in here this morning attempting to blackmail the city with Lanston's offer. Now don't get me wrong, Wes. If a company wants to move someplace else, that's their business, but this type of solicitation in another matter. After all, you know the problems we're facing. I mean, we sat together on the president's commission on cities for nearly six months. You, better than anyone, should know that the type of tactics this Lanston character is using will squeeze the life right out of us."

The conversation continued with the two men discussing the problem. At one point Garth considered revealing his association with Lanston, but at the last instant he decided against it. The revelation of the friendship might leave him vulnerable to criticism if he should later decide to side with Lanston's group. However, for the time being he had to agree with Roth that Lanston's tactic did appear somewhat questionable. "Wes," said Roth. "This isn't a problem for Washington D.C. alone. Every major city in the country faces it. We have to do something about it now, before things deteriorate further."

"I know, but what, Tom?" answered Garth. "Everyone knows what the problem is, but no one seems to be able to come up with the answer."

"Well, I think I've come up with an answer, but I'll need your help."

"What is it?"

"Right now I'm putting the finishing touches on a bill. It'll be finished next week, and I want you to introduce it in Congress. I think someone like yourself, from a state like Iowa, needs to sponsor this bill. It would be sort of a symbolic gesture."

"What's the bill?"

"Well, I haven't got time to go through the details, but, in essence, it calls upon the federal government to identify troubled cities, you know, the ones hardest hit with economic problems. Once this is accomplished, the government will give preferential treatment to the firms in those cities bidding on government contracts. It would act like a handicap. Since labor costs and taxes are higher in these cities, the government would take that into consideration. Also, any firm that moves out of a troubled city would be disqualified from receiving government contracts. It might sound drastic, but it's the only way we're going to save the cities in this country. What do you say, Wes? Will you introduce the bill?"

"Let me think about it, Tom," responded Garth somewhat apologetically.

"Sure, but try and let me know soon. Tomorrow, if possible, OK?"

Garth arrived at the restaurant late. Lanston was already seated. Garth pointed to his friend, and the maitre d' guided him skillfully through a maze of people and tables. Lanston smiled as Garth approached. "How'd it go this afternoon, Wes?" he asked. "Learn anything new?"

"Yeah, learned a lot, ole buddy!" Garth's expression was stern.

"Something wrong, Wes?" asked Lanston, sensing Garth's displeasure.

"Yeah, I'd say something's wrong. This whole relationship, that's what's wrong. You've been conning me. The McDrew Corporation, ever hear of it?"

"Of course, but how do you know about the McDrew deal? Did I tell you about it?"

"No, Tom Roth told me about it."

"Oh, Tom Roth. I suppose he's not too happy about losing McDrew. But I don't see what that has got to do with me conning you?"

"It has a lot to do with it. You come to my office to talk about the New York subsidy and then turn right around and play robber baron with the corporations in the city."

"I still don't understand the point."

"The point is," replied Garth, exasperated, "you're bitching about having to cough up money to pay for problems in big cities, and at the same time you're running around creating more problems for them. Doesn't that sound contradictory to you?"

"Of course not!" defended Lanston. "Every state seeks new industry. It just so happens we're a bit more assertive in our publicity."

"Aggressive is a better word," countered Garth.

"Aggressive, assertive, what's the difference? We need industry, and we're not going to get it by waiting until it suddenly dawns on someone that Iowa has a lot to offer them. Wes, be open-minded. Think about it. It's good economics."

"Good economics! How can you even make such a statement? It's crazy."

"No, it isn't. If companies like McDrew move to Iowa, they can cut their labor costs and operating expenditures by at least 20 percent. Now, it doesn't take a Ph.D. in economics to figure out who's going to benefit—the consumer."

"Perhaps," muttered Garth, trying to think through Lanston's argument logically.

"You know damn well it's true. And for the companies that do business abroad, their goods will be more competitively priced."

"But the cities?"

"They'll benefit too. They just don't realize it yet. When companies move out, the labor will follow. Before long, instead of everyone running to places like New York City, they'll find their way to smaller communities. It'll help distribute people more evenly across the country."

"I don't know. It sounds nice and neat, but I have my doubts if it'll work in practice," Garth answered reluctantly.

Lanston sat looking at Garth, unsure that he had convinced him. Reaching into his pocket, he withdrew an envelope and placed it in front of Garth.

"What's that, Paul?" asked Garth.

"It's for you. I really didn't think I'd need it. In fact, I had hoped that I wouldn't have to use it, you know, with our being friends, but I think you'd better read it."

Garth picked up the letter and opened it. Quickly he scanned it. It was from the governor of Iowa.

Dear Wes,

Paul Lanston and the Iowan Development Committee have my total support and backing in their endeavor to fully develop the potentials of our state. It is my hope that you too will support their efforts....

Without finishing it, Garth folded the letter and placed it in the inner pocket of his jacket.

"Listen, Wes," said Lanston, "Iowa is on the move. We have a lot to offer this country, and I think it's time we let people know just how much. What do you say, ole buddy? Will you help us?"

Name _____

Read each statement before coming to class. To the left check whether you agree or disagree with this statement. After discussing the statement with your group in class, record the total number of members agreeing and disagreeing in the boxes to the right and explain your position in a few sentences below.

A D   A D

☐☐   1. Paul Lanston's method of luring businesses out of other cities and states for the   ☐☐
         benefit of Iowa is wrong.

☐☐   2. Clare Williams was right when she stated that New York City was unique.   ☐☐

☐☐   3. You have to expect some corruption and waste in the management of large cities.   ☐☐

☐☐   4. The national government should nationalize New York City and run it like   ☐☐
         Washington D.C.

☐☐   5. Mayor Roth's plan will only encourage waste and inefficiency.   ☐☐

Name _____

☐☐   6. Federalism might have been a workable concept when the Constitution was
written, but times have changed. It's now time for this nation to consider a
unitary system of government.   ☐☐

☐☐   7. Since the rest of the nation benefits from New York City's trade, technology, art,
etc., they should expect to pay some of the cost.   ☐☐

☐☐   8. Most members of Congress would probably sell out the long term interest of the
nation for the short term benefits of their own constituents.   ☐☐

☐☐   9. Garth's chances for reelection will be seriously threatened if he supports House Bill
358.   ☐☐

☐☐   10. When the national government bails out one state or city, it only encourages others
to be wasteful and inefficient.   ☐☐

Name _____

If you were Representative Garth, would you sponsor Mayor Roth's legislation?

_____

_____

_____

_____

_____

_____

_____

_____

_____

_____

_____

_____

_____

_____

_____

_____

_____

_____

_____

_____

_____

_____

Name _____

If you were Representative Garth, would you vote for House Bill 358?

_____

_____

_____

_____

_____

_____

_____

_____

_____

_____

_____

_____

_____

_____

_____

_____

_____

_____

_____

_____

_____

_____

_____

Letters

Dear Professor Wattenberg,

Greetings from a politician. That's right, a politician, full-fledged and certified! Now Professor, I know what you must be thinking but don't get excited. I am not running for office. No one knows better than I that I have neither the experience nor the backing to trek off in that direction, at least, not yet anyway. But, as luck would have it, a marvelous opportunity has fallen into my lap. Yesterday while pondering exactly what I was going to do with my life now that I have graduated, I received a call from Jack Timberly. I don't know if you recall Jack, but he was in your political science class last fall (seat B-12). Anyway, Jack's father works for a young district attorney by the name of Randal Hunington who apparently, after ten years in the D. A.'s office, has decided to make his move in politics. Since this is his first showing, he'll need lots of experienced help. Now stop for a moment, and think Professor. Of all your students, who has had the most field experience? That's right, me! Remember how I helped with the Fehrman campaign last year. Without exception, it had to be the most well-organized campaign in the state. Of course, some of the credit has to go to your exceptional advice, but I would like to think my contribution was a substantial one too. Jack told his father about my political experience, and he, in turn, told Hunington who hired me at $1500 a month. It's not much money, but, if Hunington gets elected, I get a one-way ticket to the land of "MILK AND HONEY."

I suppose by now you're wondering who's Hunington. To be quite honest with you, I'm not sure myself. The only thing I know is that when Wilbert Norridge announced he was giving up his congressional seat to retire, Hunington decided to make a run for it. As Jack tells it, Hunington would have preferred to have waited for a few more years, but, then, he decided if he didn't run now, he'd be facing an incumbent later. We both know how hard it is to unseat someone already in office. So rather than fighting with his back against the wall, he decided to charge ahead. Sounds like a gutsy guy, right? I can't tell you much about the man politically, but Jack knows where I stand on most issues, and he has personally assured me that I'd have no trouble supporting the man.

Well, I must sign off for now as I am still packing. Tomorrow I leave for the trenches. Once I arrive, I will write again.

Yours truly,
Michael

Dear Professor Wattenberg,

Yesterday I moved into a small, three-story, apartment building right in the middle of the district. My landlady, Mrs. McClaridy, is a wrinkled old widow with a tongue sharp enough to cut through a four-inch steel girder. She took one look at my trunk, you know, the one with all the fraternity and travel stickers pasted on the lid, and launched into a tirade on left-wing radical students and their communist pinko professors. And that wasn't all. Immediately following her commentary on the university, I was forced to submit to a ten minute recital of the house rules—no drugs, no booze, no parties, no animals, and no girlfriends shacking up overnight! Good God, you'd think she was running a monastery instead of a boarding house.

Mrs. McClaridy gave me a room on the top floor with a window overlooking the district I'll be working for the coming months. That's what I'm doing now, looking out the window and writing this letter. Believe me, the people certainly look different from the ones I'm used to associating with at the university.

Tomorrow I'm supposed to meet Hunington and the rest of his staff. Perhaps then I'll be able to tell you more about him and his prospects for election. Someone's banging on the door now. It's probably Mrs. McClaridy coming up to tell me another rule she forgot earlier. Must go.

Yours truly,
Michael

Dear Michael,

Pleased to hear you're settled. Don't be too condemning of old Mrs. McClaridy. Before this election is over, you may well thank her for the rigidity of her house rules. Remember: Discipline is the watchful companion of success.

As always,
Professor Wattenberg

Dear Professor Wattenberg,

I met Hunington for the first time last Thursday. As you well know, I am not some starry-eyed kid on the block. Quite the contrary, I'm a devoted realist so you will believe me when I tell you that this guy is going to be the candidate of the year. He has all the qualities. He's about six-one in height, sandy colored hair, and wears a smile that could melt a 25-pound block of ice fifty feet away. If he weren't running for politics, I'd say he'd have to be the perfect double for the next Robert Redford movie.

In addition to having all the right physical qualities, he also just happens to have what I consider the right political views. He's a liberal, not a radical but a liberal. On almost every issue we talked about, he was slightly to the left of dead center. Now you're probably thinking to yourself that this is just too good to be true, but wait. There's still more! The man has a family that looks as if it popped out of a storybook— a beautiful wife, three gorgeous kids, and a magnificent golden retriever whom he jogs three miles with every morning before coming to work. I tell you the photo opportunities are virtually unlimited. If there ever was a perfect candidate, he's it! When the primary rolls around in March, it'll be like selling candy to kids.

Incidentally, I met Mrs. McClaridy in the hall yesterday, and she asked me what kind of work I did. I told her I was a professional campaign worker. Apparently she wasn't too pleased because she immediately launched into another one of her tirades calling politics the devil's work and Satan the first politician. I'm not quite sure how she arrived at her conclusions, but when she left, she was muttering something about Adam and Eve, an apple, and some unfulfilled promise. I'm really not quite sure about Mrs. McClaridy.

Yours truly,
Michael

Dear Michael,

According to statistics, the average height of a politician is six feet. You have one inch to work with. In regards to Mrs. McClaridy, believe it or not, she's what the politician calls the "silent majority."

As always,
Professor Wattenberg

Dear Professor Wattenberg,

Today we finalized staff organization charts. We have talented people; the trouble is that we don't have enough of them. I suppose most organizations feel the same. The thrust of the campaign will center around four key staff members: Tom Brady, Peter Wade, Paula Frette, and myself. Of course, Tom Brady, who has the most experience and is a close friend of Hunington, will be campaign manager and chief strategist. Paula Frette was assigned to publicity. Paula owns an advertising firm so she was a natural for the spot. Peter Wade was asked to handle funding, and I was given two slots to fell: precinct and issue research. I can't tell you how surprised I was when Hunington handed me the assignment. According to the overall campaign chart, I'm now second in line, just under Brady. Quite a promotion considering I've only been on the job a week, wouldn't you say? However, I do get along with Brady, and he informed me Hunington was quite impressed with my work. In fact, in so many words, he told me if Hunington were elected, I'd go to Washington while he ran the district office. That's OK with me. He can have the district. I want Washington! By the time I arrived at the boarding house, I was so excited I had to tell someone the news. Unfortunately, the first person I encountered was Mrs. McClaridy. When I told her I had been promoted, she just shrugged her shoulders and told me not to get excited. The world of politics she says is like a mirror. It reverses everything. Strange woman that Mrs. McClaridy.

Yours truly,
Michael

Dear Michael,

I was pleased to hear of your promotion. Pay no attention to McClaridy. Always remember: The measure of a man's success is the distance he places between himself and the crowd.

As always,
Professor Wattenberg

Dear Professor Wattenberg,

Thank you for your kind words of encouragement. They are much needed around here. For the last week everyone in the office has been sitting around biting his/her nails. In two days we go before the Democratic committee for the endorsement. I have to admit things look pretty good for Hunington right now. Only two other candidates are seeking the endorsement, a middle-aged woman by the name of Patricia Quinn and Daniel Warner, a newcomer active in some sort of expressway project in the district. Neither one has much support. According to Tom Brady, the only possible threat is Pat Quinn because of her membership on the East Suburban School Board. It's my understanding that she has vehemently opposed busing and as a result of that opposition has been able to put down a strong political base in a few of the fringe neighborhoods who are currently fighting integration. However, since the party is reluctant to jump into a racial fight at this time, I don't think Hunington need worry too much about Quinn. Interestingly enough though, I have heard a rumor that Quinn and Warner plan to run in the primary with or without an endorsement. Oh well, this is America, isn't it! I'll write you tomorrow and let you know the outcome of the vote.

Yours truly,
Michael

Dear Michael,

Be thankful Patricia Quinn and Daniel Warner are running. No one likes the winner in a one-horse race. It's un-American.

As always,
Professor Wattenberg

Dear Professor Wattenberg,

Disaster! Hunington didn't get the endorsement. I can't believe it! Everything was set. Only twelve hours prior to the meeting, Chairman Vozella assured us he had talked to a majority of the other members of the committee, and their votes were committed to us. As expected, we arrived early, greeted everyone, seated ourselves, and then it happened. Wilbert Norridge, Jr. strolled down the aisle wearing a smile that would make a movie star green with envy and stole everything. I didn't even know Norridge had a son! No one bothered to tell me because they didn't think Norridge's son, who happens to be an ordained minister, would be interested in politics. But as Norridge himself put it in his endorsement speech, "God's chariot travels all roads in search of salvation." Although Norridge may sound like a kook, let me tell you, he's slick, and, what's more, his father plans to help grease the way for him with a lot of personal campaigning in the primary and general election. Apparently, that's the reason many of the other members of the committee decided to switch their support to Norridge.

After the meeting broke up, we met at the office to re-evaluate Hunington's chances. I made a few quick calculations based on your research of political support factors and found that Norridge can expect a 15% advantage in the primary with his father's help. We feel that with a little luck and a lot of hard work we can overcome that advantage. So, Hunington is still in the race. God only knows why, but Quinn and Warner have remained steadfast in their plans to run too. I'm sure Warner's only interest in this campaign is in testing the water for something in the future. It's Quinn I feel uneasy about. I have this sneaky feeling that she is after something else. I guess I'll just have to wait and let time judge my intuitions.

When I arrived back at the boarding house, McClaridy was sweeping the walk. I couldn't bring myself to tell her what had happened. Lord only knows what she would have said. Tomorrow I start the heavy stuff: research and polling. I'm exhausted now, so I must sign off.

> Sincerely,
> Michael

Dear Michael,

A man can look upon failure in two ways: as permanent or as temporary. It is to Hunington's credit that he chose the latter.

> As always,
> Professor Wattenberg

Dear Professor Wattenberg,

Sorry I haven't written sooner, but, as you well know, this business of politics does have a way of keeping one busy. For the last three weeks I've been scrounging around the area trying to get an over-all picture of the district. I must say, it does look interesting. I know of your interest in these things so I thought you might like to see what I've come up with. Besides, who knows, we might even be able to arrange a little graduate credit on the basis of my involvement in Hunington's campaign. I'll talk to you about it after the election.

Inside I've enclosed a diagram of the district along with some statistics. I suppose you've already come across them. As you can see, it looks pretty much like any other district. I've divided it according to municipalities. For some strange reason the divisions between the cities appear to be sharp with different socioeconomic, ethnic, religious, and racial differences well defined. So, even though our strategy will resolve around precincts, the municipalities can be used as a rough estimate to obtain a quick picture of the district. Also, note the over-all slight majority for the Democrats. But unfortunately it is a slim margin, and, from looking back into the records of previous elections, I am afraid it appears to be a classic textbook example of a "swing district." Basically, with the exception of Darian, the northern cities are Republican, and the lower ones are Democratic. Oh well, those worries are for the election. It's the primary that we are presently concerned with.

Tomorrow I start looking into the issues. I have this uncanny feeling that it's going to be like sticking my hands into a beehive. But then, it is the only way to get a little honey on your fingers, right!

> Yours truly,
> Michael

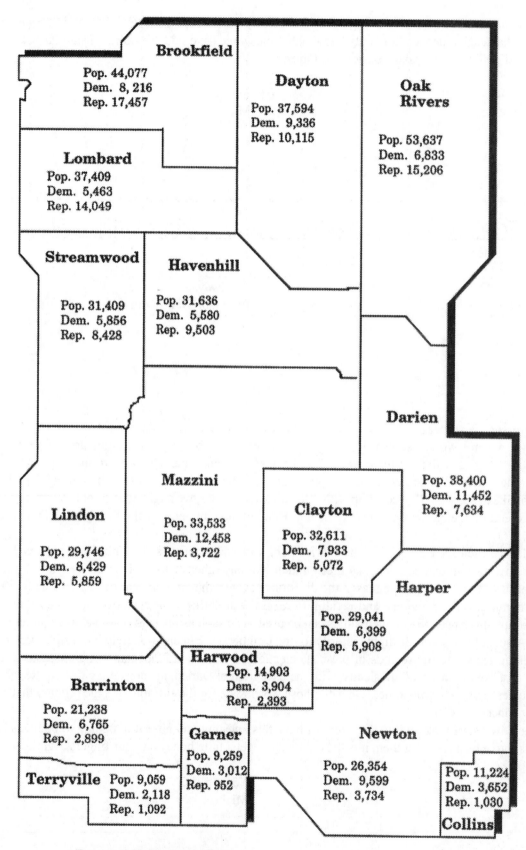

Brookfield

Pop. 44,077
Dem. 8, 216
Rep. 17,457

Dayton

Pop. 37,594
Dem. 9,336
Rep. 10,115

Oak Rivers

Pop. 53,637
Dem. 6,833
Rep. 15,206

Lombard
Pop. 37,409
Dem. 5,463
Rep. 14,049

Streamwood

Pop. 31,409
Dem. 5,856
Rep. 8,428

Havenhill

Pop. 31,636
Dem. 5,580
Rep. 9,503

Darien

Pop. 38,400
Dem. 11,452
Rep. 7,634

Mazzini

Pop. 33,533
Dem. 12,458
Rep. 3,722

Clayton

Pop. 32,611
Dem. 7,933
Rep. 5,072

Lindon

Pop. 29,746
Dem. 8,429
Rep. 5,859

Harper

Pop. 29,041
Dem. 6,399
Rep. 5,908

Harwood
Pop. 14,903
Dem. 3,904
Rep. 2,393

Barrinton

Pop. 21,238
Dem. 6,765
Rep. 2,899

Garner
Pop. 9,259
Dem. 3,012
Rep. 952

Newton

Pop. 26,354
Dem. 9,599
Rep. 3,734

Terryville Pop. 9,059
Dem. 2,118
Rep. 1,092

Pop. 11,224
Dem. 3,652
Rep. 1,030

Collins

Democratic Vote = 149,371
Republican Vote = 148,705

	Voting Age Population	Percent Voting	Numbers Voting	Percent Democrat	Percent Republican
Brookfield	35,262	61	25,673	32	68
Dayton	29,837	65	19,451	48	52
Oak Rivers	42,910	51	22,039	31	69
Lombard	30,599	63	19,512	28	72
Darian	29,539	64	19,086	60	40
Streamwood	24,161	59	14,282	41	59
Havenhill	24,469	61	15,083	37	63
Clayton	22,894	52	13,005	61	39
Lindon	22,882	62	14,288	59	41
Mazzini	25,795	62	16,180	77	23
Harper	22,169	56	12,307	52	48
Terryville	6,969	46	3,210	66	34
Barrinton	16,337	59	9,664	70	30
Harwood	11,377	55	6,297	62	38
Garner	7,068	56	3,964	76	24
Newton	20,273	65	13,333	72	28
Collins	8,634	54	4,682	78	22

	Median Income	Professional / Management	White Collar	Union Worker	Nonunion Worker	Unemployed	White	Minority	Protestant	Catholic	Jewish	Other
Brookfield	$46,137	54	20	19	5	2	96	4	91	8	1	0
Dayton	$42,947	38	35	15	9	3	94	6	88	12	0	0
Oak Rivers	$45,749	40	31	19	8	2	97	3	88	10	2	0
Lombard	$45,219	39	37	14	7	3	93	7	87	8	5	1
Darian	$27,439	20	25	34	19	2	88	12	82	17	1	0
Streamwood	$29,613	23	27	15	21	4	85	15	89	9	2	0
Havenhill	$25,476	33	29	18	17	3	91	9	85	14	1	0
Clayton	$22,745	15	20	39	23	3	83	17	73	13	10	0
Lindon	$19,934	5	20	25	44	6	88	12	78	20	2	0
Mazzini	$23,854	9	27	46	12	6	96	4	34	63	3	0
Harper	$18,257	11	34	25	24	6	84	16	83	15	1	1
Terryville	$9,238	2	16	20	43	19	64	36	81	9	5	5
Barrinton	$19,238	8	32	31	22	7	84	16	73	24	1	2
Harwood	$14,948	4	19	19	42	16	83	17	76	21	1	2
Garner	$18,297	13	21	33	26	9	81	19	82	16	1	1
Newton	$19,735	9	24	27	33	7	86	14	67	31	0	2
Collins	$17,298	8	26	26	34	6	80	20	75	23	1	1

Dear Michael,

I have taken the liberty to enroll you in a graduate course: PSC 561 Field Research. I shall be your adviser. Your fee slip will arrive shortly. Do be prompt, and return it straight away. I will base your grade on the election. I know that you would want it that way.

As always,
Professor Wattenberg

P.S. How is Mrs. McClaridy?

Dear Professor Wattenberg,

Unbelievable, simply unbelievable! The woman is a contradiction to rational behavior. Today, after 12 grueling hours of working the district, I returned to the boarding house to find Warner's picture plastered all over the front of the building. I couldn't believe it. At first I thought it might be some sort of prank, you know, the kind McClaridy would pull just to badger me a bit. But before I could even get into the house to find out, down the steps struts the old bat leering from one corner of her mouth to the other. I told her I was working for Hunington, not Warner. Then in that catty voice of hers she scoffed, "I know. It is I who work for Mr. Warner!"

It truly is amazing. Of all the apartment buildings in this district, I had to pick McClaridy's. And, as it so happens, Warner is McClaridy's first cousin on her mother's side. I know, because I had the unique pleasure of listening to the whole story in excruciating detail. So that's how it now stands: a house divided. It should make for interesting dinner conversation, don't you agree? But then, perhaps I should look on the bright side. There is one, you know. Now that we have politics to discuss, I shall be spared from her insufferable gabble about neighborhood gossip and the local church group.

Must go. McClaridy is ringing the dinner bell. Its ringing sounds unusually solicitous tonight. I wonder what's on the menu, or should I ask?

Yours truly,
Michael

Dear Michael,

The ironies of human existence defy comprehension by mere mortal intellect. But, do not despair. It is only he who surrenders up hope that is lost. Continue on. Your reward awaits.

As always,
Professor Wattenberg

Dear Professor Wattenberg,

I barely have the strength to lift this pen, but I feel the need to write. Perhaps it will help to sort things out in my own head. From what I can ascertain, there are five real smokers in the upcoming primary: the Greater Metropolitan Expressway, abortion, women's rights, integration, and welfare. All five issues have the potential of being real burners if not handled properly.

The first issue I mentioned, the Greater Metropolitan Expressway, sounds more like a state issue than one for a congressional campaign, but it isn't because the federal government is funding the project. Therefore, whoever goes to Washington will have considerable influence on where it is located. Presently two routes have been proposed. I've enclosed a map to illustrate them. Of course, none of the communities involved want it mainly due to the homes and businesses it will displace; but then, too, everyone is convinced that it will funnel many undesirables from the city into the community. Norridge and Warner have announced their support for plan #2. Quinn favors plan#1, and we have yet to decide.

As you might guess, the issue of abortion looms big in Mazzini. Undoubtedly this is due to the large Catholic population. It is my understanding that the church's influence is quite strong. In fact, there are almost as many kids in the parochial schools as the public schools. So, any stand on this issue is going to mean votes and lots of them. Norridge is really wringing his hands on this issue. In all of his early campaign speeches he has promised the voters that he supports his father's record and intends to follow in the same footsteps. Well, even though he is personally known not to favor liberal abortion laws, the records clearly indicate that his father voted consistently in favor of such legislation. His strategy for dealing with it thus far is not to talk about it. I guess he figures that since he can't buck his father's voting record, he'll keep his mouth shut tight and hope the people in Mazzini are aware of his personal beliefs. Quinn and Warner have gone on record as favoring the current abortion laws and the use of public money in welfare abortions. Hunington's liberal instincts tell him to announce in favor of the status quo, much like Quinn and Warner, but I have convinced him to hold off on making any public statements. We might be able to squeeze Norridge in Mazzini if the need should arise.

Here is an interesting twist. Where do you think the staunchest and most politically active women's rights groups are located? That's right—Mazzini. Can you believe it! Right now there is a 60-30 split among Mazzini women. Thirty per cent of the women favor strong federal legislation to protect women's rights, and sixty per cent want to leave well enough alone. As one might also expect, the abortion issue is also involved with the women's rights groups strongly favoring abortion rights. So as far as Mazzini is concerned, it looks as if you can't have one group liking you without the other hating you. Of course, Quinn and Warner have little trouble supporting the women's rights groups, because they also support abortion. Again Norridge is boxed in since his father voted against all "lib" legislation. He's handling this issue like the abortion one; he's simply not talking. And then too, I've got Hunington's lips sealed on the issue, at least until the first polls come out, and we know where we stand.

As usual, integration is going to prove to be the most volatile issue. There have been attempts to integrate city schools with some of the border suburban communities. Garner, Newton, and Collins would be most affected. As I told you in one of my earlier letters, Quinn is the number one barnburner on this issue. She has led the fight against integration with enormous popular support. In fact, I believe the polls will show that she has got things locked up pretty tight in these three communities. All of the other communities have adopted a wait and see attitude. Oh, incidentally, there is one more interesting facet to this issue. Terryville, with its large minority population, would naturally benefit from any integration plan, but then you can't have Terryville without alienating the other communities. Nice, right?

The last issue is welfare. Terryville and Harwood Heights receive substantial welfare payments. The rest of the communities are tired of footing the bill and oppose any increases. Of course, both communities favor such increases. Quinn has openly opposed increasing welfare payments. Nothing has been heard from any of the other camps on the issue.

Well, for now that's how it stacks up. Everyone is out campaigning hard. A lot of jaw banging and tongue slapping are going on, but, for the most part, the candidates are dancing around as many of the tough issues as possible. But then, it's too early to commit oneself anyway. I suspect once the first polls are released, everyone's positions on these issues will begin to solidify.

Yours truly,
Michael

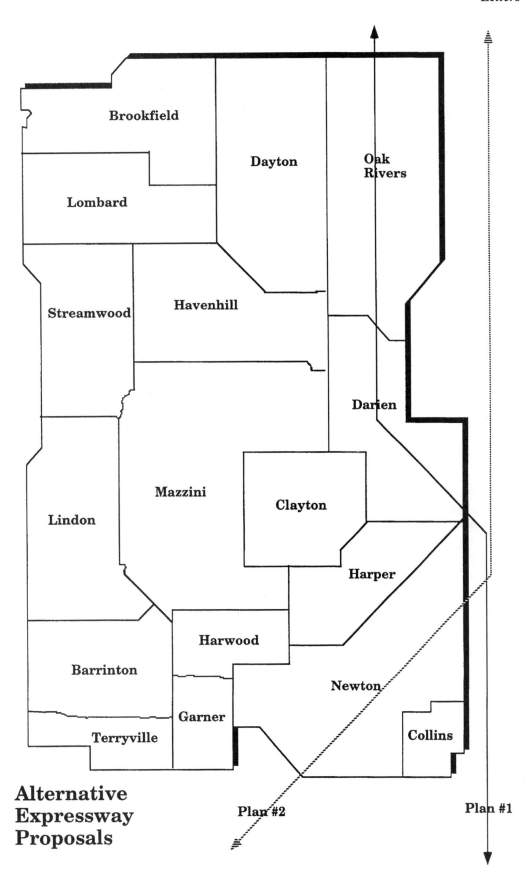

Alternative Expressway Proposals

Plan #2

Plan #1

Dear Michael,

    Only a fool is quick to surrender his thoughts. It is a wise man who chooses to listen first and speak last.

              As always,
              Professor Wattenberg

Dear Professor Wattenberg,

    Strange things are occurring about the boarding house. As you well know, I have been rather tired lately. In fact, during the last week I have averaged less than five hours of sleep a night. So today when there was an unexpected lull at the campaign headquarters, I decided to sneak back to my room and make up some of the lost time. When I arrived, I hurried up the stairs with keys in hand ready to unlock my door when I discovered it already open. This struck me as rather odd since I am in the habit of always locking my door. I opened it cautiously, and whom should I find but McClaridy hovering over my desk. She appeared some-what surprised but quickly recovered to explain that she had begun her spring cleaning early this year and needed to move the furniture about so that she could clean properly. In fact, it appears to me that she has taken an unusual interest in her household chores as of late. Every time my phone rings she suddenly appears with broom and dustpan to sweep the hall outside my door. I suspect espionage. Perhaps it is my imagination, but I have nevertheless taken precautions. I now keep all campaign communications under lock and key in my trunk. The phone just rang, but it was a wrong number. Good Lord! I hear McClaridy trudging up the stairs with her cleaning materials again. Better go.

              Yours truly,
              Michael

Dear Michael,

    Do not judge Mrs. McClaridy too harshly. Her sin is one impelled by the passion of politics, but surely it must be considered venial in comparison to those of other politicians.

              As always,
              Professor Wattenberg

Dear Professor Wattenberg,

    Unpredictable! That's what politics is—unpredictable. In fact, the following is so unpredictable that I doubt that you will really believe it. I would not have believed it myself if I hadn't been there to see it with my own eyes. We were just getting ready to close up shop for the night when the door opened and who should walk in but Patricia Quinn, her campaign manager and three staff workers. At the time I was so dumbstruck I didn't know what to say—but she did. For the next three hours we negotiated. I haven't got time to tell you everything, but, in a nutshell, this is what's going on.

    Patricia Quinn wants to drop out of the race. According to her, the handwriting is on the wall. By her own calculations she has neither the votes nor the resources to continue the race. To demonstrate her point she shared with us the results of a straw vote she commissioned last week. It clearly showed that the bulk of her support is located in three communities: Garner, Newton, and Collins. In the rest of the district she has virtually no support at all. Therefore, she feels it would be best if she dropped out in support of Hunington. But as one might assume, her support of Hunington is not totally altruistically motivated. In return she wants Hunington, if elected, to nominate her to the state board of education. This is not an impossible request since members of Congress do have a great deal of influence in the board's selection. In this state it is an unwritten rule that each member of congress has one appointment. Anyway, a place on the board would give her considerable influence and a springboard for any future election at the state level. Also, it would allow her to continue her integration battle. It's my understanding she selected Hunington because Norridge has already committed his nomination for that position to one of his financial backers. Naturally, we told her that before we could commit ourselves we would want to look at the results of the first poll coming out next week. Being a politician herself, she understood, but I must admit she looked very confident when she walked out the door.

My earlier instinct about Quinn was right. She never really expected to get the nomination. Her goal was the state board of education, and the congressional race was her ticket. Oh, I almost forget. Before Quinn left, she dropped some interesting news about Warner. As the two underdog candidates, she and Warner frequently conferred on mutual problems. On most of those occasions the major topic was campaign funds. According to her, he's having serious financial problems and getting desperately close to folding. But she also stated that it was her distinct impression that he is intent on continuing if he can come up with the funds. Apparently he wants to put on a good show for the party so next time they'll give him more than a passing glance. But then, as Quinn puts it, he's close to going "belly up."

Of course we are not sure how reliable the information is. It could be that Warner deliberately misled Quinn. Or, it could be that she is trying to mislead us. With all the heavy politics, it's anybody's guess who is trying to mislead whom or if, in fact, it's true. All I know is that I'd give a lot of course credit hours to really know. Wait one minute—I hate myself for what I'm thinking, but I think I know how to find out. That's right. You guessed it—McClaridy!

Yours truly,
Michael

Dear Michael,
From the mouths of babes—comes truth! If you must, you must!

As always,
Professor Wattenberg

Dear Professor Wattenberg,
This morning I had my first opportunity to speak with McClaridy about Warner's financial troubles. She was in the kitchen scrambling some eggs when I came down for my orange juice. I waited until the right moment and then asked her straight out if Warner was catching any splinters reaching into the bottom of his campaign chest. I was a bit surprised at her reaction. She threw the pan off the burner, turned on me with flashing eyes and demanded to know why I was asking. I told her that I just heard a rumor and was curious. She replied that if I was so damn curious, I could drop Hunington and switch over to Warner. Then, I'd be able to find out for myself.

That told me everything I needed to know. First, McClaridy has never told a lie in her life and since she wouldn't deny the accusation, it has to be true. Second, it also told me things must be pretty grim in Warner's camp since that's about the first time I've ever heard a swear word pass McClaridy's lips.

I must admit I felt somewhat guilty about setting the old woman up like that. I guess I've come to like her, but, then, politics are politics, right?

The first poll results are due tomorrow. In honor of it we've scheduled a nail biting session tonight. At this rate, by the time the election is over, I'll need a good plastic surgeon to restore my fingers. Must go now. As soon as the results are in, I'll pass them along for your viewing pleasure.

Yours truly,
Michael

Dear Professor Wattenberg,

Here it is—the poll. I picked it up this morning from the research center and have been pouring over the results ever since. I suspect you've already noticed that Norridge has the edge. Simple subtraction reveals the raw naked truth—we trail by 10,431 votes. I knew we would place second, but I had hoped for a smaller spread. Apparently Norridge's name recognition among voters, coupled with his father's campaign support, is proving more formidable than I first anticipated.

My political instincts tell me something has to give because, as much as I hate to say it, I don't think we can overtake Norridge in a campaign blitz. Hunington and Norridge are ardent campaigners and have matched each other dollar for dollar and speech for speech. So if we put on a blitz, Norridge would simply counter with his own. In fact, I am somewhat reluctant to recommend the blitz to Hunington because it might well backfire. Right now I'm certain that Norridge feels comfortable with his lead and would prefer to save the heavy stuff for the election. However, if we trigger a blitz, we might force his hand and get buried in the onslaught. After all, Norridge did inherit his father's campaign organization and thus is better equipped with volunteers and financial backers. I'm not taking anything away from Hunington's organization. We have a great staff, but, unlike Norridge, we're on a budget, and money is getting pretty tight this close to the primary. Most backers are now waiting to see who the candidate will be and then spend their money in the actual election.

No, the more I think about it, I don't think we can out-muscle Norridge. Instead, we are going to have to outmaneuver him. It's time for me to be getting down to the headquarters. Hunington and the others are waiting for the results. I don't think they'll be too pleased.

Yours truly,
Michael

Dear Michael,

Do not despair. Raw vote counts are often misleading. I have examined the over-all vote while returning back to information relayed to me in previous letters. If all that you have written is correct, the answer is obvious, and Hunington's nomination is secure.

As always,
Professor Wattenberg

P.S. A conference will pass me by your way in two weeks. It would be nice if we could meet for tea, don't you agree? Perhaps that dear sweet woman, McClaridy, would care to join us. Please extend an invitation on my behalf.

	Wilbert Norridge JR.	Randal Hunington	Patricia Quinn	Daniel Warner	Uncommitted
Brookfield	2,680	4,445	76	121	811
Dayton	3,658	4,749	39	259	731
Oak Rivers	2,819	571	81	2,601	673
Lombard	1,721	2,717	64	432	559
Darian	5,641	486	117	4,047	1,141
Streamwood	3,439	1,421	38	219	717
Havenhill	3,774	1,005	113	146	839
Clayton	4,392	2,070	56	453	1,003
Lindon	4,423	3,012	102	312	563
Mazzini	3,083	3,510	1,510	846	3,490
Harper	2,577	2,696	99	256	946
Terryville	964	1,007	118	34	76
Barrinton	2,797	2,675	101	256	914
Harwood	1,383	1,513	153	296	531
Garner	248	251	1,998	219	301
Newton	1,676	2,312	3,886	416	1,364
Collins	460	864	1,428	382	705
TOTALS	**45,735**	**35,304**	**9,979**	**11,295**	**15,364**

Name _____

1. Identify the positions of each candidate on the following issues:

Greater Metropolitan Expressway

      Norridge

      Quinn

      Warner

Abortion

      Norridge

      Quinn

      Warner

Women's Rights

      Norridge

      Quinn

      Warner

Integration & Welfare

      Norridge

      Quinn

      Warner

Name _____

2. What are some of the advantages an incumbent might enjoy over a challenger? Can Norridge be considered an incumbent? Why?

3. Explain the offer Quinn extends to Hunington. Should he accept?

4. What is the major objective of Daniel Warner in this campaign? What is his major problem?

5. Where should Hunington concentrate his efforts in the district during the primary? During the general election?

6. Do you feel that it would be justifiable for Hunington to compromise his personal beliefs on the major issues in this case solely for the purpose of gaining votes? Explain.

Name _____

Professor Wattenberg believes Hunington can win. Devise a winning strategy, complete with stands on the major issues.

_____

_____

_____

_____

_____

_____

_____

_____

_____

_____

_____

_____

_____

_____

_____

_____

_____

_____

_____

_____

_____

_____

_____

Name _____

List some of the things that you have learned about campaigning as a result of planning Hunington's victory.

_____

_____

_____

_____

_____

_____

_____

_____

_____

_____

_____

_____

_____

_____

_____

_____

_____

_____

_____

_____

_____

_____

_____

_____

_____

_____

The Late, Great Professor
Bain's Brain Machine

Neal Ridgeway and Paul LaFrance sat in the back of a lecture hall at Marion State Penitentiary. The room was medium in size, like that of a basketball court, rectangular in shape, and void of any decorative wall hangings. Peter LaFrance, a national columnist, scanned the sterile appearance of the room briefly before turning to his friend to comment in a low, sarcastic whisper, "Wouldn't you love to know the name of their decorator?"

"Hey, it's a prison, not an art museum," replied Ridgeway.

"I know, I know, but it's too awful to be a mere accident. Decor such as this can only be achieved through years of practice."

"Do you have to be so negative all the time, Paul? What is it with you columnists anyway, an occupational hazard?"

"Occupational hazard!" laughed LaFrance. "Neal Ridgeway, famed state's prosecutor, talking about negativism and columnists! Listen buddy, when it comes down to negativism, you prosecutors have us columnists beat hands down."

Ridgeway was about to counter the remark but stopped short as he saw a man enter the room from a side entrance. Quickly he nudged LaFrance, "Hey, he's here."

LaFrance peered across the long hall to where he saw a gaunt, bespectacled, middle-aged man walking across the floor. "That's Bain?" whispered LaFrance astonished.

"Yeah."

"I don't believe it," he mumbled.

"Believe what?"

"Bain. I don't believe Bain. Just look at him."

"What's wrong with him?" asked Ridgeway.

"Are you serious? A gray pinstriped suit jacket and green plaid trousers. It's offensive. And that tie. Just look at that tie. He couldn't have bought that thing—he had to inherit it!"

"Hey, don't judge the man by his dress," commented Ridgeway. "C'mon, I want to introduce you to him."

"I can't believe I let you talk me into this," moaned LaFrance as he grudgingly made his way with Ridgeway through the aisle now filled with others who had likewise come to view Professor Bain's demonstration. "Say," called LaFrance from over Ridgeway's shoulder, "who are all these people?"

"Associates and colleagues of Professor Bain and local newspeople," answered Ridgeway while continuing to push his way through the crowd. "And then too, some are prison officials."

"I wonder if they're all as crazy as us?" grumbled LaFrance.

"For Christ's sake, Peter, would you just shut up until the man's had a chance to demonstrate his machine? Then you can work your mouth until it falls off your face."

"OK, but if you ask me, it sounds pretty crazy—a brain machine!" LaFrance laughed again but stopped when Ridgeway turned with a disapproving look. "All right, all right," capitulated LaFrance with his hands held up. "Let's meet your Professor Bain."

Professor Bain was busy sorting through papers in his briefcase as the two men approached the platform. His bald head glistened under the harsh overhead lights. Catching sight of the two men approaching, he quickly extended his hand and said, "Ah, Neal, I'm so glad you could make it." Then turning to LaFrance, "And this must be your columnist friend, Peter LaFrance, correct?"

"Yes, Professor. Let me introduce you." With that Ridgeway preceded with what was now the unnecessary amenities. Professor Bain stood patiently by, smiling politely as Ridgeway forced his way through the introduction. LaFrance, somewhat more reluctant, warily scrutinized the professor.

"Let me compliment you on your column, Mr. LaFrance," commented the professor. "I am one of your most avid readers. That's why I was so pleased to learn of Neal's acquaintance with you. I don't mind saying a man of your stature could be of great help to our efforts."

"Our efforts?" repeated LaFrance confused.

"Certainly. Didn't Neal tell you? Well, it doesn't matter. You shall soon see for yourself and that will be compelling enough."

"Compelling?" replied LaFrance, obviously still confused. "Say, what...."

"Excuse me," interrupted the professor. "I must attend my machine. We will have sufficient time to discuss your support after the demonstration."

"Support?" cried LaFrance to the professor, who by this time was already walking back behind the platform to the experimentation room. Turning back to his friend Ridgeway, he again repeated, "Support? What the hell does he mean by support?"

"Now, Peter," said Ridgeway, attempting to calm LaFrance. "Don't go working yourself into a contortion before you know what's going on."

"That's what I'm trying to find out. What's going on here? Why am I here?"

"You're here because the professor needs the support of the media to sell his machine to the public."

"Why me?"

"Come now, Peter. Your modesty is absolutely nauseating. You know very well why you were selected. As one of the most well-read syndicated columnists on the judicial system in America, Professor Bain considers your support vital to his efforts."

"Bain! Me support Professor Bain. Good Lord, Neal," exclaimed LaFrance. "The man is a crackpot!"

"He is not!" countered Ridgeway in a strained whisper as he pulled LaFrance back to two chairs in the front row. "He's a highly respected scientist. And could you please keep your voice down? Everyone here is going to think we're the crackpots."

"Excuse me, ladies and gentlemen," called a tall thin man from the platform. "May I have your attention?" The lights in the room dimmed slowly, but the noise of the people talking and shuffling about continued.

"Who's that?" asked LaFrance, nodding in the direction of the speaker.

"Bill Wardle," answered Ridgeway. "He's assistant warden here at Marion."

Wardle rapped the wooden mallet on the table in front of him and again pleaded for cooperation. When the room was absolutely quiet, he spoke, "Thank you. Today it is my pleasure to welcome you here for a demonstration of what I consider to be one of the most revolutionary discoveries in crime prevention in the history of man. I can only say that we here at Marion State Penitentiary are pleased to be of assistance to Professor Bain." Wardle turned to the professor and smiled affably. "I would now like to take a minute to explain a few policy matters so as to avoid any possible misunderstanding. As with all experiments conducted within the jurisdiction of this correctional institution, the inmates were informed that their cooperation was strictly voluntary. No coercive measures whatsoever were taken to induce any inmate to participate against his will. In this particular case, a simple announcement was read to all inmates stating that an experiment was to be conducted and that those participating would receive special considerations in their upcoming parole hearings. In all, thirty-nine inmates volunteered. Each was screened for suitability and, eventually, twenty were selected for the experiment. Then, each inmate, in the presence of an attorney, was advised as to the nature and purpose of the experiment. And finally, we guaranteed that our questions would be confined only to those crimes of which they were presently convicted. Such a guarantee insured that no inmate would be exposed to the danger of self-incrimination. Now, at this time let me introduce Professor Bain."

A polite applause rose from the audience as the professor stepped forward. Ridgeway and LaFrance joined in, with LaFrance being somewhat less enthusiastic than his friend. Professor Bain smiled amiably and waited until the last spectator finished clapping. The professor's nervousness was evident in his voice that was pitched unusually high. "First, let me thank all of you for attending our demonstration today. Before we actually begin, it might be interesting to review briefly...."

"Oh Christ," moaned LaFrance softly as the professor continued. "We're going to have to sit through his life's story." Ridgeway nudged an elbow into LaFrance's ribs, who recoiled in a low, wincing groan. Turning to protest, he was met with a disapproving expression. Ridgeway raised his finger to his lips, cautioning LaFrance to silence.

"Actually," spoke Professor Bain, "much of the credit for this instrument belongs to my father, the eminent Professor Henry Bain, Sr. It was he who pioneered most of the neurological research necessary for the development of the instrument. After his death, I continued and ultimately succeeded on behalf of his efforts." Professor Bain poured a small amount of water into an empty glass and sipped from it. He was more relaxed now.

Turning again to Ridgeway, only this time protecting his ribs, LaFrance replied, "Absolutely thrilling, wouldn't you say?"

Professor Bain stepped behind the table on the platform to bring forward what appeared to be a large multi-colored diagram of the brain that was attached to an easel. Pushing the easel forward somewhat awkwardly, the professor unfortunately lodged the front leg of the structure into a crack in the floor of the platform. Suddenly, the entire easel collapsed, sending it tumbling off the platform onto the concrete floor with a loud crash. A woman in the third row who had been busily scribbling notes on a pad leaped to her feet in a startled scream.

"Oh, Jesus!" moaned LaFrance, turning to view the pandemonium breaking out in the room. Professor Bain stood helplessly by as two attendants retrieved the easel and returned it to an upright position on the platform. Meanwhile, Bill Wardle jumped in quickly to grab the gavel. Striking it sharply on the table in front of him, he continued until the audience was again brought to silence.

Once order was restored, the professor moved forward to the front of the platform. He blotted his forehead with a clean white handkerchief. After recapturing his composure, he apologized and then moved to the easel to continue his discussion, "Let me first begin by saying that the mind is an exceedingly wonderful and complex instrument. Even to this day its secrets have eluded our most meticulously designed experiments. My father, from the outset of his investigation, knew that his task would not be a simple one. "Yet," emphasized the professor, raising one finger, "he reasoned that while he undoubtedly would not be able to free all of the mind's mysteries, he might, through hard work and perseverance, be capable of inducing this marvelous organ to surrender up just one of its many precious secrets."

LaFrance turned to Ridgeway and simply groaned in utter disgust. The professor continued, "Now, my father began with a rather elementary hypothesis, namely, that the act of lying is of a higher order in the mental process than that of telling the truth." The professor laughed amusingly, tugged downward on his vest, and straightened his tie before beginning again. "Perhaps that might sound strange to many of you, but if you stop to consider it, it really is not as strange as you might first think. You see, telling the truth is a relatively simple process. A question is asked. The mind first receives the message in the form of sound waves that it subsequently converts to electrical impulses that then travel along specially designated nerve routes to the appropriate decision-making spot in the brain." The professor moved a pointer along the pathway outlined on his chart until he came to the decision-making spot he referred to earlier. "Here the mind decodes the electrical impulses through a complex biochemical process that we do not fully understand as of yet. Once broken down and recognized, the brain creates new electrical impulses that travel to the portion of the brain responsible for warehousing all knowledge. Then in a truly amazing process that makes the computer look like a child's toy, the brain begins sorting through literally billions of bits and pieces of information until it comes upon the exact one it is searching for and, once found, an electrical message is again sent back along the same route signaling that the information has been located and is ready for release. The mind then simply sends the appropriate signals back and the information is again converted to sound waves we all understand—speech."

"You taking notes?" whispered LaFrance to Ridgeway.

"Why?" inquired Ridgeway.

"I think we're going to get a 'pop' test later."

Ridgeway leaned closer to LaFrance about to reply when the professor continued, "Now that, I repeat, is a simple process. My father, through his experiments, found telling the lie is considerably more complicated. In the lie two additional steps are needed between finding the information and relaying it to the outside environment." The professor pointed to each of the two sites outlined on his chart and then repeatedly tapped the pointer between them to emphasize his statement. "The first is the decision not to relay the correct information, and the second is the construction of the lie to be conveyed. My father discovered that the creation of this false information takes place in another sphere of the brain and is relayed through different nerve routes. In years of painstaking work he mapped these nerve routes out for us. Unfortunately he died before the advent of the computer technology necessary to devise audiovibratory systems needed to block nerve passages. We continued his work and eventually succeeded." The professor paused to change charts on the easel. This time a chart superimposing new nerve routes on the old system was displayed. "What occurs in our process is that through a computer, we first pinpoint the exact location of the nerve passages for both the truth and the lie. This is necessary because the exact routes are different for each individual. We accomplish this through the use of two computerized audiovibratory hookups that are attached to the subject in the following manner." The professor carefully attached two, small, round, black cardboard demonstrators to the chart. "Once these are located we then, on the audiovibratory hookups leading to the lie route, initiate a series of pulsating sound frequencies designed to interrupt the electrical flow along the neurons. These serve to block any attempt to create lies. Along the truth routes we likewise initiate sound frequencies. However, unlike those along the lie route, these serve to increase the electrical flow, much like a booster in an electrical circuit. In this way the desire to tell the truth is irresistible on the part of the subject. His will is muted, and he is totally unable to break the truth circuit in his own head. Thus, he answers any question put before him willingly and truthfully. Now," said the professor, putting the pointer aside, "some of you might be concerned about the health of the subject. We have researched this issue thoroughly and have found no ill side effects from being on the machine. In fact, all subjects have reported feelings of extreme pleasure while on the machine. I myself have been on the machine several times and have found it very relaxing." The professor paused to search his audience. "Is everyone clear as to how the machine works?" he asked rather confidently. "Good. We shall continue then." The professor raised his hand signaling two assistants in the back of the room. Immediately they came forward and began distributing to each observer a stack of papers neatly collated and bound by a ringed folder.

"My assistants are now distributing for your examination the results of our experiments at Marion." The professor waited until everyone had his/her copy in hand before proceeding. "As you can see for yourself, we have presently processed nineteen subjects. The last one, and the one I believe will prove most interesting, has been reserved for our demonstration today." The professor moved over to a curtain behind him and pushed a large green wall button. The curtain slid back in the gray steel track revealing a square interrogation room shielded from the audience by a large viewing window with thick plate glass. A table dominated the center of the room with four wooden chairs surrounding it. Along one side of the room were two smaller tables each holding large and expensive scientific instruments. This is where the last experiment will take place today," said Professor Bain. "You will be able to view and hear what occurs in the experimental room, but the one-way mirror and sound proofing will make it impossible for the subject to hear or see you." The professor checked his watch. Looking up at his audience, he said, "It is time for the experiment to begin. If you have any questions, I will be more than happy to answer them following the conclusion of the experiment." The professor turned and left quickly.

While waiting for the experiment to begin, LaFrance flipped casually through the pages of his folder until he came upon the incomplete form of the twentieth subject, inmate 437842—Stuart Drennan. Quickly LaFrance nudged Ridgeway. "Hey, Neal, look at this," he said, pointing to the name at the top of the page. "Isn't this the guy who was involved in that big jewel heist about five years ago?"

"Yeah," replied Ridgeway. "That's why it should be so interesting."

"Why?"

"Because they never recovered the jewels—a million and a half worth of them. Also," whispered Ridgeway, leaning closer to LaFrance, "Drennan has been steadfast in his claim of innocence."

"What do you think, Neal?"

"About what?"

"His innocence."

"Oh, that," replied Ridgeway nodding. "Personally I think he's guilty. I did when we prosecuted the man, and I still do."

"Then why do you think he volunteered for this experiment?"

"He had to."

"Had to?"

"Sure. Drennan is facing a twenty-five year stretch in this hole, and with the jewels still missing, he'll serve every day of it unless he gets special consideration from the parole board."

"Still," replied LaFrance, "it seems like a big risk on his part."

"Listen. Drennan's convinced he can beat this machine. When we arrested him, he requested a lie detector test. We tested him seven times."

"And?"

"Inconclusive, all of them. Drennan's power of concentration is phenomenal, absolutely phenomenal. That's why this should be such a great demonstration," added Ridgeway almost gleefully. "Drennan against the machine. Believe me, it's the classic confrontation." Ridgeway raised his hand to LaFrance and then pointed to the large plate glass window of the experimentation room. "Quiet! Here comes Drennan now."

Ridgeway and LaFrance watched the man through the window as he entered the experimentation room through a side entrance. LaFrance, unfamiliar with Drennan, was surprised at his appearance. He was tall, approximately six feet in height, and lean but with a muscular build. From what LaFrance could ascertain, he appeared to be in his early forties and were it not for the prison blue uniform with the number taped above the right pocket, he might well pass for a lawyer rather than an inmate.

The side door opened again. Outside in the observation room the audience watched as the professor entered to confront Drennan. Bain walked over to the table and seated himself opposite to Drennan. Extending a hand to the man, he introduced himself, "Good morning, Mr. Drennan. I'm Dr. Henry Bain. I'll be conducting the research this morning. On behalf of the research staff and myself I would like to thank you for your participation in this project. Before we actually proceed, I need to ask you a few questions. They might seem redundant to you by now, but, nevertheless, I am compelled to ask."

Drennan nodded.

"Mr. Drennan," asked Professor Bain, "do you understand that your participation in this experiment is strictly voluntary?"

"Yes."

"And, it is also true that you have consulted with your attorney and fully understand the nature and purpose of this experiment?"

"Twice."

"I'm sorry?" asked Bain confused with Drennan's answer.

"I spoke with my attorney twice."

"Oh, I see," replied Bain a bit flustered. Regaining his composure, he continued, "And realizing the nature and purpose of this experiment, it is still your desire to proceed?"

"Yes."

Professor Bain motioned to his two assistants standing in the background. Immediately they proceeded to ready the experiment. A series of electrodes were brought forward and placed in front of Drennan. As one assistant spread a clear jelly substance on the flat underneath part of the electrode, the other prepared Drennan by similarly lubricating two spots on each of three sections of his body: the back, the chest, and the neck. Finally, on two spots located just above the eyebrows on the forehead two smaller electrodes were carefully set in place. Professor Bain, having completed the initial calculations at the computer terminal, returned to his seat in front of Drennan. In his hand he held a small instrument, which he explained to his subject as a remote control programmer that allowed him to feed commands to the terminal that in turn fed data to the computer back in his laboratory. Drennan's attorney, who was seated to the left of the professor, looked anxiously on as Bain made a few last second adjustments to the electrodes on his client's forehead. All was ready now.

Professor Bain looked up directly at Drennan and smiled. "Before we begin, Mr. Drennan," he said, "I want to reassure you that you will feel no pain whatsoever. On the contrary, you should feel, once you are properly programmed, complete and utter relaxation, like that of a deep satisfying sleep. Also, let me repeat. You needn't be concerned about any damaging effects to your physical or mental health. All effects are temporary, lasting only while the instrument is in operation. Once it is switched off, all effects disappear. Is that understood?"

Drennan remained perfectly still.

"Mr. Drennan, is what I just said understood?"

"Yes," answered Drennan tersely annoyed that his concentration had been interrupted.

"Good. Then let us begin. Now, Mr. Drennan, I am going to ask you a set of programmed questions. I want you to lie to each of them. Do not tell me the truth, understand?"

Drennan nodded awkwardly with the cords dangling from his head.

Professor Bain quickly blotted his forehead with the crumpled white handkerchief again and then punched a four-digit code in the remote control programmer. Instantly Drennan's eyes bulged from his head as if he had been deathly startled. Simultaneously from the opposite end of the room a series of lights flashed across the screen of the terminal, first in horizontal rows and then vertical. A second later, the patterns of lights were no longer discernible but flashed sporadically rapid movements across the screen. Drennan's expression relaxed, his eyes dulled, and the lids covering them grew heavy.

"Mr. Drennan," called Professor Bain softly, "you needn't be so tense. Relax." Almost on command Drennan's eyes closed, and the tenseness in his face eased. "That's better," responded Bain. "Can you still hear me, Mr. Drennan?"

"Yes."

"Good. How do you feel?"

"Wonderful."

"Can you describe it for me?"

A slight smile emerged from Drennan's almost muted expression. "Yeah, I feel light, like a cloud, and I'm...I'm drifting...yeah, that's it, a warm gentle breeze is carrying me along."

Professor Bain again pressed a series of digits on his remote control programmer before again addressing his subject. Drennan's smile faded. "Mr. Drennan," called the professor. "This is Professor Bain. Recall our earlier conversation. Your answer to all my questions will be a lie. Do you understand that, Mr. Drennan?"

"Yes," answered Drennan. His voice was heavy and dulled.

"From this point forward, Mr. Drennan, I will refer to you not by your name but only as subject 319. Is that understood?"

"Yes."

The professor readied the set of prepared questions to be asked of Drennan. An assistant delivered to him Drennan's biostatic printout. He studied it momentarily, made calculations, and again entered a series of numbers into the remote control programmer. Drennan's expression remained unchanged.

"Subject 319," called the professor, "what is your name?"

"319."

"No, subject 319. That is your code number. I want your name. Who is 319?"

"Professor Bain," answered Drennan. "My name is Professor Bain."

Laughter rumbled through the observation room with Drennan's reply. LaFrance leaned closer to Ridgeway to remark, "He's toying with the professor."

"The experiment isn't over, you know!" retorted Ridgeway.

"Nevertheless," responded LaFrance, "round one—Drennan!"

Professor Bain wiped his forehead again and then motioned to his assistant who immediately ripped a page from the printer and delivered it to him. He scrutinized it momentarily and then hurriedly made more calculations before entering new data into his remote control unit. Drennan's expression remained unchanged. Turning to the window, Professor Bain announced, "I now wish to inform you that I have programmed our subject to relay truthful information." Turning back to Drennan, he asked, "Subject 319, what is your name?"

"Stuart Drennan."

"Very good," rewarded Professor Bain. "Now subject 319, I want you to think back. It is five years ago. It is winter, and the month is February. Do you understand?"

"Yes."

"The time is 10 o'clock in the evening. What are you doing, subject 319?"

"I'm entering a building."

"What kind of building?"

"An apartment building."

"The name? What is the name of the building?"

"The Garden Towers."

"Why are you there?"

"Jewels. I'm there for jewels."

"Who do the jewels belong to?"

"Sylvia Thayer."

Professor Bain flipped through the pages of questions before laying them aside. He stared into the eyes of his subject. Getting up from his chair, he moved over to Bill Wardle who was seated in the back left-hand corner of the experimentation room. Together the two men conferred in muffled whispers.

"What's up?" asked LaFrance of Ridgeway from the observation room.

"Don't know," he answered. "We'll just have to wait and see." Together they watched as the professor returned to Drennan.

"Subject 319," alerted Professor Bain. "It is now 9 o'clock in the morning. The date is February tenth. Do you understand?"

"Yes."

"Where are you?'

"I am at the police station."

"Do you have the jewels with you?"

"No."

"Where did you hide the jewels, subject 319?"

"I OBJECT!" screamed Drennan's attorney, springing from his chair. "Your guidelines stated that no questions would be asked unless it had prior approval from either myself or Mr. Drennan. That question was not approved. As such, you have no right to ask it!"

"Mr. Rosati," replied the professor to Drennan's attorney, "often during an experiment, conditions change, thereby necessitating slight modifications in procedures."

"But you agreed not to...."

"We agreed," interrupted Bill Wardle, "not to question subjects about crimes other than ones for which they were already convicted. I see no conflict with the question asked."

"I totally disagree!" persisted Rosati almost shouting. "And furthermore, I refuse to allow my client to answer your questions."

"The right to answer or not answer is not yours to decide, Mr. Rosati. That belongs to your client, Mr. Drennan," answered Wardle, pointing to Drennan.

"My client is incapable of answering!" screamed Rosati, shaking with rage. "He's under the influence of that damn machine!"

"Mr. Rosati, if you don't control yourself, I'll be forced to have you removed from this room," stated Wardle firmly.

"Like hell I'll leave," defied Rosati.

Rosati and Wardle continued their verbal battle with the confrontation swelling to near violence. As the two men shouted and screamed their protests and banged their fists on the table, Professor Bain attempted to continue his questioning of Drennan. However, due to Rosati's and Wardle's angry exchanges, no one in the observation room, including LaFrance and Ridgeway, could pick up the conversation between the researcher and his subject. Finally Rosati, frustrated in his verbal attempts to halt the experiment, lunged toward Professor Bain sending him wheeling back against the glass window and then madly began ripping the electrodes from his client's body. Immediately Drennan's eyes popped open wide; his expression was one of bewilderment. In the background the terminal lights flashed erratically across the board as a guard wrestled Rosati to the floor. Professor Bain recovered and moved quickly to restore order to the chaos. "It's over!" he shouted. "The experiment is finished. Everyone, please remain calm! I have ended the experiment!"

In the observation room everyone was standing now, helpless spectators to the madness within. Once order was restored, however, the stunned silence that had held the audience captive suddenly collapsed, giving way to an explosion of excited voices.

"Christ, can you believe that?" said Ridgeway nearly shouting into LaFrance's ear. "He went nuts!"

"Who?"

"Rosati," replied Ridgeway.

"What'd you mean? Wardle's the one who flipped out."

"C'mon, you don't really believe that."

"Of course. Look...."

"Hey," interrupted Ridgeway. "They're leaving."

"Yeah and look at Drennan. He's grinning from ear to ear," commented LaFrance.

"Why?"

"Because he just put one over on the professor."

"How do you mean?"

"I mean, Drennan played along just to discredit the professor. When they check the record, you're going to find out all the information he gave is going to have no relation to the crime at all. The professor and his brain machine are going to be the laughing stock of the political and scientific community. No one will ever believe him again. Just wait—you'll see."

"Even so, what about the others?"

"Listen. Unless it's 100 percent, it will never be admissible in court. You know that. It'll be like the lie detector test."

A rapping on the front table in the observation room interrupted LaFrance and Ridgeway's conversation. It was assistant warden Wardle. He shook his head. "Let me apologize for the disruption. Believe me, I'm as shocked and appalled as you must be." He shook his head again and then continued, "Professor Bain has asked me to convey to you that he will hold a press conference shortly in the conference room down the hall, third door to the left." He checked his watch. "Shall we make it in twenty minutes. That should give the professor a few minutes to refresh himself."

"I don't care what you say," said LaFrance after Wardle had left, "he put one over on the professor."

"We'll see," replied Ridgeway. "C'mon, let's get down there. I want a good seat."

Twenty minutes later, almost to the second, Professor Bain entered the room. He seated himself at the table in the front. Neal Ridgeway and Peter LaFrance were positioned front row center of the professor. Approximately thirty people, mostly reporters, attended the meeting. Professor Bain looked over his audience, stopping only when his eyes fell upon Peter LaFrance. He smiled with delight and then remarked, "Mr. LaFrance, I'm so pleased you could join our press conference." Then, without acknowledging anyone else in the room, he turned to confer with two of his assistants who had arrived earlier.

Ridgeway nudged LaFrance. "Talk about the 'fair-haired boy,'" he chided. LaFrance's only reply was an annoyed shrug.

The professor rose from his chair. "Ladies and gentlemen, I trust that you have had sufficient time to review the data we distributed earlier. Therefore, I am now available for your questions. Who would like to begin?"

"Professor Bain," questioned a woman, springing to her feet. "How does your machine differ from the polygraph or lie detector as it is more commonly called?"

"Good heavens," laughed the professor, as if amused by the question. "The two machines aren't even comparable. The lie detector operates only on a feedback system. That is to say, it records electrical changes on the skin's surface produced by stress—the type of stress produced when one knowingly tells a lie. However, there are some individuals who possess enormous powers of concentration or who have learned to control their neurological responses through such methods as biofeedback. In either case the results of polygraphs are distorted. On the other hand," boasted the professor, "the criminal cannot escape the truth with my machine. It's foolproof because it neurologically blocks the lie. It is only possible to tell the truth."

"Then," questioned another member of the audience, "you think evidence obtained from your machine should be admissible in court?"

"Definitely," stated Professor Bain. "However, I must add that while I still believe there should be a court of law for the defendant, I feel its structure will be drastically altered with my machine."

"In what way?" asked another man.

"Well, for one, the jury system would undoubtedly be abolished."

"But the Constitution guarantees that every person has the right to a trial by jury," added the same man.

"True, but the Constitution can be amended when it becomes obsolete. That's why our Founding Fathers gave us the amendment process."

"Then you're saying the jury system is obsolete?"

"Most certainly. The jury system was designed to determine guilt or innocence, and, as a method, it served us well. But let's be honest. It's far from perfect. However, the same is not true of my machine. It is absolutely perfect in ascertaining guilt or innocence, and since that is what the jury system is all about, it's obsolete and should be replaced immediately."

"Why have courts, then?" asked another member of the press.

"The courts would be for sentencing. Again, guilt or innocence is not the question. The only people appearing before the court would be the guilty. Consequently the only burden of the court would be to assess penalties."

"How do you think the accused will feel about your method, Professor?" asked an older woman from the back.

"If they're innocent, they'll love it, because again it's a guaranteed way to prove their innocence. No longer will those falsely accused of crimes be forced to endure the mental and financial agonies of an imperfect judicial system. As for those who are guilty, I suspect they will be less than enthusiastic with the new system. But then," shrugged the professor, "I'm not concerned about their feelings."

"Not concerned?" replied LaFrance, speaking up as he repeated the words back to the professor. "A bit callous, wouldn't you say, Professor Bain?"

"Perhaps, Mr. LaFrance," replied the professor. "But then, sometimes it's possible to be too concerned about the rights of the guilty."

"Really?" commented LaFrance with raised eyebrows.

"May I explain, Mr. LaFrance?" requested the professor.

LaFrance shrugged reluctantly suggesting he continue.

"Three years ago a young man was riding a commuter train on his way to work in the city. About midway through the trip a group of seven teenagers between the ages of 17 and 19 boarded the train at one of its inner city stops. Also riding on the train was a lovely young woman with a small child. The teenagers began taunting the woman with obscenities. Their laughter became louder, their taunts bolder. Finally one of the teenagers grabbed the woman and forced her to the floor. That's when the young man intervened. By the time the train arrived at its next stop that same young man had a total of 23 broken bones. An unidentified witness reported on the train that one of the youths repeatedly kicked the young man in the back until he heard the spine snap. The teenagers were apprehended but never brought to trial because all the youths testified in behalf of each other that they acted in self-defense. None of the other witnesses would testify because they were too terrified." The professor's voice was strained with anger. "Want to know how I know about this." LaFrance sat quietly by, not answering the challenge. "It's because," continued the professor, "the young man is my son-in-law. And for the last three years I've watched the quiet agony in the eyes of my daughter as she wheels his broken body about the house. Their young lives are ruined, and it angers me to the point of rage because I know that those animals who did it are still running loose in the streets."

"Eventually the law will catch up with them. It always does in cases like this," commented Ridgeway, eager to console the professor.

"That's not the point," he retorted tersely. "The point is that had they been put away the first time they did something like this, my son-in-law wouldn't be in that damn chair today. But no, the judicial system doesn't work that way. It's too inadequate so Jerry had to suffer and so will a lot of other innocent people before those animals are locked away for good. I tell you it's time we begin to pay some attention to the rights of law-abiding citizens: the right to feel safe and secure in your own home, the right to walk the streets at night without fear of being mugged or murdered, and the right to have your children protected from the child abusers, the pimps, and the pushers. These things will never happen unless we perfect the judicial system. That's what I'm trying to say here today. With my machine we can do it now!"

"What about the Fifth Amendment?" asked LaFrance. "A defendant cannot be compelled to testify against himself."

"That portion of the Fifth Amendment should be stricken from the Constitution!"

"Really?" replied LaFrance.

"Of course. Like the jury system it's obsolete. I believe our forefathers included that portion of the Fifth Amendment in our Constitution to guard against the potential danger a defendant might be forced to testify against himself falsely. With my machine that's simply not going to happen."

"Forgive me, Professor," quipped LaFrance. "But aren't you a little ahead of the game plan here?"

"How do you mean, Mr. LaFrance?"

"I mean, you have yet to demonstrate conclusively that your machine is error free in its analysis."

"But, I don't understand?" responded Professor Bain confused. "You have the data right in front of you."

"Yes, yes, I understand. But don't you see? The tests were on men who were willing to confess to crimes of which they were already convicted. They had nothing to lose and everything to gain by cooperating even if it meant falsifying their statements."

"There was the demonstration today. Drennan was not cooperative," countered the professor.

"True, but then I'm not altogether sure you were successful with Drennan. How do you know he wasn't conning you? I mean," concluded LaFrance, "you can't seriously suggest that we revamp the entire judicial system on the evidence you've given us today."

The conversation between LaFrance and the professor continued with the former adamant in his demands for more conclusive evidence and the latter insistent that such evidence existed in the present experiment. During this conversation Bill Wardle entered the room and stood by patiently listening to the two men. Finally he walked over to Professor Bain and softly whispered something into his ear. The professor smiled. The room suddenly stilled.

"Mr. LaFrance?" called the professor.

"Yes," he answered.

"Mr. Wardle has just reported to me that only moments ago he received a call from Captain Jerome Hartigan of the Evansville police force. From our information obtained from Drennan while on the machine, they have located the jewels. All of them!"

The room erupted as those present turned expressing their surprise to each other. Very little could be heard now from a distance due to the noise. Professor Bain approached LaFrance and Ridgeway. "Mr. LaFrance, will you join us now? We can free people from their fear. With your help people can walk the streets in safety once again." The professor paused looking directly at LaFrance. An intenseness engulfed him as he continued, "Mr. LaFrance, the essence of democracy is freedom—freedom from the fear of the tyrants of the street as well as the tyrants of the government. With your help I can free people of their fears; I can give them back the streets." The professor paused again and then passionately pleaded, "Mr. LaFrance, I implore you to join us."

Peter LaFrance turned to see the excitement of those about him. He felt Ridgeway pulling at the sleeve of his coat.

"Peter, Peter," he questioned excitedly, "what do you say? Will you join us?"

Name _____

> Read each statement before coming to class. To the left check whether you agree or disagree with this statement. After discussing the statement with your group in class, record the total number of members agreeing and disagreeing in the boxes to the right and explain your position in a few sentences below.

A D   **A D**

☐ ☐   1. Professor Bain's brain machine would infringe on the protection of the Bill of   ☐ ☐
        Rights.

☐ ☐   2. Professor Bain's brain machine would make the streets safer to walk at nights.   ☐ ☐

☐ ☐   3. Bain's brain machine is far superior to the jury system.   ☐ ☐

☐ ☐   4. Drennan's constitutional rights were violated when he was connected to the   ☐ ☐
        machine.

☐ ☐   5. Newspaper men like LaFrance do more harm than good to the society.   ☐ ☐

Name _____

□□ 6. As crime rates increase, the courts must start considering the rights of society more than the rights of the criminal. □□

□□ 7. Technological progress will soon make the courts obsolete. □□

□□ 8. In the long run technological innovations produce more harm than good. □□

□□ 9. It is not the responsibility of scientists to be concerned with ethics. □□

□□ 10. The only people who would be afraid to submit to Professor Bain's machine are the criminals. □□

Name _____

If you were Peter LaFrance, would you lend your support to Professor Bain and his brain machine?

_____
_____
_____
_____
_____
_____
_____
_____
_____
_____
_____
_____
_____
_____
_____
_____
_____
_____
_____
_____
_____
_____
_____

Secrets

Jack Wilmont finished dictating the letter to his secretary and pushed the recorder aside. Easing himself back into the soft cushions of the high back chair, he removed his glasses and rubbed his eyes. They were tired and bloodshot, and the soft caresses brought welcomed relief. Suddenly he stopped. His hand fell to his lap, and he sat silently in the room as if he were but another of its fixtures. The stillness surrounded him ringing silently in his ears like background music to the events he now recounted.

It was a little more than seven months ago that Jack Wilmont entered the primary race in an attempt to capture the Republican nomination for a congressional seat in the fifth district. Five other candidates also ran, each seeking the opportunity to challenge the Democratic incumbent, Rodney Norsek. From the outset of the race, Wilmont felt his chances were excellent. Of the five candidates on the primary ballot he was the only moderate—two were conservatives and two were liberals. This presented a unique opportunity for Wilmont. For, as the only moderate, he was in a pivotal position of being able to draw votes from both sides of the political spectrum in a highly competitive and stratified district.

Wilmont's early inclinations of advantage proved prophetic for soon the Republicans came to see him as their only hope of unseating Norsek. Drawing votes from conservatives, liberals, and moderates, Wilmont won an easy primary victory and then launched immediately into an active and aggressive campaign against Norsek. However, despite his valiant efforts, Wilmont continued to lag behind in the polls throughout the campaign. Norsek's conservative views, in a district long known for its conservatism, coupled with his four-term incumbency, proved unbeatable. Now with less than five days remaining before the election and with the latest polls revealing a ten-point spread to be closed, Wilmont and his campaign staff were on the verge of desperation. Wilmont was still lost in thought recounting the past when he was suddenly jolted out of his mesmerized state by a crash in the adjoining office. He sprang from his chair and headed for the door. In the reception room outside he could hear two men screaming, cursing, and fighting. He grabbed the door and pushed. The furniture that had fallen against it tumbled aside. As the door opened, he saw his young campaign manager, Miles Henning, struggling on the floor with another man who was from what Wilmont could tell somewhat older. Rushing over to where the two men were locked in combat, he grabbed the stranger by the coat collar and pulled him off Miles. Then, with a heavy shove he pushed him across the room. Stumbling over an overturned chair, the man lost his balance and fell against the opposite wall. Quickly Wilmont turned to his aide who was scrambling to his feet. His face was bloodied and bruised. Screaming an obscenity at his assailant, he lunged forward on the attack. Wilmont caught him in mid-air as he attempted to pass. Miles struggled in Wilmont's grasp, attempting to free himself. Finally Wilmont overpowered the young man, and with a heavy-handed swing he forced him back in the opposite direction onto the couch. Standing between the two, Wilmont screamed at the top of his voice, "HOLD IT! DON'T ANYONE MOVE!"

Wilmont's arms were outstretched warning the two men to stay put. Neither moved. The fight was over. Wilmont's will had prevailed. Miles sat on the couch, wiping blood from his split lip. The other man was picking himself off the floor while holding a handkerchief to a gash on his face. "Now, just what the hell is going on here?" gasped Wilmont, breathless from the excitement.

The young man whose identity left Wilmont baffled, straightened his coat and then grabbing the door to leave shouted in a defiant tone, "Ask your keyhole peeking pervert!"

Anger flashed in Miles' eyes, but as he started to get up, Wilmont pushed him back. "Easy now, Miles," cautioned Wilmont again. "It's over, OK!"

Wilmont turned back to the other man, but he was gone. "I'll call the police," said Wilmont, moving to the phone. He straightened his clothes and took a deep breath to regain his composure.

"No, no," interrupted Miles hurriedly. "Don't call the police."

"Why?" exclaimed Wilmont. "You've just been assaulted. We have to call the police."

"We can't!"

"Why?"

"Because this isn't a matter for the police, that's why," said Miles still blotting his swollen lip. "Just give me a minute, and I'll explain."

Wilmont was exasperated. He started to speak but was silenced by Miles' outstretched hand.

"In a minute, OK, Jack?" Miles said, stalling Wilmont.

"OK, have it your way. Pull yourself together and then come to my office immediately, hear?" Wilmont headed out of the door, but before leaving, he turned back to Miles and said, "All I can say, Miles, is you'd better have one hell of a good explanation—or I'm phoning the police!"

"Yeah," muttered Miles confidently while gingerly checking his damaged nose.

As Wilmont passed back through the reception room, he saw his secretary huddled in the corner behind her desk. Even from a distance, he sensed her fright. "It's OK, Helen. Believe me, everyone's all right. Just go back to work for now, and I'll fill you in later." With that, Wilmont turned and headed for his office.

"Oh, Mr. Wilmont," called his secretary. "I almost forgot. You have a call; it's Congressman Norsek."

"Damn," muttered Wilmont, "of all times to call." He started for the phone but stopped when he saw Miles turn the corner and rush into his office. He glanced back at Helen who was holding the phone. On the panel below he could see the light blinking. "Damn," he muttered again. He hesitated for a moment and then stomped into his office.

"What about Congressman Norsek?" asked the woman pleading.

"Tell him I'll call him right back, Helen," called Wilmont over his shoulder as he hurried into his office.

Miles was sitting in a chair before the desk nursing his lower lip when Wilmont entered. His handkerchief was soaked with fresh blood.

"OK, Miles," demanded Wilmont. "Let's have it. Who was that man and what's going on here?" The pitch in Wilmont's voice betrayed his excitement.

Miles' composure was incredibly calm as he looked up at Wilmont. He smiled but the thinning of his lower lip widened the split, and he grimaced with pain.

"C'mom, Miles!"

"OK, OK," responded Miles capitulating to Wilmont's impatience. "The man you saw in my office was Henry Tuffleman. Know him?"

"No," answered Wilmont. "Should I?"

Miles shrugged his shoulders. "I guess not. I just thought you might because he's one of Norsek's staff members. But then," he added, upon reflection, "he's not on the campaign staff. He's listed as a research assistant in D.C." With that Miles returned his attention, much to Wilmont's displeasure, back to his lip.

"OK, so he's Henry Huffleman. But that...."

"No, Jack," interrupted Miles, "not Huffleman—Tuffleman—it's T-u-f-f-l-e-man not H-u-f-f...."

"Who cares!" screamed Wilmont. "Huffleman—Tuffleman, what difference does it make?"

"It makes a lot of difference!"

"Why?"

"Because Tuffleman is your ticket to Washington D.C."

Wilmont slumped into his chair behind his desk. "I don't understand," he confessed. "I just don't understand what's going on here."

"Listen," said Miles, removing the handkerchief from his mouth. He scooted his chair closer to Wilmont's desk. "You remember about a month ago I introduced you to that friend of mine from Montana?"

"Vaguely," replied Wilmont. "Wasn't his name Terry?"

"Right, Terry Henson. He's a nature freak—about twice a year he packs his wife and kid up, and they all head out to some wilderness resort area up in the mountains. Anyway, when he stopped by to see me this year, they had just returned from the Big Horn country. Now get this," leered Miles. "Terry's profession is photography. Now what do you suppose that means?"

"What?" asked Wilmont unable to anticipate Miles' desired response.

"Pictures!" exclaimed Miles. "Everywhere Terry goes he shoots pictures, hundreds of 'em, and every time he visits he makes me sit for hours looking at them. I tell you, even though I sometimes get sick of looking at all those pictures, I have to admit the man's fantastic with that damn instrument."

Wilmont stared blankly back at Miles. "What's all this have to do with the man in your office?"

"I'm getting there. Be patient, huh? Just give me time."

Wilmont slumped back into his chair.

"Anyway, this time Terry hadn't time to develop his pictures, but he was insistent that I see his shots anyway. So he selected a couple of rolls, we borrowed the darkroom at school one afternoon, and he started pouring 'em out, roll by roll." Miles' voice tightened slightly. His mood became serious. "At first, it didn't strike me, but for some reason I was drawn to this one picture of a mountain resort area where Terry and his family stayed. It was like there was something in it I was familiar with, but I couldn't put my finger on it. And then," said Miles, striking his fist hard against the table startling Wilmont, "it came to me!"

"What?"

"Henry Tuffleman."

"Tuffleman?"

"Yeah."

Wilmont thought for a moment before finally saying, "So what? The man's taking a vacation."

"No," exclaimed Miles, "that's not the point. In the picture Tuffleman has his arm wrapped around another man."

"A homosexual?"

"Yeah, but that's not all," said Miles, his voice quivering with excitement. "At first I couldn't make out the other man because his back was slightly turned, and he was wearing a hat and sunglasses. So I had Terry blow the picture up and guess who?"

"Who?"

"Rodney Norsek."

Wilmont's eyes widened from the disbelief. Both men sat staring at each other. Wilmont was the first to break the silence. "Well, let's not jump to a hasty conclusion here," he stammered. "I mean, lots of men embrace today—it's the changing time."

"No," stated Miles emphatically. "Not in this case. I checked it out myself."

"How?"

"When I saw the picture, I couldn't help it. I threw Terry in the car along with his camera, and we headed back up to Big Horn country. We drove straight through all night but when we got to the resort, Norsek and Tuffleman had already left."

"So how can you conclude...."

"Wait, there's more," said Miles, cutting off Wilmont. "I talked to one of the cabin maids and found out that Norsek and Tuffleman visit the resort about twice a month, on the average. Of course, they use different names."

"Why would they risk going back to the same place?"

"Why not? You should see this resort—it's in the rugged backcountry. It's huge! Anyway, I slipped the maid a hundred bucks to call me the next time they checked in. Sure enough, two weeks later I got the call. I took my camera and headed back up to Big Horn. For two days I crawled around in the bushes snapping pictures of Norsek and Tuffleman. I tell you there's no doubt Norsek and Tuffleman are lovers!"

Wilmont was stunned, numbed by the revelation. He sat conspicuously silent while contemplating the situation. "How did Tuffleman find out you had the pictures?"

"I don't know," admitted Miles. "I've been trying to figure that out myself. No one else but Terry knew," suddenly he stopped short, "except, that is, the maid. Of course, she probably leaned on Tuffleman for money, you know, playing both ends against the middle. After all, she had my number and description. It had to be her."

"My God, it's hard to believe. Norsek doesn't look the type. I mean he's so—so—conservative."

"Yeah," laughed Miles somewhat cynically. "That's what his voters think. At least," he added, "until we set the record straight."

"What!" cried Wilmont appallingly. "You don't seriously think we should exploit this for our own personal gain?"

"Of course," countered Miles, "why do you think I spent a weekend crawling around in bushes—for my wood lore merit badge? Hell no, man. I did it to nail Norsek. I tell you, with the shots I got, we can blow him right out of the water?"

"But it's not right!"

"Why?"

"Because this is his personal life. It has nothing to do with whether he's a good legislator or not."

"That's not altogether true, Jack," replied Miles. "I mean, there are times when the public has a right to know about the private lives of their legislator especially when it could influence how they vote in Congress. I think what we have here is a classical case of conflict of interest."

"On homosexuality?" laughed Wilmont, as if amused with Miles' analogy. "You're reaching pretty hard, aren't you?"

"Not really."

"Come on, Miles. You can't be serious."

"I am, really. Listen to me, Jack. For the last six months I've done nothing but issue research so that we'll be on top of things when we get to Washington. I know what's going on, and I can tell you that without a doubt gay rights are definitely going to be on the calendar for consideration this next session. Right now, the gays are in Frisco drawing up the bill."

"Who's going to sponsor it?"

"Who cares," yelled a frustrated Miles, "that's not the point. The point is the voters have a right to know about Norsek's relationship with Tuffleman because it's going to affect his decision."

"I see your point, but I don't know," hedged Wilmont.

Miles was exasperated with Wilmont's indecision. "Listen," he said, moving quickly again to the offense. "There's also a matter of morality."

"You mean whether homosexuality is right or wrong?"

"I suppose that could be another angle, but, no, that's not what I mean."

"What then?"

"Listen, let me lay it out for you. Tuffleman is on Norsek's staff, right?"

"Right."

"And who," continued Miles convincingly, "pays his salary?"

Wilmont shrugged. The answer was all too obvious. "The public, of course."

"Right. Now doesn't that sound a bit suspicious to you? I mean, using public money to payroll your lover."

"That's assuming Tuffleman was hired because he was Norsek's lover. It could be he was hired because he was qualified for the job."

"Perhaps," countered Miles. "But then maybe the public should have the right to find out, huh?"

"Norsek has a wife, a family—it'd ruin his life."

"Come on, get off it, Jack," yelled Miles. "That's his problem. Politics is like that. It goes with the territory. Every politician knows his life is subject to public scrutiny. Norsek knew the risk when he ran for office. Besides, you have no right to worry about Norsek."

"Why?"

"Because your sole responsibility is to the people who support you." With that, Miles tossed a folder across the desk to Wilmont. "Look at this."

"What is it?"

"The latest straw poll. Our research people gave it to me this morning. You're still nine points behind. Do you know what that means? If you don't use this against Norsek, all of our work has been wasted. It's all been for nothing! You can't let that happen. You have an obligation to us, your supporters." Miles' voice cracked under the strain of desperation.

Wilmont opened his mouth about to speak when his secretary burst through the door near hysteria. "Mr. Wilmont," she cried, "it's Congressman Norsek on the phone again!"

Wilmont turned back to Miles and read the wanton look he had seen so often in the eyes of his supporters the last few weeks. He had come so far, but yet he still had so far to go—perhaps too far.

"Mr. Wilmont, please, you'd better hurry," pleaded his secretary. "The congressman says it's urgent."

Wilmont stood positioned between the two—the symbolic middle. He had to move, but which way....

Name _____

Read each statement before coming to class. To the left check whether you agree or disagree with this statement. After discussing the statement with your group in class, record the total number of members agreeing and disagreeing in the boxes to the right and explain your position in a few sentences below.

A D   A D
☐☐ 1. Because of his sexual preference, Norsek will be biased toward voting for   ☐☐
         legislation favorable toward homosexuals.

☐☐ 2. Norsek's hidden sexual preference makes him a security threat in our government. ☐☐

☐☐ 3. Wilmont has a responsibility to his supporters to use this information to win the ☐☐
         election.

☐☐ 4. Even if Wilmont won't use the information, Miles should still reveal it.   ☐☐

☐☐ 5. Voters have the right to know about their legislators' private lives.   ☐☐

Name _____

☐☐ 6. The fact that it is nearly impossible for a gay politician to be elected to a public office demonstrates how bias Americans are to this group in our society.   ☐☐

☐☐ 7. If Wilmont believes Norsek's sexual preferences should be revealed, he should do it after the election.   ☐☐

☐☐ 8. Norsek probably hired Tuffleman because of their relationship.   ☐☐

☐☐ 9. Norsek lied to the public by presenting a heterosexual image. Therefore, he should be exposed.   ☐☐

☐☐ 10. In a political election there is no room for morality. One simply does what's necessary to get elected.   ☐☐

Name _____

If you were Jack Wilmont, would you expose Rodney Norsek? If so, how and when? If not, why?

_____

_____

_____

_____

_____

_____

_____

_____

_____

_____

_____

_____

_____

_____

_____

_____

_____

_____

_____

_____

_____

_____

_____

Back Alley

A lone figure lay pressed against the pavement in an African city, his frail body protected by a few inches of rough stone curbing and the dense gray darkness of the night. Slowly the man raised his head to search the surrounding area. Except for the police located on the rooftops above, the streets seemed deserted. Carefully he lowered his head and shoulders back into the crevice of the gutter so as not to create any noise. Twice before he had created noise by calling out—once to seek help, once to surrender. Each time the police's response was the same—gunfire. He was trapped; there was nothing left to do but wait.

He lay staring down the street. Suddenly ahead, in the gutter, he saw movement. Breaking through the blackness of the night moved a small gray creature. It was a rat. At first the man was unsure of its direction. The darkness and thick gray clouds of fog obscured his vision. Intently he watched its short jerky steps until its path was unmistakable; it was headed toward him. Closer and closer it moved, obviously unaware of his presence, until finally, a mere foot from the tip of his nose, the creature caught sight of him. For a brief stunning moment the rat peered into the eyes of its intruder. Then, reeling back on its hind legs, nostrils flaring, the creature let go a series of shrill shrieks that pierced the silence of the night. Unable to defend himself, the man lay helplessly, looking down into the creature's mouth. Two sharp fangs dominated, surrounded by thick layers of pink fleshy tissue covered with a white, pasty substance. Back and forth the small body jerked, sucking air in and pushing it out with an unnerving shrillness. Again and again the animal shrieked, each time louder than before. Finally, when the man thought he could stand no more, the rat lunged. Catching him in the face, the fangs tore deeply into the fatty portion of his left cheek. Instantly he rolled, screaming and yelling in an attempt to shake free of the animal. Immediately the gunfire started. Chips of concrete, rock, and gravel covered him as the bullets tore at the earth. Again he rolled, this time back toward the gutter. The gunfire ceased. Over the beating of his heart, he could hear the small creature scurrying down the street, dragging its coarse stringy tail behind, shrieking its last indignant protest before disappearing into the darkness.

In the still of the night the man cursed silently. He cursed everything: the darkness in which he was lost, the police who held him pinned in the street, and the country for its ignorant and primitive ways. But, most of all he cursed himself, for he had no one else to blame for the insanity of the moment. Had he stayed back in the States, none of this would have happened. But, no, he had to run off halfcocked to some backward country in search of that one story that would almost certainly guarantee him the Pulitzer Prize. Now, with his informant lying dead in the street less than five feet from him, it was doubtful if he could even salvage his own life, much less the story. Over and over he repeated to himself, "Dumb, dumb, dumb...."

The stench of the coarse rock, stained with the day's garbage, filled his head. He felt faint, dizzy. The hot liquid in the pit of his stomach began to stir. Attempting to force its way to the surface, it surged repeatedly up and up. For a brief second his eyes rolled loose in their sockets—nausea overcame him.

An hour passed before Burchett awoke to find himself still in the gutter. It was 3:00 a.m. now. Soon the morning sun would replace darkness with light. What then, he thought. The police would surely find him. Would they kill him? Yes, the answer was unavoidable. In this country they would.

Suddenly, in the darkness the man could hear the footsteps of someone running in the distance. Slapping against the pavement with increasing frequency, the steps grew louder. His body stiffened with terror. He could barely bring himself to turn his head in the direction of the sound. The fog clouded his vision. Squinting, he could make out the figure of a man, large in frame, moving quickly toward him. Gunfire and flashes of fire erupted from the building above. The figure closed in on him rapidly. Less than twenty feet from him the man plunged to the earth as if hit, rolled three times, and landed squarely on top of him. He rocked violently, trying to shake the man off. Grunting and groaning, both men struggled. Finally Burchett was overpowered. The man grabbed him by the hair and pulled back his head as far as possible while jamming a gun barrel up under his chin. Burchett could hardly bear the pain without crying out.

Leaning as low as possible to avoid the sporadic gunfire, the man hissed through clenched teeth, "OK, Buddy, let's have it. Who are you?"

Though in pain, he was relieved. Not only were the words spoken in English, but also they were unmistakably American. Half choking and straining to force the words from his mouth, he spoke slowly, "I'm James Burchett, a member of the American diplomatic corp."

"Like hell you are," the man charged, jerking back on Burchett's head. "I know every diplomat in this country, and you're not one."

Burchett could stand no more, "OK, OK, I'm not a diplomat."

The man eased his grip. "Then who are you?" he demanded.

"My name really is Burchett, but you're right. I'm not a diplomat. I'm a reporter for the *New York Chronicle.*"

"Damn, wouldn't you know it," responded the man, releasing Burchett, "a reporter. That's all I need. Trapped in the street, the police trying to blow my ass off, and, of all things, I get a silly snot-nose reporter from the *Chronicle* to wet-nurse. Hell, I don't even subscribe to the damn paper."

Before the man could maneuver his body back into the gutter for protection, a shot rang out. He grimaced in pain while grabbing his left arm. Burchett could see blood pouring out from between his fingers.

"Oh, God! NO! Are you hit? Is it bad?" Burchett was frantic as he moved toward the man to help. The man reached up, grabbed Burchett by the hair again, and with one powerful stroke he shoved his head back into the gutter.

"You wanna get your fool head shot off?" he hissed.

"I just wanted to help."

"Good, then shut up and stay down. The fewer problems you cause me, the better off we'll both be."

Burchett watched the man as he slowly raised his head to survey the situation. He was a large black man with a broad, flat nose and rough facial features.

Another shot rang out, and quickly the man ducked his head back into the gutter. "Damn, we gotta get the hell outta here," he said, cursing. "The police here are the worst shots in the world, but you never can tell when they'll get lucky."

The man huddled closer to Burchett. "Now listen. Behind you, about fifty feet, is a blind alley. If we can make it there, we can shield ourselves from all this loose lead flying around."

"But the police," questioned Burchett, "what if they're waiting in the alley?"

"They won't be, not at this time of night."

"How do you know?"

"Because they're cowards, every last one of them. The most they'll do at night is sit on the rooftops and shoot at anything that moves."

"Are you sure?"

"Trust me."

"I don't know."

"Then stay here," the man said as he threw his leg up over the curb.

"No, no. I'll come."

"I thought so," the man said, grinning back at Burchett. "Now, follow me and be careful not to make any noise. With the fog they can't see us, so they'll shoot at anything making a sound. Got it?"

"Yeah."

"OK, then let's go." With that the man lifted his body up onto the sidewalk and started crawling for the alley. Close behind, on the man's heels, Burchett followed. Slowly the two men dragged themselves toward the opening in the building. Burchett could feel his raw knees and elbows scraping against the top of the rough brick. They burned, and he winced with each thrust of his legs. By the time the two men reached the alley, Burchett was near exhaustion. Crawling over to the left side of the alley, he rested his back against the exterior wall of the building. Below him the pavement was wet, and he could feel the moisture seeping up through the seat of his trousers. It didn't matter; nothing mattered but life itself.

Burchett looked to his left. The man who had led him to this alley was seated next to him, peering out into the darkness of the street.

"Well," he said to Burchett while reaching into his pocket for a cigarette, "it ain't home, but it's better than the gutter, right?"

Burchett nodded.

"At least now," he continued, "we don't have to worry about stray bullets." From the rooftops above the sporadic shooting continued. It would continue that way all night.

The two men sat next to each other. Burchett was terrified. With his face still bleeding and his neck stiffening, he could barely speak.

"What happened?" the man asked, looking at the blood on Burchett's face. "Catch a little lead?"

"No," answered Burchett, "a rat."

"Hum," laughed the man, white teeth gleaming against his black face, "territorial bastards, aren't they? Back home, the only way a rat will fight is if you corner him, but here they'll fight you for the damn garbage if they think you're on their turf. Damn," he said, shaking his head, "I've never seen anything like it."

Unconcerned about his face now, Burchett asked, "What do you think our chances are of getting out of here?"

"Not good, but then not hopeless either," responded the man. "Over there across the street," he said, pointing, "I've got some friends who own a building. I'm suppose to meet them there in 'bout an hour—if things work out, that is. You haven't helped matters any, ya know. With all this gunfire they might be inclined to forget the whole thing now."

Burchett still couldn't help but feel somewhat uneasy. Finally he asked, "Even if we do make it to your friends' place, how will that help? The police are patrolling the street behind the building. In fact, the police have us boxed in. So even if we do make it, they'll find us when they search the buildings in the morning." Burchett's voice quivered, revealing the desperation he felt.

"No, no!" the man replied, trying to calm Burchett. "My friends are members of the underground. There's a trap door in the building leading to the sewer system. Once we're in it, we can follow it to the river beyond the reach of the police. The problem is getting to the building. It's about 500 feet across the square. That's a pretty big killing zone for the police, but I figure we can make it if this fog holds out."

Burchett relaxed. Hope was in sight for him now. The two men began to pass the time with small talk, both knowing that the moment would soon come when each would have to take his chance in the street.

"Say, I haven't had the chance to ask, but I'm curious. How in the hell did you wind up getting stuck in this part of the city at this time of night? Don't you know there's a curfew?" asked the man.

"Yeah, I know about the curfew," came the response.

"Then why in God's name are you out?"

"I was looking for you."

"Me? You don't even know who I am."

"Sure I do. You're David Hill, CIA agent first class, or should I use your code name, 'Python'?"

Hill reached out and grabbed Burchett by the collar, dragging him closer. "How did you know that. No one knows!"

"No one but the underground, of which he was a member," Burchett said, pointing back to the corpse in the street.

Hill leaned around Burchett for a closer look. Turning back toward the man he held in his grasp, he demanded, "Who's he?"

"My informant. It appears he needed money desperately; however, his loyalty to the movement prevented him from turning you over to the police. So, instead, he came to us. We rewarded him handsomely in return for your story."

"What story?"

Burchett laughed. "You people really play it down to the wire, don't you? I know all about you and why you're here, so knock off the dummy routine. You came here tonight to deliver the assassin's fee—you know the blood money to kill the leader of this country, Ali Masudi. I hear the price is a half million American dollars. Care to confirm that for me?" Burchett could feel Hill's hot breath blowing across his face.

"OK," Hill said resignedly. "No sense in me trying to bullshit you. It's true, all of it. But listen, Burchett," Hill said adamantly, "this is strictly off the record. I...."

"No way," interrupted Burchett. "No way in hell! If you think you can run all over the world trying to kill people and we'll keep quiet about it just because you're the CIA, you're crazy. What do you think we're running, a newspaper or radio free Africa?"

"Hey, you're really carrying a heavy load around. What have you got against the CIA?"

"They don't play by the rules, you know, International Law, Geneva Conventions, UN resolutions regarding sovereignty and acts of terrorism—ever hear of any of them?"

"Yeah," replied Hill, "I've heard of some of them, but out here they don't mean a damn thing."

"Obviously not, at least where you're concerned," countered Burchett.

Hill shook his head. "Listen," he said, "it's not like that at all. Maybe I can explain it better this way. Do you know anything about Chicago?"

"Yeah, I know a lot about Chicago. I lived there for a few years when I was a kid."

"You know where Brookside East is located?"

Burchett nodded, indicating he did.

"Know what kind of place it is?"

"Well, it's not the best," replied Burchett.

"Hey, man," drawled Hill, "let's be fair—it's the worst, and you know it!"

"OK, so it's the worst. Get on with the story, will ya?"

"Well, that's where I grew up. Now there aren't too many good things about growing up in that neighborhood, except that you have a front row seat to life, you know, stripped of all its frills and lace. Well, I remember when I was around ten, this old Jewish immigrant from Poland moved into the neighborhood and set up a little shop. He was a tailor, best tailor in the whole damn city. I swear, no kidding, he could fit a suit in one glance without even touching the customer with a tape measure. Man, was he ever good. But he had one problem."

"What—discrimination?" asked Burchett.

"Hell, no. No one in Brookside East cared about what you were or where you came from. Everyone in the neighborhood was already so gutter-low that knocking someone else down would be ridiculous."

"So what was the problem?"

"Morality," responded Hill emphatically. "Morality was his problem. See, in nice white middle-class neighborhoods you can afford the luxury of being moral but not in neighborhoods like Brookside East. Well, see, just after Wifkowski moved in and set up shop, he was visited by the local representatives of the mob who wanted to sell him some insurance. They don't call it insurance. They're not that sophisticated. To them it's just protection, but it all works out to the same thing. Well, Wifkowski couldn't bring himself to buy it. It wasn't the money. It was a matter of moral principle. In less than three weeks he was robbed twice and mugged once. Each time that he went to the police, they promised him they'd get right on it. But nothing ever happened. It wasn't that they didn't want to do their job. It was just that they were backlogged with about a hundred other cases just like it. About a week after he reported the last crime to the police, some sixteen-year-old kid walks into his shop and begins beating on the old man. As it happened, an off-duty cop was in the shop at the time and nailed the kid to the wall right in front of three witnesses. You know what?"

"What?"

"The judge let the kid off, something about the kid being a minor and the way the police questioned him. But that wasn't the half of it. Not only did he let the kid go, he even gave him cab fare back to the neighborhood. With all the expense of being robbed and the medical bills, Wifkowski couldn't afford to ride. He had to walk. When he got back home, he found his shop vandalized."

"Oh, no," moaned Burchett.

"Yeah, that's what Wifkowski said too. It's the first and last time I ever heard the man swear. God, did he ever curse up a storm. That very day he delivered the first installment on his protection policy. About a week later some young punk walks in, sticks up the place, and pushes him around just for a little fun. You're going to find this hard to buy, but, believe me, it's true. I swear to God. Two days later a big guy, about six-four, walks into Wifkowski's shop carrying a small brown bag."

"The guy was a mob man, right?" asked Burchett curiously.

"Right, only we called them hammers or enforcers, depending on who they worked for. An enforcer was higher than a hammer because the enforcer employs a hammer. It's like an apprenticeship."

Burchett was growing impatient with Hill's long explanation. Finally, unable to contain his curiosity any longer, he blurted, "Come on, what the hell was in the bag, money?"

"No!"

"What then?"

"Thumbs. Two freshly cut thumbs."

Burchett could hardly believe what he had heard. Images of how the thumbs were obtained kept flashing through his head in vivid detail. It was almost more than his mind could stand. "That's the most barbaric thing I think I have ever heard," replied Burchett.

"Maybe so, but it's reality, man. I did happen."

"OK, so it happened. But what's it got to do with what we're talking about?"

"The point is that the police couldn't help Wifkowski. It's not that they didn't want to help, it's just that their hands were tied with all the red tape, you know, the rules and regulations, and triplicate forms, the rights of the defendant, and all that other garbage that prevents them from helping victims. And if you don't think every punk walking the street knows it too, you're crazy. They know the cards are stacked in their favor, and, believe me, they use it to their own advantage. Let me tell you—it ain't that way with the mob.

If they catch you messing with their clients, you've had it. And you can be sure the punks know that too. You might call it barbaric, but to people like Wifkowski, who have to live in Brookside East, it works and that's all that counts. Well, the same thing is true out here. Most of the world is like Brookside East. The only thing that matters here is survival. If we played by the rules, every terrorist and rebel leader in the world would literally kick the shit out of us every time we turned around."

"So what you're saying is that since they don't play by the rules, you want a license to run around the world killing anyone you happen to think necessary."

Hill had flared to anger now. "That burns me, you know, that really burns me."

"What?"

"Your Park Avenue morality. You live in such a nice sheltered little world that you have nothing better to do than amuse yourself with these little morality games. Hell, man, you'd better wake up and look around. Three-fourths of the world never heard of that UN shit or would they care about it if they had."

"Do you care?" asked Burchett point blank.

Hill was taken back by the question. He never thought about it from the angle of whether he cared. He thought for a moment. Burchett waited, totally unable to anticipate Hill's response. No matter, Burchett thought, any response from Hill now would make good copy.

"I don't care about the rules as much as I do about the people in this country."

"Oh, sure, that's why you're out to kill one of them," taunted Burchett.

Hill managed a slight laugh while shaking his head, "Man, you really take the cake, you know. Where in the hell were you raised anyway—Disneyland?"

"No, Brooklyn."

"Well, let me assure you. It doesn't show."

"It doesn't mean I don't know what I'm talking about."

"Well, it doesn't mean that you do either!"

"And I suppose you do?"

"Yeah, I do. I know this country like the back of my hand—the people, the poverty, the hopelessness and the despair, the ignorance, and what's behind it all." Hill could feel the pouch of money pressing tight against his chest. "Ali Masudi," muttered Hill. He turned to Burchett and asked, "Do you know anything about him?"

"I know he's not too fond of us. That's why the CIA wants to get rid of him, to swing the country around to the West."

"Is that all you know about Masudi?"

"Well, I understand that he's pretty much of a dictator."

"Dictator!"

"Well, yeah," hedged Burchett. "What would you call him?"

"Butcher, that's what I'd call him. That's what the Zulia call him too. Did you know that?"

Burchett said nothing.

"Didn't think so," Hill finally said. "But then, you've only been in the country two weeks. Know why they call Ali Masudi the butcher? His father was a butcher at the Bagami stockyards. When Masudi grew up, he followed in his old man's footsteps. Instead of butchering cattle, Masudi decided to butcher Zulia."

Burchett appeared confused, and Hill sensed it. "My God, it's true. You're going to write this story, and you don't even know what the hell's going on, do you?"

"So educate me," replied Burchett.

Hill released a deep sigh. "OK, in this country there's two dominant tribes," explained Hill, "the Zulia and the Walaga. Technically the two have been at war with each other since the fourteenth century. That's when the Zulias were forced up into Central Africa by a more powerful tribe that no longer exists—compliments of the French," Hill added sarcastically. "Well, the Walaga laid claim to the country in the fifth century and were inclined to believe they possessed exclusive rights to the territory. However, being somewhat smaller than the Zulia, they were unable to force them out. In fact, even though they've warred all this time, the Zulia have pretty much had things their way. Even when the war stopped and politics took over, the Zulia still dominated because they had more votes. Of course, the elections were rigged, but it wouldn't have made much difference. The Zulia still would have won. As time went on, some of the more liberal-minded Zulia became guilt-ridden over the plight of the Walaga, so they convinced the Zulia's leading political party to adopt a reform program whereby a few Walagas would be selected for entry into high-ranking occupations."

"Ali Masudi," Burchett said, catching the drift of Hill's story.

"Right, Ali Masudi. That's where it all began. At age sixteen he entered the country's leading military academy and graduated four years later a commissioned officer. Young, bright, and ambitious as hell, nothing could stop him. When the southern border war broke out ten years back, it was Masudi that pushed the invaders out, saving a substantially large portion of the country's iron ore deposits. He became a symbol of salvation to his people and a national hero to boot. Musladi Muringi, the former leader of this country, personally promoted him to rank of Field General, the first Walaga ever to hold the rank. Ali Masudi repaid Muringi's generosity five years later by hanging his head, neatly detached from its body, of course, out in the public square for the whole world to see. He's been in power five years now, and over 30,000 Zulias have been slaughtered. I tell you, this guy has a monstrous thirst for efficiency. Not only were his political enemies placed on the death list, so were their families. He just rounded up all the women and children, some no more than babies, and slaughtered them all. I guess he didn't want any revengeful orphans running loose in the country." Hill's voice hardened as he spoke, "Rumor has it that Ali Masudi personally took part in the killings—for the sport of it. That's why we want to get rid of him, so we can restore some stability to this part of Africa. With Masudi gone the Zulia would have a good chance of regaining the government. Don't you see? We have to stop this bloodshed."

"I had no idea," Burchett said.

"Few people do, but then most people could give a shit about this country or the people in it. I hope this means you won't screw everything up by printing your story," said Hill.

Burchett just looked at Hill. "I can't do that. It's my job to print the story."

Again Hill was moved to anger. "You're just like any other reporter. A story—that's all you care about. The whole damn country could go down the toilet, and the only thing you'd be concerned with is who'd get the by-line."

"Hey, don't lay that guilt on me. It's not me running guns all over the world, spreading revolution and chaos."

"Chaos?" repeated Hill. "Is that what you think we're doing? We're...."

"Yeah, chaos," said Burchett, cutting Hill off. "You think you're saving everyone with the crap you're pulling here. What do you think the Walagas are going to do when Ali Masudi is shot—lie over and play dead while the Zulia take over the government? Hell no, they're going to start shooting. And before long, everyone will be trying to blow each others' heads off. And who can blame them? It's the only way they know how to deal with problems because it's the only thing we're teaching them. Isn't it about time we showed them how to understand?"

"We will," replied Hill, "when the world is safe to talk in."

"Oh, no, the old balance of power bit, huh? Don't you guys ever update your politics? Can't you see what you're doing? You've been so busy trying to balance one country against another by giving everyone guns that the world can never be safe. Too many people have too many guns! When is it going to stop? I...."

"Quiet," interrupted Hill. Silence fell between the two men. Even their breathing stopped as they both listened to the night.

"Time's up," whispered Hill. "It's now or never."

"How do you know?" asked Burchett.

"The signal."

"Signal?" questioned Burchett. "I don't hear any signal."

"Well, shut your mouth and listen."

Burchett closed his eyes, thinking it might help. He had once heard someone say that people don't hear because they have a tendency to be distracted by their sight and that accounted for the fact that blind people often heard things others didn't. He strained to listen. Across the square he could hear a faint tapping, as a rope or cord slapping against a brick wall—nothing unusual. The city was filled with ropes dangling from buildings. Nearly all second-floor tenants who occupied these slums hung ropes out their windows. It was their only fire escape except the front stairs, which were usually the first to go up in flames.

"No, I don't hear anything," replied Burchett, "except the ropes."

"Doesn't that strike you as a bit odd since there's no breeze?"

"Yeah, you're right!" Burchett's voice perked up at the thought of getting out of the alley and away from the police. But then, for a brief second, his hopes were dashed as doubt filled his mind. "How do you know it isn't just a rat or a cat messing with the ropes?"

"Listen again," Hill said. "Listen to the rhythm."

Burchett closed his eyes again. If it worked before, it would work this time too.

Slap...Slap...Slap
Slap...Slap
Slap...Slap...Slap
Slap...Slap

The sounds were faint but unmistakable. Looking at Hill, Burchett was so moved with happiness and relief he choked on his words. Nodding, he let Hill know he understood.

"Good," answered Hill. "It's time to move. We haven't got long before they bolt the door and leave. You know, they're not going to risk staying around too long."

"How do we get across the square?" asked Burchett, excited with the anticipation of danger.

"We don't," Hill responded bluntly. "I do."

"What about me? You're not going to leave me?"

"No, but the underground is expecting one man, not two. If they see two of us racing like hell toward them, they're likely to gun us both down. They get a little edgy about surprises. And I don't blame them. After all, too many of them have been killed lately. I'll go across first and negotiate your passage. Besides, it'll work out better this way. If we both go running across the square at the same time, it'll give the police twice the chance of hitting one of us. You get their attention while I make it across. Then I'll decoy for you. All right?"

"Maybe, but I hate to be the one left behind," Burchett said grudgingly.

"It's the only way," responded Hill.

"OK, let's get with it. The longer I stay out here, the slimmer my odds."

Hill rolled over onto his side. Reaching into his jacket, he pulled out a small revolver and laid it in front of Burchett.

"Listen carefully. I don't want you screwing up. I'm going to make my way down the street about a hundred feet. You make your way up the street about the same distance. That'll give me enough distance so when you draw their fire, I won't run the risk of being hit by a stray bullet. While they're returning your fire, I'll make it across, establish contact, and then get you across. Remember. Don't start across until we open up on the other side. And don't, for God's sake, run in the direction of the fire. Just run straight across and then make your way to us when the firing stops. Got that?"

"Yeah. But why do I have to go back into the street? Can't I do it here?"

"Hell, no. You got to give 'em something to shoot at. Ya know, divert their attention away from me. You can't do that stuck back here, can you?"

"I guess not," reluctantly agreed Burchett. "But I don't like it! When do I start firing?"

"Just give me time to get into place. Now, remember," Hill said, turning so that he could start down the street, "stay calm. Don't panic. We'll be all right."

Burchett watched Hill slowly make his way out into the street and down the gutter. Placing the gun in his pocket, he rolled over onto his stomach and started for the street. Again the raw tissue surrounding his knees and elbows began to burn. There was no time to think about it. Hill would be waiting. He was in the gutter now, approximately one hundred feet from Hill. He could hear nothing but the night. He retrieved the gun from his pocket and held it for a brief moment while attempting to calm his racing heart. He hated guns. Even as a young boy, when most of his friends were getting their first shotguns, he hated them. Slowly he raised the gun up over the stone curbing, pointing it in the direction of the police. Then in rapid succession, he jerked off three quick shots. Immediately the police responded. To Burchett it felt as if the ground beneath him had suddenly opened up, dropping him onto the doorstep of hell. What appeared to be sounds of a thousand guns pounded his ears. Flashes of fire poured brilliantly from the muzzles of gun barrels lighting up the night. Pieces of stone and dirt torn from the ground sprayed past him. Then it was over. Darkness and silence reclaimed the night. For a second Burchett almost forgot about Hill. Had he made it? Looking out across the street, he searched in vain. There was nothing, nothing but emptiness.

Across the square Hill stood in the doorway while a member of the underground tended his wounded arm. About to speak, he stopped short, hesitating. Silently he cursed the God that had filled his head with such unthinkable doubt. Should he save Burchett or leave him for the police? If he did leave him, they would surely kill him. That's the way all curfew violators were handled. It was Ali Masudi's direct orders: "Kill all curfew violators immediately and without exception." And that's exactly the way the police would do it. Nobody disobeyed an order from Ali Masudi. Besides, the police, ignorant and brutal, enjoyed every opportunity to kill. It was like a savage rite of manhood.

But how could he not save Burchett? Hill agonized over his decision. If he did save Burchett, there was little doubt the story would be printed, thus revealing the assassination plot. Such a revelation would produce catastrophic problems for the agency. Racing through his mind were the events surrounding the publications of the CIA's abortive attempts to assassinate the Cuban leader, Castro. That, Hill recalled, had led to an almost total collapse of intelligence operations. Closing his eyes, he could recount every event down to the last detail. First, the newspaper stories. Reporters who knew nothing of the agency portrayed themselves as experts, distorting everything they wrote. One newspaper even reprinted a list of suspected operatives working abroad. Within three months, left-wing radicals shot seven of these men.

Then came the public's reaction to the news stories. Indignation, swelling like a huge eruptive volcano, spread from coast to coast. For years the same agency that had protected the freedom Americans so dearly cherished was cruelly cartooned as the villain in a scenario that pictured every half-crazed military butcher as a victimized symbol of national liberation.

And finally, there were the politicians. Ah, yes, Hill recalled with bitterness. At a time when the agency needed them the most, to inject reason and rationality into chaos, they abandoned their responsibility in favor of votes. It wasn't popular to support the CIA, and they knew it. It was simple math. As one politician remarked to a director of the agency, "There are more votes on the other side." Opening his personal campaign with a vicious attack on the CIA and fanning the fires of public resentment, he won in a landslide, a landslide that burned the CIA.

Paralyzed by political entanglements, the CIA stood helplessly by as terrorists and rebel leaders opposed to Western values and interests stepped up their own covert activities, gaining new footholds in countries once thought solidly pro-American. How ironic, Hill had thought. The American public actually believed they were crusading for democracy, and all the time they were cutting their own throats. Now, years later, the CIA was able to regain some of the ground they had lost during those awful years but not without enormous sacrifices. If Burchett printed the story, everything gained might be lost. How could he let that happen?

And what of the Zulia? Reports of an attempted assassination would bring new purges and more bloodshed. Is it right for one people to save their freedom at the expense of another people? How could he stand idly by and let Masudi continue his merciless vendetta? It somehow seemed unforgivable to do so. Pressing his mind further than he ever thought possible, he considered the alternatives.

It was raining now. The fine wet particles drifted through the thick air like leaves in an autumn breeze. Across the square he could hear Burchett's raspy voice, desperately pleading for his life,

> "Hill...Hill, where are you?
> Hill, you out there?
> Come on, Hill, for God's sake, answer me."

Motionless he stood, like a marble statue, peering into the night. The young African tugged at Hill's coat sleeve. Motioning in the direction of the voice, he asked, "The man in the street, is he your friend?" It was as if God had abdicated the very power of life and death....

Name _____

Read each statement before coming to class. To the left check whether you agree or disagree with this statement. After discussing the statement with your group in class, record the total number of members agreeing and disagreeing in the boxes to the right and explain your position in a few sentences below.

A D   A D
☐ ☐   1. No country, under any conditions, has the right to interfere in the internal affairs   ☐ ☐
          of another sovereign nation.

☐ ☐   2. When measured against all the lives that will be lost when the assassination   ☐ ☐
          attempt is revealed and foiled, Burchett must die.

☐ ☐   3. Because of the atrocities Ali Masudi has inflicted on his people, he deserves to die.   ☐ ☐

☐ ☐   4. Even though some people complain about the CIA, we'd be in serious trouble with-   ☐ ☐
          out it.

☐ ☐   5. Even if Burchett promises not to print the story, there is no way Hill can trust him.   ☐ ☐

Name _____

☐ ☐ 6. When it comes down to a choice between national security and the rights of the press, national security should prevail.   ☐ ☐

☐ ☐ 7. Economic security is important to the survival of a nation. Therefore, the use of military force to secure it is sometimes justifiable.   ☐ ☐

☐ ☐ 8. In order to preserve freedom and democracy, America has a right to interfere in the affairs of other countries.   ☐ ☐

☐ ☐ 9. In this world you can't always play by the "rules."   ☐ ☐

☐ ☐ 10. This country would be better off if we disbanded the CIA.   ☐ ☐

Name _____

If you were Hill in this case, would you attempt to save Burchett's life?

_____

_____

_____

_____

_____

_____

_____

_____

_____

_____

_____

_____

_____

_____

_____

_____

_____

_____

_____

_____

_____

Name _____

Assume you were Burchett and Hill saved your life. Would you print the story? Why?

_____

_____

_____

_____

_____

_____

_____

_____

_____

_____

_____

_____

_____

_____

_____

_____

_____

_____

_____

_____

_____

_____

A Truly Magnificent Machine

August 9, Camp David

Peter Harrinton stood alone in a grove of pines watching the sunset. It was beautiful, more beautiful than the human artist could possibly conceive. Like a huge ball of fire it seared its way between the earth and the sky, painting the horizon with a brilliant, spectacular array of colors: reds, pinks, and oranges. It was peaceful, and he welcomed the solitude. For the decision he was about to make as President of the United States would affect not only Americans but also the people of the world.

It was dark before he turned, heading back to the presidential cabin. As he walked, he contemplated his situation. It all began with his election. Yes, it was the election, he recalled. He could still remember that day. Closing his eyes tightly while pausing for a moment to recollect, he could still feel the same sense of excitement surging through his body. It was a feeling like no other human being could ever imagine. At the time he was ecstatic, not only for himself but for the whole world. For, of all the candidates that had sought office that year, it was he who had pledged himself to the task of freeing mankind from the nuclear menace. It would be a long journey and the first step, as he saw it, was an agreement by all world powers for a complete and total cessation of all military nuclear testing. It was to this goal that he had dedicated his first term of office.

But, as he was soon to discover, it wasn't all that easy. The burden of the presidency would not allow one man to pursue one goal singularly. The day to day affairs of office required unbelievable amounts of time, often leaving very little for that which the president is most interested. However, Harrinton refused to be distracted from his primary objective. His first appointment was clear evidence of his commitment to eventual disarmament. As Secretary of State, he chose his long time friend and mentor, William Wilkerson, a man with impeccable negotiating credentials.

Many political observers were surprised at the Wilkerson selection, and in the long run their surprise proved prophetic for his dovish attitudes and anti-military reputation soon became major obstacles in his confirmation by the Senate even though the cold war had ended with the disintegration of the Soviet Union.

Apparently a few senators, along with some leading columnists across the nation, felt that Wilkerson's relaxed military posture might constitute a major disadvantage for the West, particularly since a number of third world nations were on the verge of entering the nuclear age. And too, they argued, was it not America's strong military technology that allowed for the quick and decisive victory over Iraq in Operation Desert Storm? Why surrender that advantage when one could not foretell when we might be called upon again to protect our interest abroad? At one point leading members of the president's own party suggested he dump Wilkerson in favor of someone from a more moderate background. Harrinton resisted, pushing even harder for Wilkerson's confirmation. In the end Wilkerson was approved by one vote.

In the years to come Wilkerson's reputation improved as he pushed the world harder and harder on the issue of nuclear disarmament. Although Wilkerson was thoroughly devoted to the president's goal of complete and total cessation of military nuclear testing, he negotiated from strength, refusing to compromise America's security. As he repeatedly stated, any treaty between the United States and any nuclear power would be acceptable only if accompanied by an on site inspection agreement. Only through such an agreement could the fears and suspicions of all sides be put to rest. At first the former Soviet republics, now the Commonwealth of Independent States, and the Chinese balked, fearful of each other and the real intentions of their long time adversary. Wilkerson persisted. One plan after another was presented. Each time, at least one nuclear power found fault. Finally, hard-line attitudes began to soften with all sides desiring an end to the escalation if for no other reason than to escape the immense economic burdens of nuclear weaponry. After almost three years of continuous negotiations, victory was within reach. In May, Wilkerson laid his final proposal on the table. Through diplomatic channels the Chinese were first to give tentative approval but only, they stipulated, if the Commonwealth of Independent States also agreed.

It was now left to the Commonwealth of Independent States. Among the Americans, the Commonwealth, and the Chinese there was enough power to persuade all other countries possessing nuclear energy to join with them in search of a better world. The president, the Chinese, and the whole world waited while the Commonwealth debated. But now, even if the Commonwealth did accept the treaty, it might all have been for naught. For a day earlier, General Tyrone Pace, the Chairman of the Joint Chief of Staff, had presented a report that threatened the peace initiative.

Back at the presidential cabin, the others waited for Harrinton's return. There was William Wilkerson, General Tyrone Pace, and Dick Reid, the president's chief political strategist. For each the impatience was almost unbearable.

When the president walked in, all of the men stood. Harrinton waved them down and then proceeded to his desk where he again began to thumb through the report General Pace had brought to him only hours before. It was this that now lay between the president and his goal. The president slammed the report shut, startling those in the room. "Damn," he cursed out loud. "Why wasn't I informed of this earlier?" He was up, out of his chair, pacing about. "How is it possible to have research like this going on and the president not be aware of it?"

"Mr. President," answered General Pace, "that's what I've been trying to explain. We didn't know. I only found out about the possibilities of this new weapon myself a few days ago."

Wilkerson groaned at the general's explanation. "My God, General, you mean to tell us that you run a multimillion dollar facility for nuclear war research and you don't know what's going on in there. God help us all!" he said, throwing up his hands in disgust.

General Pace turned glaring at Wilkerson. "No, Mr. Secretary, that is simply not true. I am aware of everything under my supervision."

"Everything except the Iubar project," countered Wilkerson, pointing to the folder on the president's desk.

General Pace slumped back resignedly in his chair. "You're right," he confessed. "I should have been on top of this. But I assure you, this is not the way things usually operate at the laboratory, except, that is, in Von Hoffstat's case."

"Alfred Von Hoffstat?" inquired the president, raising his eyebrows.

"That's correct, Mr. President," answered the general. "Iubar is his project. He's responsible. Normally, I know exactly what's going on at the laboratory, especially when it concerns nuclear research, but Professor Von Hoffstat is another story. Half the time no one knows what's going on in his head."

"Surely, he follows procedures, doesn't he? I mean," said the president, "he does have to requisition equipment and to do that he has to have his experiments approved, right?"

General Pace sighed. "True, but the problem is that Von Hoffstat is a genius. He's like an Einstein. No one even approaches his intelligence. Why, the other nuclear scientists don't know what he's talking about most of the time. So, when he requisitions equipment and submits reports, no one knows what the hell they're about."

"You're kidding," commented Reid, somewhat in awe of the man.

"No, I'm not, and to compound the problem Von Hoffstat has a secretive personality. He's paranoid someone's going to steal his work. I mean, it's not that he won't report his work. He will but only when he's finished with it."

"Then I take it, he's finished now?" inquired the president.

The general shook his head, knowing the contradiction that he was about to create. "No, he's not finished."

"Then why did he report it this time?" asked Reid.

"Because he did something he rarely ever does."

"What?"

"He read a newspaper and it just happened to be the one about prohibiting nuclear war research."

"But how could that be? The treaty is confidential. It hasn't been released yet. The Commonwealth demanded it that way!" exclaimed Wilkerson.

"I know, Mr. Secretary," replied General Pace, "but we both know there's plenty of speculation about it in the paper, and Von Hoffstat is no dummy. I guess he decided that he had better get his work out of the closet before the door was nailed shut."

Reid was sitting on the edge of the president's desk going through the Iubar folder. "My God!" he gasped. "Can it be true? Will it really do what it says here?"

"Yes," answered the general without hesitation. "It can and it does. That's why we can't sign the treaty. We have to continue the research."

"How can we not sign?" asked the president. "We've come so far with the treaty."

"Mr. President," General Pace said standing, "we are on the verge of a new frontier in nuclear weapons." He paused momentarily and then blurted out the words, "Radiated light! That's what it is: a strange new source of nuclear energy. Why, the Commonwealth and the Chinese don't even know it exists. In fact, we don't know all that much about it ourselves. The only reason Von Hoffstat even discovered it was because one of his experiments got away from him. There for a minute," the general said, rubbing his forehead, "I thought the whole complex was going to go up in one big mushroom cloud, but it didn't. Instead, we got a new nuclear compound. Of course, nobody knew about it at the time except Von Hoffstat, but that doesn't matter now. What does matter is that we have it. I tell you, it was a billion to one chance. This will put us light years ahead of everyone."

The president turned to Wilkerson. "What is the current status of the treaty, Bill?"

"Well, it's in Kiev now, and it's anybody's guess when they'll come to a decision. The new leadership is trying to convince the hard-liners in the party that the world has changed."

"Bill, level with me. Which way do you think it'll go?"

Wilkerson shrugged his shoulders and muttered, "I really don't know. The political situation is so unstable. One would think with all the economic problems the republics are having in the Commonwealth that they would leap at the chance. But then, there's the military. They're really upset. Some of the generals are spreading conspiracy rumors."

"Oh God," moaned the president. "I can't believe it."

"What?" asked Pace.

"What!" exclaimed the president. "Don't you see the irony? We've pushed the Commonwealth into this mess with their hard-liners and military, and now we're the ones who might have to back out of signing the treaty. You call that fair play?"

"Perhaps," interjected Reid, "there's a compromise solution here. It is true that the treaty bans any further testing of nuclear weapons or any testing for the development of new nuclear weapons, but it says nothing about destroying what we presently have. Now, since we already have this new energy source, why can't we just shelve it and then later, if the need should arise, we can pick up where we left off?"

"Absolutely not!" stated General Pace. "Don't you understand what I've been saying? The whole thing was an accident. We don't know how we got the stuff in the first place, and Professor Von Hoffstat is doubtful if he could recreate the exact conditions to reproduce it. If we don't continue to regenerate the nuclear material, we'll lose it."

"Why?" asked Reid.

"Because this particular nuclear material rapidly degenerates with time. We could lose it in a few years." The general paused, blotting his forehead and then added, "But that's not the only problem. There's also Von Hoffstat to consider. Right now, the man's 72 years old, and he's the only one who understands all of this. We really don't have anyone with the mind to pioneer this research. If Von Hoffstat dies before he completes his work, there's a real question as to whether we'd be able to continue even if by some miracle we could duplicate the accident and get more of the stuff."

"Come on, General," mocked Wilkerson. "You mean, we don't have anyone else?"

"Really, we don't! The guy's phenomenal. I mean, he's only been working on it less than a year, and already he's developed the hardware to control it. You ought to see what he's created. It's truly a magnificent machine!"

"Machine," repeated Wilkerson in an acid tone. "It's a weapon used to kill people. It's an instrument of war, not a machine."

"Peace!" shouted the general in Wilkerson's direction. "It may be a weapon, but its purpose is peace."

"Peace, how in...."

"Because," the general said, interrupting Wilkerson, "it has been nuclear weapons that have preserved peace. The only reason we haven't had World War III is because nuclear weapons make it unwinable."

"Well, if it weren't for you people and your continual development of superior weapons, we wouldn't be in this mess today," remarked Wilkerson. "And besides, there's no guarantee that some madman or fanatical terrorist group won't use nuclear weapons in the future. Have you seen the list of radical third world countries scrambling to develop a nuclear capability? We have to put an end to this now! Immediately!"

"Hey, let's have a little peace right here?" pleaded Reid as he broke between the two men. "Fighting among ourselves isn't going to solve anything."

"Dick's right," said the president. "What we have to do is consider all the alternatives logically and rationally and then come to a decision. What's security like on the Iubar project, General?"

"Airtight. No one knows about it except for a handful of trusted technicians and us."

"Good," commented Reid. "At least we can make our decision without everyone trying to twist our arms into corkscrews."

General Pace moved over to the president and requested, "Mr. President, might I make a suggestion?"

"Certainly, General."

"Professor Von Hoffstat has asked me to extend an invitation to you to visit the laboratory. Personally I think it would be wise before you make the decision, that is."

The president contemplated the invitation. "Yes, I think so. In fact, I feel it would be wise if we all had a look at this thing Professor Von Hoffstat has created."

The general stammered sheepishly for a second and then said, "Mr. President, the professor specifically invited you, not the others."

"General Pace," replied the president sharply, "need I remind you that it is me and not Von Hoffstat who is in command here!"

"Yes, but, of course," apologized General Pace.

"Good, then set it up, Dick. We'll leave early tomorrow morning."

August 11, Centurion Research Base

At approximately 9:15 a.m. the president's helicopter touched down. Aboard were President Harrinton, William Wilkerson, and Dick Reid. General Pace, who had arrived earlier in preparation for the visit, was on hand to meet the presidential party. Along with six security guards, all four men were quickly ushered into a sterile, gray, briefing room. Identities were confirmed, and each man was routinely searched, including the president.

After a short briefing on the facilities, General Pace excused himself to prepare for the demonstration. The president, Wilkerson and Reid were directed by several security guards down a long winding corridor to yet another checkpoint. Again identities were confirmed and searches made before they were allowed to proceed through the next corridor. On the ceiling above, the men could see cameras scanning the entire length of the hall. Finally, after several minutes of walking, the corridor ended as the party approached an elevator with thick steel doors. One guard picked up a telephone located on the wall, inserted a magnetic card into a bottom slot, and then quickly punched out a series of digits. Immediately the door opened, and the president and his guests stepped aboard. The guards remained behind. Inside the elevator, cameras scrutinized the men. As the elevator ascended, Reid joked about the president being searched. They all laughed, but as the president himself expressed, he was pleased with such stringent security precautions. From what they could ascertain, the elevator rose to a height of 5 floors before stopping.

The door opened, sliding back smoothly in the metal tracks. Outside were two security guards waiting. Again identities were checked. However, this time the men were not searched. Once accomplished, the men were led to a metal door, much like that of the elevator, only smaller. Next to the door, mounted on the wall, hung an identification coder. The guard punched a series of numbers, then inserted a magnetic card. Reid couldn't help but notice it was the exact opposite procedure that was followed previously. The door opened, and the men stepped forward onto what appeared to be an observation deck.

Reid was first to approach the railing. At first he was unable to speak. He stood there in awe, gaping at the instrument below in almost futuristic disbelief. As the president and Wilkerson moved closer, they too were struck. For swelling up from beneath the concrete below them set Von Hoffstat's machine. It was immense, so immense that it had to be housed in an enclosure the size of a football field.

From above, the men could easily view it in its entirety. Structurally it appeared as if it were vertically constructed in three parts. The base of the machine was octagonal in shape, about 60 feet in diameter and approximately 8 feet tall. From a distance it looked solid, as if forged from a single block of steel. The intermediate structure appeared similar to the base, being octagonal in form but somewhat smaller. Then too, instead of a solid appearance, it was perforated with rounded openings from which protruded a series of metallic-like cylinders. The upper structure consisted of three separate spheroid-like bodies encased in thick glass containers. The spheroids were connected to each other and to the cylinders below in the intermediate structure through a vast array of copper and glass tubing. From the top of each spheroid extended a long metal tube pitched at a slight angle so as to form a tripod when joined with the others. At the very apex of the tripod was a barrel-like device, three feet long and pointing to a platform below.

A side door slid open, and two men stepped out onto the observatory deck. One was General Pace. The other was a slightly stooped elderly man wearing a white laboratory jacket.

"Mr. President," announced General Pace, "may I introduce Professor Von Hoffstat." The two men shook hands, and the president complimented Von Hoffstat on his work. The president then introduced Wilkerson and Reid. Von Hoffstat surveyed the two men cautiously. Finally General Pace, anxious to get started, suggested that the demonstration begin. The men returned their attention to the machine below. Von Hoffstat directed the demonstration from a control panel in the observatory deck.

Von Hoffstat pressed a small button on the panel. Suddenly the lights dimmed, and red warning signals located about the building began to flash. Another button was pressed, and a shrill siren sounded the final warning. Everything was perfectly quiet. From across the far side of the room, a door opened. Two technicians gripping leather straps stepped from the opening dragging a large harnessed dog between them. The dog was muzzled to prevent injury to the technicians. Almost playfully the dog leaped up into the air and back and forth while being led up a ramp to the platform below. Finally, with the animal in place the technicians secured its straps between two posts located at opposite ends of the platform. The dog sat wide-eyed, panting with excitement.

Von Hoffstat reached up and forced a lever to the down position. Immediately a large thick, metal shield was lowered into position between the dog and Von Hoffstat's machine. The dog, terrorized by the object, jerked at its leashes. As a final precaution, Von Hoffstat passed out dark protective glasses. From below, the men could hear the frightened animal whining and yelping as it strained to free itself.

In a moment the dog lay still, exhausted by its own efforts. It was now the precise moment for Von Hoffstat's demonstration. Pushing three buttons and forcing two levers, one up and one down, the machine began to whirl, slowly at first but steadily gaining in intensity. Across the room the flickering lights on the row of computers blinked madly. The dog began to stir again. Suddenly, the men above could detect a slight rhythmic glow in the spheroid structures. The glow was amplified a hundred times over as the machine continued to whirl creating piercing noises. Then, almost unexpectedly, from the barrel-like nozzle located at the apex of the machine, a thin iridescent beam of light split the darkness, penetrated the metal shielding, and struck the dog behind the left ear.

At first nothing seemed to happen. The dog sat gazing at the large metal object dumbstruck. A moment later a soft whimper was heard from the animal as its left side started to twitch slightly. Shortly the whimper turned to a howl, as the animal was no longer twitching but jerking violently. Straining at its leases, it again attempted to free itself. It thrashed back and forth, leaping wildly into the air and landing with crushing blows. The cries from the dog were so loud now that Wilkerson was forced to reach for his ears in a vain attempt to shut them out. No sooner had he done this, than the animal collapsed. It lie there trembling, quivering, its hind legs jerking irregularly. Then quite unexpectedly, and to the horror of the three men above, the whole of the animal burst into flames.

Wilkerson turned away, refusing to watch anymore. Reid wanted to turn but couldn't. The president stood watching, shaking his head in disbelief. The stench of the burning flesh and hair rose to the observatory deck. Wilkerson had just begun to choke when General Pace ushered all of them off the deck to an adjoining conference room. All were relieved to free themselves from the sight and smell of the animal below.

A minute later Von Hoffstat, who had remained behind for shut down procedures, joined the others. Wilkerson was noticeably agitated. As Von Hoffstat took his chair around the table, Wilkerson expressed his personal feelings of hostility, "Professor, I just want you and the general to know that I resent having been made an unsuspecting participant to this appalling spectacle!"

Professor Von Hoffstat looked up from the wire-rimmed glasses perched on his nose. "Please accept my apology, Mr. Secretary. We in the sciences experiment with animals so frequently that we sometimes forget the feelings to which the lay person attaches to these animals. For us the death of an experimental animal is...eh, how would you say...an occupational necessity. But please," he added, "don't judge us too harshly. Remember the sciences have nearly doubled the life expectancy of man through the use of experimental animals."

"Forgive me, Professor, if I missed the analogy," replied Wilkerson caustically. "Your research is not about life. It's about death and destruction."

The general sprang from his chair. "Mr. Secretary, this is deplorable. I won't have you...."

"Please," interrupted Von Hoffstat, waving the general off. "I need no defense here. Perhaps this is how Secretary Wilkerson views my work. That is his privilege. However, it is a view that I do not share. To me, my work is not about death or destruction or about life for that matter either. It is simply about science. I am a scientist, and, as such, I seek the truth about the universe we live in. How that truth is used is not my concern. That, my friend, is your responsibility," he said looking squarely at Wilkerson. "If I had to be concerned about how my discoveries are used, I'd never research again."

"Well said," congratulated the general.

"Agreed," commented Wilkerson. "But in times as perilous as these, such specialization can be very dangerous."

"Perhaps," responded the professor. "Only time shall tell."

Instinctively Dick Reid broke into the conversation attempting to steer it away from politics and back to the safer territory of science. "Professor," he inquired, "I saw the beam of light pass through the metal shield. Did it pierce it—burn a hole through it?"

"No, it passed through the metal object much like conventional x-rays. The only difference is that it leaves no radiation behind."

"Do heavy metals, like lead, stop it?"

"No, only animal flesh. In some way that we are unsure of yet, the radiation is absorbed into the tissue of the animal."

"And humans?" inquired Wilkerson.

"But, of course."

"What about plants, trees, or vegetation in general?" asked the president.

"No, only animal tissue."

"How?" asked Reid.

"Again," explained the professor, "we are not sure. We only know that when the radiation strikes animal tissue, some sort of molecular rearrangement occurs. This, in turn, we believe triggers a metabolic reaction at the cellular level that produces a highly flammable substance. This metabolic reaction that produces the flammable substance also serves to increase the body temperature. As the body temperature rises, so does the level of the flammable substance. Then, when the temperature reaches 112 degrees Fahrenheit, the body literally consumes itself as you saw with the experimental dog."

"Unbelievable," murmured Reid.

"Maybe, but then you did see it," said the general obviously pleased.

"Tell me, Professor," said the president. "How far away are you from using this in a deployable weapon?"

"That will take time. I would estimate about a decade at least. You see, first we have to develop a basic understanding of this new nuclear force. Then, we have to simplify the process so we can move it out of the laboratory, and, of course, I suppose we will have to find some way to miniaturize the process so it can be used militarily. These are problems, but I am confident that we can overcome them with time."

"Tell them about the satellites, Professor," requested the general.

"Well, General Pace and I have speculated about the deployment of the instrument in a satellite. One day it will be possible, you know. From there it would be possible to hit any target in the world."

"Oh God, no!" exclaimed Wilkerson. "You can't possibly mean it!"

"Good heavens, Wilkerson," shouted General Pace. "Just because we put the damn thing up there doesn't mean we'd use it. It would be a defensive weapon, acting to preserve peace. Do you think we're some kind of monsters?"

"Gentlemen," calmed the president. "There will be sufficient time to discuss this later. But, for now, I think we have got what we came for—a first hand look at the Iubar project."

August 12, White House

It was 4:15 a.m. when the president was awakened from his sleep and handed a plain, unmarked, white envelope. Inside, a card informed the president that the ambassador from the Commonwealth of Independent States wished to confer personally with himself and Secretary of State William Wilkerson. The exact nature of the conference was not revealed. The communication read simply that such a meeting was in the best interests of both countries. Immediately the president recognized the intended message; the Commonwealth was ready to respond to the proposed Helsinki Treaty. Without hesitation Wilkerson, Pace, and Reid were informed, and a meeting was arranged for 1:00 p.m., a time convenient to all.

At exactly 12:51 p.m. a long black limousine pulled through the gates of the White House and after checking through security rolled slowly up to the front entrance. The president and Wilkerson waited upstairs. General Pace and Reid passed the time in another room. In a few minutes the Commonwealth's ambassador, Leonid Clazov, was led into the oval office where the president and Secretary Wilkerson stood to greet him. The atmosphere was tense, and Clazov's face was expressionless.

The president guided the ambassador over to a chair away from the formality of the desk. Clazov seated himself and then began shuffling through the papers in his attaché case. The president and Wilkerson watched intently. Finally, Clazov came upon the paper he wished. Speaking to the president in fluent English laced with a heavy accent, he said, "Mr. President, to ensure that there is no misunderstanding, please allow me to read to you the following message my government wishes to communicate to your government regarding the Helsinki Treaty Proposal." He began:

"To the President of the United States...."

Clazov slowly read the message. His thick coarse voice lightened as he rolled off the words. The tense facial expression relaxed, and a smile formed across his thin lips as he read the words accepting the proposed treaty. As he finished and looked up, his eyes sparkled from the tears filling them. "Mr. Wilkerson," he said, gazing across the table at the Secretary, "we have finally arrived."

For the next two and a half hours the three men talked. Although the basic agreement was acceptable to both sides, differences over minor technicalities remained. These, it was agreed, would require the collective bargaining efforts of all three superpowers. Clazov indicated that his government would wait for the Americans to contact the Chinese and set the date for further talks. At 4:00 p.m. the black limousine rolled back down the drive and into the street.

General Pace and Dick Reid were summoned immediately to the oval office. Reid was first to enter followed closely by the anxious general.

"How did it go?" asked Reid before seating himself.

"The Commonwealth have accepted the agreement," answered the president.

"Damn," replied General Pace. "Then we'll have to find a way to pull out."

"Pull out!" lamented Wilkerson. "Why, such action would be unconscionable. We simply can't do it. What would the Commonwealth and the Chinese think? What would the world think?"

"We have to pull out, don't you see? The Iubar project is too damned important to the security of this country."

"Security," laughed Wilkerson. "We don't need your kind of security. We've reached an agreement, remember?"

"To hell with your agreement. The world has had thousands of agreements. Each one of them promised love and happiness forever, but not one of them has lasted. The only peace that lasts is the one maintained through strength. Don't you see? The Iubar project provides us with the opportunity to guarantee peace for at least three generations, maybe longer. We can't throw it away. It wouldn't be right to the citizens of this country. They are the ones who are going to have to pay for this treaty when it's broken, just like all the rest, or when we have to go into another country like Iraq."

"No, you're the one who's wrong, General!" challenged Wilkerson. "It's people like you and that machine Von Hoffstat has developed that's the real danger, not the treaty. Once we call off the treaty, the Commonwealth and the Chinese are going to suspect that we've gained superiority. That's when it's time to worry, when they begin to worry. When they feel that their security is threatened, they'll begin to think and act irrationally. Why this could be the edge the hardliners in the Commonwealth need to re-establish the Soviet Union. Then it'll be the cold war all over. That's the real danger, the real threat to democracy and world peace. Mr. President, surely you can see it even if the general can't," pleaded Wilkerson.

The rest of the afternoon and early evening the men debated. The general and Wilkerson remained steadfast, arguing vehemently at times in support of their beliefs. Finally, when all had seemingly been said, Reid suggested that the meeting be adjourned so that each man could search his own conscience. Exhausted, the president agreed. A new meeting was set for the following morning at 8:00 a.m. It was then that the decision was to be made.

August 13, White House

At 7:55 a.m. Wilkerson entered the oval office. The president was at his desk. Wilkerson looked haggard, as did the president.

"Get much sleep?" he inquired of the president.

"Not much, about 2 hours. How about you, Bill?"

"About the same. Say, where are the others? I thought they'd be here by now."

"Yeah, I thought so too. I'm sure they'll be along shortly."

Just then the door into the oval office burst open. Both men looked up to see Reid hurrying toward them clutching a newspaper. "Dick, in God's name, what is it?" asked the president rising.

Reid was out of breath; he couldn't speak. He pitched the paper at the president and slumped into a chair. The president took the paper and unrolled it. He read the bold headlines. "Oh, God! Please say it isn't true."

Wilkerson unable to contain himself any longer reached up and grabbed the paper from the president's hands. The headline was bold and clear: **General Pace Reveals Death Ray**

Name _____

Read each statement before coming to class. To the left check whether you agree or disagree with this statement. After discussing the statement with your group in class, record the total number of members agreeing and disagreeing in the boxes to the right and explain your position in a few sentences below.

A D   **A D**

☐☐ 1. Even if the Commonwealth and Chinese do sign the treaty, they'll still continue   ☐☐
         their own weapon research. They'll just do it surreptitiously.

☐☐ 2. Regardless of what some people say, good will hasn't preserved world peace—it's   ☐☐
         been sophisticated weapons.

☐☐ 3. If we achieve military superiority, we will probably exploit our adversaries.   ☐☐

☐☐ 4. We should sign the treaty and then continue our work on the weapon in secret.   ☐☐

☐☐ 5. Not building the weapon will damage the president's chances for reelection.   ☐☐

Name _____

☐☐ 6. General Pace was wrong in revealing the weapon to the press. ☐☐

☐☐ 7. To demonstrate our own good faith, we should share our discovery with the world. ☐☐

☐☐ 8. One clear advantage to developing weapons is that they eventually produce research that can be applied to peaceful purposes. Therefore, we should build the weapon. ☐☐

☐☐ 9. It is impossible to stop research once an idea is conceived; therefore, we might as well continue our own research on the weapon. ☐☐

☐☐ 10. Now that the Soviet empire has collapsed, we have nothing to fear abroad. Consequently, we do not need any new weapons. ☐☐

Name _____

If you were President Harrinton, what would be your decision?

_____

_____

_____

_____

_____

_____

_____

_____

_____

_____

_____

_____

_____

_____

_____

_____

_____

_____

_____

_____

_____

_____

_____

The Endorsement

A tall lanky figure stood impatiently on the corner trying to stamp the numbness from his feet. His warm moist breath rose up about his face hindering his vision. A lone traffic light beamed its ever-changing message across the street. Once threatening, it now beckoned him to cross. Instantly he lunged forward, almost slipping on the icy pavement.

In spite of the crowded sidewalk, the bitter cold, and his numbing feet, Jeff Hartley was undaunted. Nothing could daunt the keen sense of excitement he felt. In a few minutes he would be seated before the local Democratic committee, ready to accept the party's endorsement for State Representative.

Finally, he thought, after seven long years of ringing doorbells, mailing letters, and answering telephones, he now had the chance to begin his own political career. No longer would he have to work for someone else's campaign. Now that one of the two Democratic Representatives was retiring, it was time for the party to repay his years of loyalty.

A smile spread across his face as he contemplated his situation. An endorsement from the Democratic committee would ensure his primary victory. And, of course, there was no doubt that he would receive the endorsement. Jim Delano, the most powerful member of the committee, next to Chairman Frank Polinski, was from his township and sponsoring his candidacy. Also, Jerry Price, a young and aggressive committeeman from the neighboring township, was firmly committed to him. However, Jeff had always been somewhat leery of Price's support, especially since the relationship between Price and Polinski bordered on hostility. Nevertheless, Delano assured him there was a movement underway to close ranks within the party so as to present a united front in the upcoming elections. This would work to Jeff's advantage since Polinski would be eager to compromise in order to gain Price's support. Price might be young, but as Delano indicated, he was well entrenched in his township, and Polinski knew it. Consequently, between the two of them they had little trouble in securing a commitment from Polinski to use his influence in Jeff's behalf. In fact, only last week Delano called to inform him that everything was set. As Delano said, "The only thing left for you to do, Jeff, is show up at the meeting with a smile on your face and be ready to shake a lot of hands."

Even if someone would be foolish enough to challenge him, he thought, they wouldn't stand a chance. After all, no one had ever won a primary election in this district without the support of the committee. And since the district was overwhelmingly composed of Democratic voters, his election was inevitable. How could he lose!

As he turned the corner and walked down the narrow entrance leading to the Democratic headquarters, his mind drifted to his relationship with Jim Delano. Delano was like a father to him. Ever since his own father passed away when he was fifteen, Delano was always there ready to help the family. Without Delano's help he never would have made it through college, much less law school. And now, once again, Delano was in there pitching for him.

As Jeff approached the headquarters building, he paused briefly to admire its architectural features. It was a beautiful building, he thought, not large but unique within its own surroundings. Anyone familiar with architecture would immediately recognize that money had been no object. He wondered how the Democrats were able to surround themselves with such an ornate setting. In addition, he was somewhat curious about the seemingly endless campaign chest in the building. Only once in his seven-year association with the party could he recall the Democrats being short of funds. Certainly, one could not classify Jefferson as a wealthy community, and with a population of only 35,000 it was difficult to conceive of so much cash flowing through the treasury. If the citizens of Jefferson were politically active, one might be able to understand exactly how the Democrats found themselves in such an opportune position. However, one could not make such an assertion. The average citizen of Jefferson was not politically concerned. The majority of the population, roughly 60 percent, were blue-collar workers with strong union affiliations. As long as they received adequate pay increases each year and were able to put three meals on the table every day, they were content. Though Jeff realized it was unfair to equate contentment with apathy, nevertheless, as far as he was concerned, it produced the same outcome—noninvolvement!

Once, while discussing campaign tactics with Delano over a drink, he casually brought up the question. However, Delano appeared somewhat reluctant to pursue the matter in much detail. Nervously, he assured Jeff that he didn't have to worry about the legality of the party's activities. "Besides," he inserted, "your job is campaigning; ours is providing you with enough money to do a decent job of it. Anyway, it's impossible for one person to handle the whole campaign, so let us worry about the cash, and you concentrate on convincing the people that you're the best man for the office."

From the expression on Jeff's face it must have been evident to Delano that he wasn't satisfied with the answer, so Delano continued, "Listen, Jeff, you know if I could tell you where the money came from I would, but I can't. At least not now, anyway. It's not that I don't trust you. It's just that many people who contribute substantial sums to the party expect us to keep quiet about it. They have a right to privacy; you can understand that. Many of our contributors are business people who don't want to mix their political beliefs with their business life. If they did, it might prove disastrous."

Jeff looked up from his drink and responded, "I can't believe anyone could be so petty."

"Don't kid yourself," said Delano. "Remember when you first started to work on my campaign? That's the year old man Hoskin dropped five thousand dollars on the party, right?"

Jeff nodded, indicating that he recalled the contribution.

"Well, somehow the information leaked out, and the Hoskin Corporation lost two of their largest accounts. If you also recall, it took Hoskin three years before he could get those accounts back. There's no telling how much money he lost! You might also be interested to know that Hoskin hasn't contributed one damn dime to the party since then."

Delano paused while lighting his cigarette and then, in a voice barely audible, said, "You have to be patient, Jeff. One of these days you'll be in a position to find out exactly what I'm talking about, and you'll realize it just has to be this way."

Delano's answer failed to appease Jeff's curiosity, but he was relieved to learn there was nothing illegal in the party's financial transactions. Naturally, he had only Delano's word for assurance, but if there was one person he could trust, it was Delano.

Jeff stepped into the building and hurried up the stairs that entered into the large meeting hall. No sooner had he past through the corridor when someone grabbed his arm from behind. He turned and found himself staring into Price's face. Quickly Price maneuvered Jeff to the nearest corner and said, "Something has gone wrong. I think they cut a deal, but I'm not sure with whom or where!"

"Cut what?" asked Jeff.

"A deal," stammered Price. "They cut a deal!"

"What do you mean, they cut a deal? Who are they?"

Jeff tried to question Price further without much success, because Price kept breaking in with bits and pieces of information that didn't make sense. To confuse matters, Price's eyes continually scanned the hall while talking to Jeff, as if searching for someone. Finally, he broke off the conversation by saying, "Listen, kid, I have to talk to some people fast. Don't worry. I'll get back to you later, and we'll cut a deal of our own." Then, almost as fast as he had pushed Jeff into the corner, he left.

Jeff stood there alone for a moment, attempting to unravel what Price had said, but it still didn't make any sense. He looked up and saw Delano scurrying across the hall toward him. When Delano was close enough to hear him, Jeff said, "What the hell's the matter with Jerry? He was saying something about, 'They cut a deal. We're going to cut a deal.' I couldn't make out a thing he was saying." But before Delano could answer, the haggard voice of Polinski boomed over the speaker, directing everyone to his/her seats. Quickly Delano indicated that he had to leave, but before going, he turned around to Jeff said, "No matter what happens, be calm. Just hold tight, and I'll explain everything to you later, OK?"

At this point Jeff was totally bewildered and didn't know what to do other than take his seat with the rest of the party hopefuls. He knew something was going on, but what? As he took his seat, he once again tried to fit the pieces together. Then it came to him. He wasn't going to get the endorsement. That's what Price meant when he said they had cut a deal. As the endorsement for State Representative for the Sixth District moved closer, Jeff grew tenser and tenser. He could feel the muscles in the back of his neck grow tighter by the minute until he thought they would snap. He heard his nervous stomach slowly growl as it turned over, and he was convinced everyone sitting near him heard it too.

Instantly, as if an unconscious alarm inside him triggered, he heard Polinski announce that the nominations for State Representative of the Sixth District were open. The first nomination came from John Owens, a regular party member in good standing with the organization. Owens confidently placed into nomination the name of Allen Lampolie. Jeff had heard of Lampolie before, but he knew he didn't live in the Sixth District. In fact, he didn't even live close to the Sixth District, so how could he be nominated? Surely Delano would object, he thought, but when he looked up and saw Delano sitting there passively, waiting for the nominations to close, his initial fears were confirmed. He had been dumped!

Once again Polinski called for nominations from the Sixth District. Then, just before the final call, a young woman Jeff recognized as one of Price's campaign workers stepped forward to the microphone and nominated Jeff. Speeches for both candidates were given and the vote taken. A tally of the ballots revealed Jeff had received barely one-fourth of the votes cast. Allen Lampolie would be the party's standard-bearer in the next election.

Total disbelief flooded Jeff's mind as he walked back down the stairs and into the street. He couldn't believe it. For seven years he had worked diligently for the party's candidates, only to be betrayed when it was his turn. And Delano, he thought. How could Delano sit by and let it happen? The more he thought about it, the more confused he became. He knew a decision would have to be made soon, but he couldn't do it now. Mentally, he was just too exhausted.

For the next two hours Jeff drove through the winding streets of the city, trying to collect his thoughts. He wanted that nomination more than he had wanted anything for a long time. And now that he had lost it, he wanted it even more. It was growing dark by the time he headed home to unload the news on his wife, Nancy. Nancy came from a long line of politicians, and instinctively he knew she would be disappointed. On more than one occasion, often late into the night, they would sit up trying to anticipate what life would be like when Jeff became a State Representative. He thought of all the plans they had made. Now it was doubtful whether any of them would be realized.

When he pulled up to his house, he was surprised to find Delano's car sitting in the driveway. Before he could reach the front door, Nancy stepped out onto the porch and whispered to him that she knew what had happened and that Delano was waiting inside to talk to him. Jeff gave her a reassuring smile and then entered the house to confront Delano. At first, Jeff didn't bother to sit down but positioned himself next to the large picture window with his back to Delano and waited.

Delano attempted to break the ice by saying, "You look like you're taking this pretty hard, Jeff."

"Well, what do you expect?" Jeff responded tersely. "This isn't exactly what you would call my finest hour."

"I looked for you after the meeting but couldn't find you."

Jeff turned to Delano and in a sarcastic tone replied, "I suppose I should have stayed so that I could have smiled and shook a lot of hands, right?"

"That's hitting pretty low," Delano said as he was looking up at Jeff intensely.

"You've got to be kidding me," laughed Jeff. "You're complaining about me hitting below the belt. I suppose you consider that fiasco this afternoon a model for righteous behavior?"

Shaking his head, Delano replied, "You know better than that. If there was any way I could have prevented it, I would have. Personally, I think you deserve to know what happened, so I'm going to let you in on it. Maybe I shouldn't, but I'm going to anyway. As you know, there's bad blood between Price and Polinski. What you don't know is that Price is planning to unseat Polinski as chairman. From the meeting you could probably tell Price has a substantial following. That's why you received quite a few votes in spite of the fact that Polinski backed Lampolie. Polinski knew you were Price's candidate, and this happens to be the only district that Polinski felt strong enough to challenge him."

"Why Lampolie?" objected Jeff. "Why, he doesn't even live in the district. How can he possibly represent the people in this district?"

"But don't you see?" said Delano. "That's all part of the package. Lampolie is well known around the state capital and is part of the regular organization. There was no way they could fit him in their organization because they're loaded with incumbents. That's why they traded their support to Polinski for your position. That's why Polinski had to sacrifice you. It's the only way he could maintain the chairmanship and keep peace within the party. What it all boils down to is that Polinski and Price are fighting, and you were caught in the crossfire. I wasn't even aware of the arrangement until an hour before the vote. I tried to call you at home, but you had already left."

"That still doesn't answer my question," said Jeff. "How can Lampolie run for the sixth district if he doesn't live here?"

"Don't be so damn naive, Jeff," replied Delano. "Lampolie has already contacted some local realtors, and before the end of the week, he'll probably live down the street from you."

"Where does that leave me now?" questioned Jeff.

Delano sank back into his chair and said, "I talked to Polinski, and tentatively we've agreed to slate you for a county office. It's not a glamorous job, but it'll be a good springboard for you when the next vacancy occurs."

"Yeah, in another seven years, I suppose," quipped Jeff.

"Oh, I doubt that," replied Delano. "Lampolie is too ambitious. Once he gets elected, he'll start looking around for a seat in the state senate. I'll be surprised if he's a representative for more than two terms."

"Well, here we go again, all the maybes and ifs. I can't wait around for another seven years with nothing more than wishful thinking as a guarantee." Jeff banged his fist on the arm of the couch and said, "Damn it,

Jim, I know I can do a better job than Lampolie. Even you know he doesn't care about this position or the people in it."

"There are no guarantees in this game," replied Delano. "Everyone has to take their chances."

Delano stood up and walked to the door with Jeff beside him. Before leaving, he put his hand on Jeff's shoulder and said, "You know, politics has its own purgatory, and every politician has some time to serve. That's where you're at now, Jeff, but you haven't been damned. Keep that in mind, and I'll talk to you when you've had time to think it over."

For the rest of the evening Jeff and Nancy tossed ideas back and forth across the kitchen table. At one point Jeff indicated that perhaps Delano was right. Maybe every politician does have his own special purgatory to serve out, surely this wasn't the first time a deserving candidate was deprived of an endorsement. If what Delano said was true—and there was no reason to doubt him—then the best course might well be patience.

From the direction of the succeeding conversation, it was evident that Delano's position was gaining ground, at least, that is until the Hartleys heard someone banging on their front door. When Jeff opened the door, he was surprised to find himself once again staring into Price's face.

"I know it's late, Jeff," Price apologized, "but it's urgent that I talk to you now."

"Listen, Jerry," replied Jeff. "I'm beat, and besides, we were just about to call it a night. Can't it wait until tomorrow?"

"No, it can't wait," pleaded Price. "I have to be down at the state capital early tomorrow morning to confer with some of the governor's people. If it could wait, I wouldn't be here tonight."

Realizing Price was not about to be put off, Jeff stepped back and reluctantly opened the screen door. Price stepped in, and Jeff ushered him back to the kitchen. After exchanging greetings with Price, Nancy excused herself and headed upstairs.

"Want some coffee?" asked Jeff.

"Yeah, the way I feel I could use some," answered Price as he leaned back in his chair and stretched. Price scooted his chair closer to the table and rubbed his bloodshot eyes. Jeff poured the steaming coffee into a cup and placed it directly in front of Price, who by this time was fumbling around in his briefcase. Price clutched the steaming cup of coffee with the fingertips of both hands, sipped it, and then said, "I want you to know what happened this afternoon."

"I already know the whole story," interrupted Jeff. "Delano came by after the meeting and filled me in on everything."

"I just bet he did," quipped Price.

"What do you mean by that remark?" questioned Jeff.

"I mean," said Price, "that he probably told you everything with, of course, the exception of a few important details."

"Delano wouldn't do that to me," replied Jeff. "You know how close we are."

"I bet not as close as you think," Price shot back.

Jeff shook his head, indicating that he could not accept Price's implication. Then suddenly without warning Jeff blurted out, "Come on, Jerry, you can't say that when you don't even know what he said!"

"OK, you tell me what Jim said, and I'll let you know if it's an accurate account," responded Price.

Jeff breathed a sigh of resignation and then began trudging through Delano's explanation. Somehow he knew it was the only way he could appease Price. As Jeff relayed Delano's version, Price continued to sip his coffee while occasionally drumming his fingers across the table. When Jeff finished, Price slipped out of his chair and walked over to the kitchen counter to refill his coffee cup. As he was pouring the coffee, he asked Jeff if that was all Delano had told him.

"Yeah, that's all Delano said," Jeff replied.

Price turned around and leaned on the edge of the counter and commented, "Well, that's pretty accurate except for one important point."

"And what's that?" inquired Jeff.

"The part about why Lampolie chose your district," replied Price. "Sure, it's true we're locked into a head-on battle, but that's not the only reason Polinski gave Lampolie the endorsement. Lampolie has Polinski and Delano over a barrel."

"Sure, Polinski needs the support of other townships, and the only way he can get it is to support Lampolie," explained Jeff.

"No, that is not what I'm talking about," replied Price. "About five years ago the Democratic organization in this county was in debt up to its eyeballs. The telephone company was even threatening to yank out the phones, and the worst of it was that it was an election year. I tell you we were reaching into our own pockets, and we still couldn't make up the deficit. Then, out of nowhere Delano and Polinski came up with the money to bail everyone out. No one knew where the money came from, and Polinski refused to open the books to any of us. Well, at that time Lampolie was working for the State Labor Department, investigating unfair labor practices. He was close enough to some of the union officials to discover where the money came from."

"Oh, no," muttered Jeff.

"That's right, Jeff," replied Price, "straight from the union retirement fund. Sure, the money was replaced, but that won't make much difference in court, will it? I think you can figure out the rest yourself."

"Yeah," nodded Jeff, "Lampolie stumbled onto the information, sat on it, and then when the time was right, used it to his advantage."

"Exactly," responded Price.

"But how can you prove it?" asked Jeff. "I'm sure the union officials were smart enough not to keep books on the transaction."

"Oh, absolutely," replied Price. "But Lampolie wasn't. In order to convince Polinski that he had the goods on him, he got one of his political cronies to draw up a phony indictment that he presented to Polinski. Well, Polinski caved in and promised to use his influence to get Lampolie slated. What Lampolie doesn't know is that a copy of that indictment was made, and we have one."

"When did you get it?" asked Jeff.

"Last week."

"How?"

"Through the guy who originally drew it up," replied Price.

"Through Lampolie's friend!" Jeff said in amazement.

"Of course," replied Price casually. "When Lampolie made the deal, he didn't include his friend, Bill McDaniels."

"Bill McDaniels!" exclaimed Jeff.

"That's right, Bill McDaniels," responded Price. "He's the character you've read about in the papers. Bill was employed in the States Attorney's office and was working on a campaign at the same time, at least that is before the newspapers got wind of it. The publicity got so hot they had to can him. It was then that he came to us with the indictment, hoping we would take him into our organization."

"Did you?" asked Jeff.

"No, but we did have the time to make another copy of the indictment," responded Price. Price paused for a moment and then said, "Jeff, I want you to run against Lampolie. We'll sit back and let Lampolie have the nomination. Then in the general election, with my backing and this information, you'll have a clear shot at taking the whole thing, especially if you unload the information just before everyone goes to the polls."

"I can't do that, not to Delano," Jeff said.

"Why not?" cried Price. "He cut you out, didn't he?"

"I realize that, but he has been a friend to me all my life," responded Jeff. "Why don't you use it against Polinski?"

"You know I can't do that," replied Price sarcastically. "If I did, I'd never get the support of the other members of the committee for chairman, and the first thing we have to do is unseat Polinski. The public has a right to know this information, and you're in the position to give it to them."

"Then why don't you give it to the district attorney's office?" asked Jeff.

"There's no guarantee they'll push for a full investigation, and even then, it might be too late for the both of us. Besides, if you're going to defeat Lampolie, you have to be the first to reveal it to the public. That way you'll have the publicity and the image you'll need to win. If the DA reveals it, the public will place you in the same category as they do Lampolie. Jeff, you have to do it for your benefit and the benefit of the party." Price looked at his watch disapprovingly. "It's time to catch my flight," he said slowly. "Think about it, and I'll call you tomorrow. Remember, Jeff, Polinski's getting old and can't last forever. We could make a great team."

Price and Jeff were silent as they walked to the door. Before Price stepped out, he reached into the inner pocket of his sport coat, withdrawing a long white envelope and handed it to Jeff. "There it is, Jeff," said Price. "Just be careful with it."

"What's in it?" inquired Jeff.

"The indictment," responded Price.

"Why give it to me?" questioned Jeff.

"Because if you don't use it, I can't," replied Price. "It's in your hands now."

Name _____

Read each statement before coming to class. To the left check whether you agree or disagree with this statement. After discussing the statement with your group in class, record the total number of members agreeing and disagreeing in the boxes to the right and explain your position in a few sentences below.

A D   **A D**

☐ ☐   1. Lampolie is only doing what any other politician would do.   ☐ ☐

☐ ☐   2. Jeff owes Delano. Therefore, he shouldn't reveal the indictment.   ☐ ☐

☐ ☐   3. Even if people knew about the union contribution, they wouldn't care.   ☐ ☐

☐ ☐   4. If Jeff doesn't reveal the indictment, it means he is a dishonest politician.   ☐ ☐

☐ ☐   5. Jeff's best shot is to go with Price.   ☐ ☐

Name _____

☐ ☐   6. If a politician was ever totally honest with all the people, he/she would never get elected.   ☐ ☐

☐ ☐   7. All politicians are dishonest.   ☐ ☐

☐ ☐   8. To get ahead in life, whether it's business or politics, you can't be honest.   ☐ ☐

☐ ☐   9. People don't demand or even expect their politicians to be one hundred percent honest.   ☐ ☐

☐ ☐   10. When it comes down to a choice between friends and ethics, it's better to go with your friends.   ☐ ☐

Name _____

If you were in Jeff Hartley's position, what would you do? Why?

_____

_____

_____

_____

_____

_____

_____

_____

_____

_____

_____

_____

_____

_____

_____

_____

_____

_____

_____

_____

_____

_____

_____

_____

_____

NOTES

NOTES

NOTES

NOTES

NOTES

NOTES

NOTES